Tools Quickfinder Matrix

	Page	Understand	Observe	Point of view	Ideate	Prototype	Test	Reflect	1 day	2–3 days	4–7 days	14 weeks
Problem statement	49	○	○	○					✓	✓	✓	
Design principles	53	○	○	○	○	◐	◐	◐			✓	✓
Interview for empathy	57	○	○				◐		✓	✓	✓	
Explorative interview	63	○	○				◐			✓	✓	✓
Ask 5x why	67	○	○				◐			✓	✓	✓
5 WH questions	71	○	○				◐			✓	✓	✓
Jobs to be done	75	○	○		○		◐			✓	✓	✓
Extreme users/lead users	79	○	○				◐				✓	✓
Stakeholder map	83	○	○				◐				✓	✓
Emotional response cards	87	○	○				◐					✓
Empathy map	93	○	○	○			◐		✓	✓	✓	✓
Persona/user profile	97	○	○	○			◐			✓	✓	✓
Customer journey	103	○	○	○		◐	◐				✓	✓
AEIOU	107	○	○		○						✓	✓
Analysis question builder	111	○	○									✓
Peers observing peers	115	○	○									✓
Trend analysis	119	○	○		○							✓
"How might we…" question	125			○	○				✓	✓	✓	✓
Storytelling	129		○	○		◐	◐			✓	✓	✓
Context mapping	133	○		○	○			○			✓	✓
Define success	137	○	○	○	○	◐	◐	○			✓	✓
Vision cone	141	○	○	○				○				✓
Critical items diagram	145			○		◐	◐	○			✓	✓
Brainstorming	151				○	◐	◐	○	✓	✓	✓	✓
2x2 matrix	155	○	○	○	○	◐	◐	○	✓	✓	✓	✓
Dot voting	159				○	◐	◐	○	✓	✓	✓	✓
Brainwriting/6-3-5 method	163				○	◐				✓	✓	✓
Special brainstorming	167				○	◐					✓	✓
Analogies & benchmarking as an inspiration	171		○		○	◐					✓	✓
NABC	177		○	○	○	◐	◐				✓	✓
Blue ocean tool & buyer utility map	181				○	◐	◐					✓
Exploration map	187					●	◐				✓	✓
Prototype to test	199					●	◐		✓	✓	✓	✓
Service blueprint	203					●	◐				✓	✓
MVP – minimum viable product	207					●	◐					✓
Testing sheet	213						●			✓	✓	✓
Feedback capture grid	217	○	○	○	○	◐	●	○	✓	✓	✓	✓
Powerful questions for experience testing	221	○	○				●			✓	✓	✓
Solution interview	225	○	○				●				✓	✓
Structured usability testing	229	○	○				●					✓
A/B testing	233						●					✓
I like / I wish / I wonder	239	○	○	○	○	◐	◐	○	✓	✓	✓	✓
Retrospective sailboat	243					◐	◐	○		✓	✓	✓
Create a pitch	247			○		◐	◐	○		✓	✓	✓
Lean canvas	251			○				○			✓	✓
Lessons learned	255							○				✓
Road map for implementation	259							○				✓
Problem to growth & scale innovation funnel	263							○				✓

Examples of tools applied over a typical design cycle of 1 day up to 14 weeks

Also by co-authors Michael Lewrick, Larry Leifer, and Patrick Link

The Design Thinking Playbook

Also by co-authors Michael Lewrick and Larry Leifer

The Design Thinking Life Playbook

THE
DESIGN
THINKING
TOOLBOX

For general information on our other products and services or for technical support, please contact our Customer Care Department within the United States at (800) 762-2974, outside the United States at (317) 572-3993 or fax (317) 572-4002.

Wiley publishes in a variety of print and electronic formats and by print-on-demand. Some material included with standard print versions of this book may not be included in e-books or in print-on-demand. If this book refers to media such as a CD or DVD that is not included in the version you purchased, you may download this material at http://booksupport.wiley.com. For more information about Wiley products, visit www.wiley.com.

ISBN 9781119629191 (Paperback)
ISBN 9781119629214 (ePDF)
ISBN 9781119629245 (ePub)

Cover illustrations: © Achim Schmidt
Cover design: Wiley

SKY10029101_081621

THE DESIGN THINKING TOOLBOX

A GUIDE TO MASTERING THE MOST POPULAR AND VALUABLE INNOVATION METHODS

Michael Lewrick

Patrick Link

Larry Leifer

Illustrations:

Achim Schmidt

WILEY

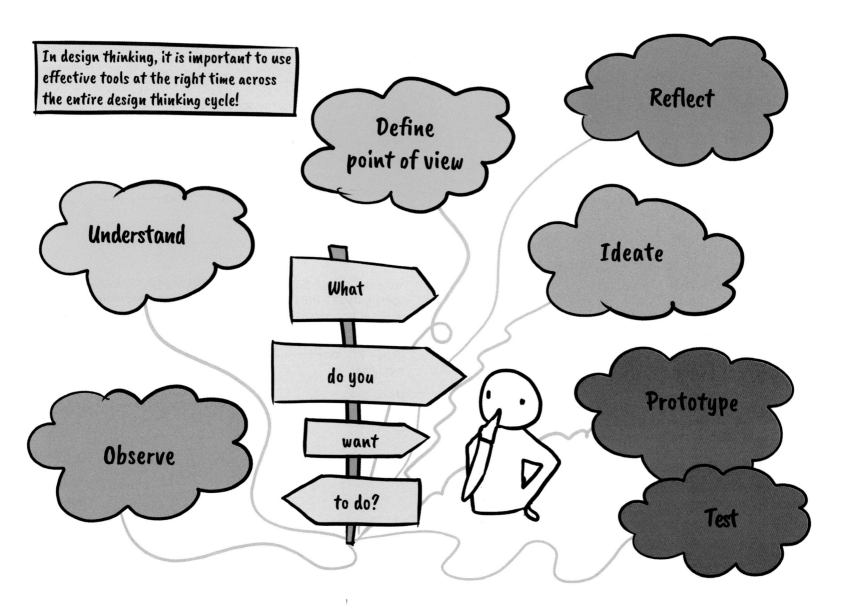

Preface

Prof. Ulrich Weinberg

HPI School of Design Thinking

Many who come in contact with design thinking for the first time search for help in applying it. New mindsets often overwhelm us because over the years we have forgotten how to solve problems with creativity on an ad-hoc assembled team without clearly defined goals.

With the international best-seller *The Design Thinking Playbook*, Michael, Patrick, and Larry have reached many innovators. The *Playbook* provides an inspiring framework for making the design thinking mindset available to a broad range of readers in the context of application.

The Design Thinking Toolbox is an excellent complement to the Playbook. Like the Playbook, the Toolbox is geared to the needs of the readers. The three editors asked more than 2,500 design thinking users from actual practice and academia about the tools and methods they prefer to use and which ones, in their view, bring the greatest benefits. From this, a unique collection of design thinking tools and methods evolved.

The experience at the HPI teaches us that the selection of the right tools across the entire design thinking cycle makes a vital contribution to success. The selection depends on the situation, the team, the possibilities, and the respective goal.

Design thinking is not a rigid concept. It should be used more playfully, that is, the sequence must be adapted to the circumstances.

The Design Thinking Toolbox encompasses, in my view, five key elements that make it an indispensable work tool, in particular for beginners and for deepening design thinking knowledge:

- Assignment of the most important tools to the design cycle
- Simple explanation on the use of tools
- Proposal of alternative tools
- Expert tips from the community
- Exemplary pictures of application

More than 100 experts from the global design thinking community contributed to the content, and show how widespread the mindset has become and how knowledge is exchanged today globally.

I hope you have fun using these design thinking tools and methods!

Uli

Driven by curiosity

We are curious, open, ask W+H questions continuously, and change the perspective in order to look at things from various sides.

Focused on people

We focus on the human being, build empathy, and are mindful when exploring his/her needs.

Accept complexity

We explore the key to complex systems, accept uncertainty and the fact that complex system problems demand complex solutions.

Visualize and show

We use stories, visualizations, and simple language to share our findings with the team or create a clear value proposition for our users.

Experiment and iterate

We build and test prototypes iteratively to understand, learn, and solve problems in the context of the user.

THE DESIGN THINKING TOOLBOX

MINDSET

Co-create, grow, and scale

We continuously expand our capabilities to create scalable market opportunities in a digital world, and especially in digital ecosystems.

with varying perspectives and frameworks

As the situation requires, we combine different approaches with design thinking, data analytics, systems thinking, and lean start-up methodology.

Develop process awareness

We know where we stand in the design thinking process and develop a feeling for the "groan zone" to change the mindset through targeted facilitation.

NEW MINDSET NEW PARADIGM BETTER SOLUTIONS

www.design-thinking-toolbook.com

Collaborate in networks

We collaborate on an ad-hoc, agile, and networked basis with T-shaped people and U-shaped teams across departments and companies.

Reflect on actions

We reflect on our way of thinking, our actions, and attitudes because they have an impact on what we do and on the assumptions we make.

Contents

We begin with the results of the global survey, an explanation of the design thinking process, and a brief checklist. In addition, warm-ups are presented that loosen up the mood and fit the respective situation. In terms of content, the presentation of the tools follows the logic of the design thinking micro-process. At the end of the Toolbox, we will present initiatives that show how design thinking can herald in a cultural transformation in the context of the company and beyond.

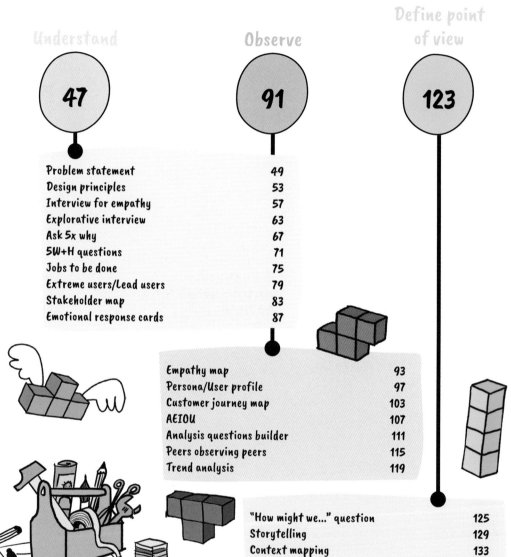

Understand

47

Observe

91

Define point of view

123

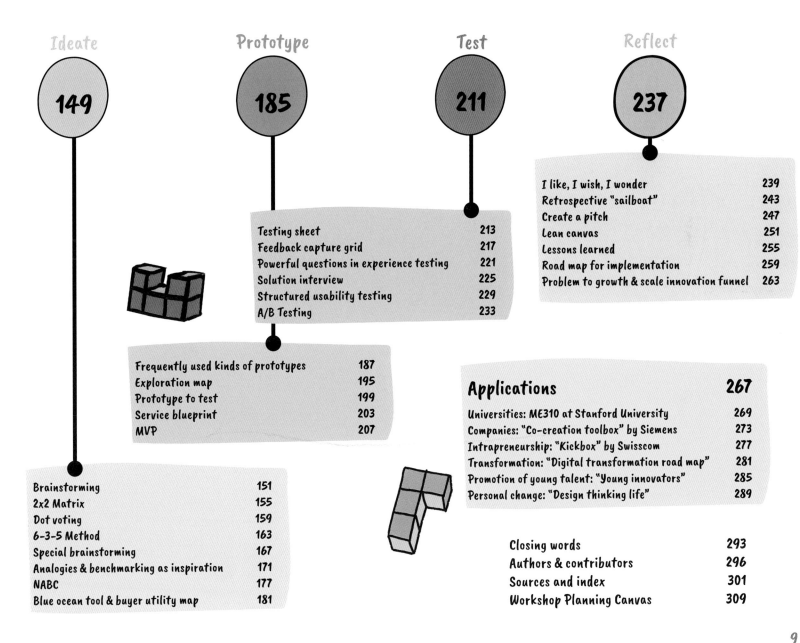

The Toolbox in a nutshell

Briefly and to the point, we will present the framework in which we move in this Toolbox and how we can use it most efficiently.

In design thinking, we adapt methods that are commonly applied by designers. This is why we make use of an iterative procedure in design thinking, from the problem statement right up to problem solution. The objective is to generate as many ideas as possible, including "wild" ones, with the help of various creativity techniques. The creative working method aims to trigger both halves of our brain. On our "journey" to a solution, iterations, leaps, and combinations of ideas are desirable in order to obtain a solution that in the end meets the needs of users (desirability). The solution must then also be economically viable (viability) and technically feasible (feasibility); see page 20. On the way to the solution, a high level of error tolerance is of great value, particularly in an early phase.

The tools and methods presented in this book are a means to an end, that is, we always customize the tools to our situation. If you try to explain design thinking in a few words, you must add that, with design thinking, the work is done on interdisciplinary teams, if possible. This is best done with a sufficient number of "T-shaped" team members, who possess not only the depth of knowledge in a certain domain but broad general knowledge as well. A diverse composition of teams (area, culture, age, gender) help in the process and also aid in breaking silo mentality. A central aspect of the design thinking mindset is to build on the ideas of others and not focus on ownership or competition. We deal with the design thinking process and the design thinking mindset in greater detail later.

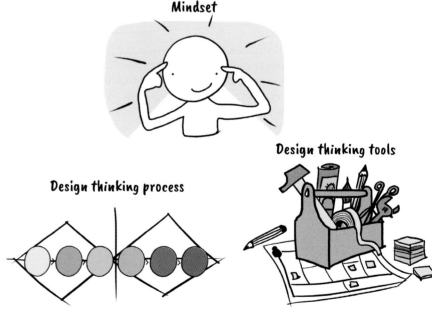

Mindset

Design thinking process

Design thinking tools

What tools are in the Toolbox?

The Design Thinking Toolbox aspires to present in a concise way the most important methods and tools in design thinking. To this end, we interviewed over 2,500 design thinkers in order to find out which tools yield the greatest benefits and are preferred by the design thinking community. A total of 150 tools were included in this survey and allocated to the individual steps in the design thinking cycle. At this point, we want to express our gratitude to the international design thinking community, whose members motivated one another to take part in this survey. We are particularly pleased that design thinkers from every continent participated. The survey enabled us to discuss in this Toolbox all those tools that are valuable in the eyes of the design thinking community for living the design thinking mindset.

In collaboration with companies and universities, we have found that users wish a quick reference book, particularly when they are just taking their first tentative steps with design thinking. Thus a selection of just over 50 tools came into being, described by more than 100 experts.

How is the Toolbox structured?

By way of introduction, we first discuss in the Toolbox the design thinking mindset and the design thinking process. The process is used as a reference to classify the individual tools and methods. In addition, a tabular list is integrated in the book cover. It helps with the navigation and with putting workshops together. At the end of the book, the "Quickfinder Tools" and the "Agenda canvas" workshop also helps to turn workshop preparation and workshop planning into a positive experience at an early stage.

What the Toolbox is not.

What we absolutely didn't want to do is publish a "cookbook." It is important for us to describe the application of the individual tools and point out in which phases these tools yield great benefits. These pointers are visualized as one full or half-full Harvey ball per process step in the table as well as at the beginning of each tool description.

Every moderator of design thinking workshops should develop his own sense of how and when the individual methods and tools are used, and adapt them to the individual situation of each design thinking workshop and each individual design challenge.

What additional value does the Toolbox offer?

We have made the working tools available online in the form of well-known canvas models, lists, and empathy maps (see www.dt-toolbook.com). Because warm-ups have proven their value for a positive start of a design thinking workshop, six of these ice breakers are also included in the Toolbox.

Love it, change it, or leave it!

As already mentioned, we did not want to write a cookbook for design thinking. **This is important to us:** The individual descriptions of the tools and methods are merely intended as a guide. Hence the Toolbox also shows how other design thinkers use them and what insights they have garnered. After all, the tools and methods must fit the setting of the workshop, the problem statement, and the participants.

We ourselves had to experience only too often how a detailed agenda without any flexibility and the wrong methods at the wrong time not only turned the workshop into a lousy experience for participants but, far worse, there was no viable solution in the end, nor had the actual problem been dealt with. After such an experience, the likelihood is high that we did design thinking exactly once with our team, and that a defensive reaction against design thinking must be expected.

This means that although design thinking needs tools and methods, experience and a sense of applying it in a targeted way and in sync with the situation are far more important. Some of the methods and templates can and must be adapted.

Love it! Change it! Or leave it!

It is quite instructive to take part in many design thinking workshops yourself in order to learn from others or reflect on the application of the tools together with the workshop participants. A design thinking facilitator and user never stops learning!

A design thinking workshop is not conducted in a way we are familiar with from the explanations in a cookbook!

The global survey

Results of the survey

Who participated in the survey?

To learn more about the relevance and popularity of design thinking tools, we started the first global survey on "Design thinking tools & methods" in the spring of 2018. The aim of the survey was to find out which methods and techniques are used in actual practice and at universities. The survey was distributed virally throughout the world, mainly via social media. This way, we were able to reach more than 2,500 people with varying levels of knowledge in design thinking who completed our online questionnaire.

Most of the participants in the survey had experience with the mindset, meaning that 85% of them had worked with design thinking for more than two years. There were 23% with more than 7 years of design thinking experience.

In which sectors do participants work?

In terms of affiliation with a particular industry or sector, it is remarkable that most interviewees (30%) were from the consultancy sector. A large proportion (18%) of them were dealing with digital solutions or were working in the IT industry; 12% specified that they came from the education sector; followed by banks, insurance companies, and service providers (10%), as well as in production, supply chain management, and logistics (7%). Other industries claimed 23% of interviewees, including pharmaceuticals and biotech at 4%, or NGOs at 2%.

Experience in design thinking

	<1 year 14%	2–3 years 33%	4–7 years 30%	>7 years 23%

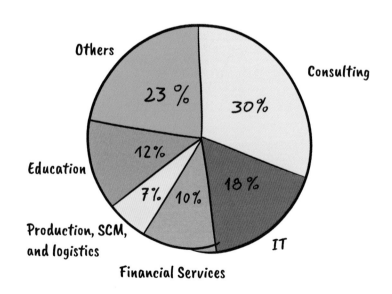

Others 23%
Consulting 30%
Education 12%
Production, SCM, and logistics 7%
Financial Services 10%
IT 18%

How is the distribution across the globe?

In view of the global reach, the survey included participants from 44 countries. The majority came from Europe (65%), followed by North America (16%), South America (7%), Asia (7%), Australia (3%), and Africa (2%).

The global design thinking community

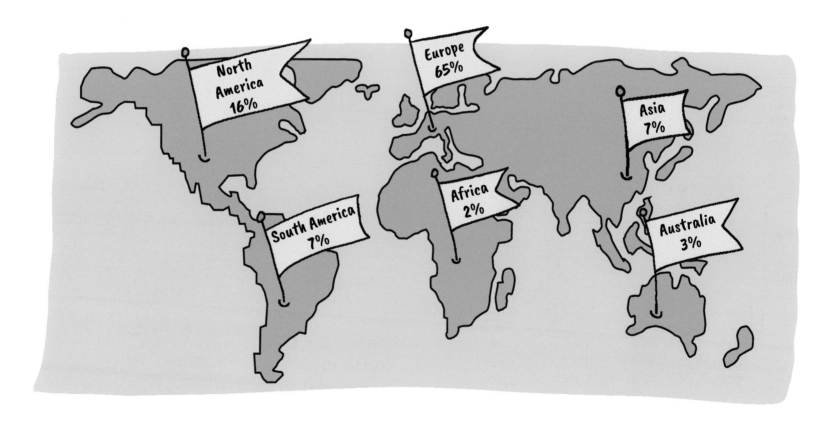

North America 16%

Europe 65%

Asia 7%

South America 7%

Africa 2%

Australia 3%

The best-known tools

In the global survey, we asked participants if they knew the respective tool and if so, how they rate it. **Awareness [%]** represents the percentage of individuals who know the tool. **Popularity [%]** indicates how many people rated the tool as very useful or stated that it's their favorite tool. The basis for the popularity rating was the basic population of participants who are familiar with the respective tool.

It was no surprise to us that the better known tools are also the most popular, as shown in the Popularity/Awareness plot chart. The following applies in general: **The simpler and more user-friendly the tools, the more often they are applied.**

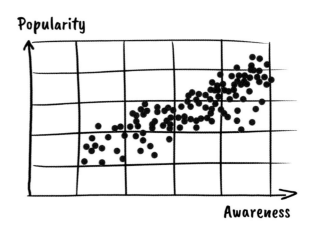

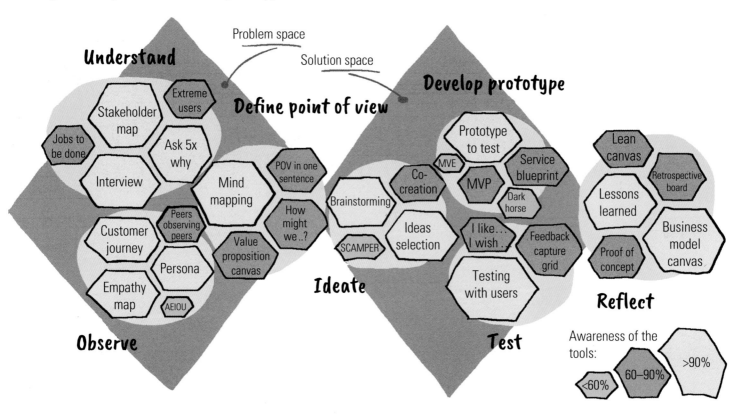

Problem space
Solution space

Understand
- Extreme users
- Stakeholder map
- Jobs to be done
- Ask 5x why
- Interview
- Peers observing peers
- Customer journey
- Persona
- Empathy map
- AEIOU

Observe

Define point of view
- Mind mapping
- POV in one sentence
- How might we ..?
- Value proposition canvas

Develop prototype
- Prototype to test
- MVE
- Service blueprint
- MVP
- Dark horse
- Co-creation
- Ideas selection
- Brainstorming
- SCAMPER

Ideate

- I like... I wish ..
- Feedback capture grid
- Testing with users

Test

Reflect
- Lean canvas
- Retrospective board
- Lessons learned
- Proof of concept
- Business model canvas

Awareness of the tools:
- <60%
- 60–90%
- >90%

16

What is design thinking?

Design thinking?

"The beginner's mind"

People who have never dealt with design thinking often ask for simple analogies to help envision it better.

We have had good experiences with taking these people on an imaginary trip to their childhood. Especially at the age of 4, all children have something in common – they ask many 5W+H questions in order to learn and understand situations.

Nor do children know any zero-error culture. For them, doing, learning, and trying again stands in the forefront. This is how children learn to walk, draw, and so on.

Over the years many of us have forgotten this ability to explore and this type of experimental learning, and our education in schools and universities has taken care of the rest so that we do not question and investigate facts and circumstances in a big way.

With the "beginner's mind," we want to encourage people to ask questions as though we didn't have the slightest idea as to their answers. Like an alien from outer space who sets foot on Earth for the first time and asks himself why we throw plastic into our oceans, work during the day and sleep at night, why we wear ties all the way to rituals that seem strange indeed to an outsider, such as looking for eggs at Easter time.

"If your mindset is unprejudiced...it is open to everything. "In the beginner's mind, there are many possibilities, but in the expert's mind there are few." — Shunryu Suzuki

A "beginner's mind" as the basis for our attitude:

- Free of prejudices about how something works
- Free of expectations about what will happen
- Filled with curiosity to understand things more deeply
- Open to a world of possibilities since we do not yet know at the beginning of our "journey" what is possible and what is not
- Fail early on and often; learn quickly

How we behave in order to apply design thinking successfully:

- We bid farewell to prejudices on "how things work."
- We put aside expectations about what will happen.
- We strengthen our curiosity to understand facts and problems in depth.
- We open ourselves up to new possibilities.
- We ask simple questions.
- We try things out and learn from it.

Success factors of design thinking

In addition to the "beginner's mind," which constitutes an excellent starting point, a number of core propositions and success factors have become established in the design thinking community. We will describe them briefly.

1. Starting with human beings

People with their needs, possibilities, experience, and knowledge are the starting point for all considerations. People know pleasure (gains) and frustration (pains) and have tasks to be fulfilled (see Jobs to be done, page 75).

2. Create awareness of the problem

In design thinking, it is of crucial importance to understand what we work on and what greater vision ought to be pursued. In order to find a solution, the team must have internalized the problem and have understood it in depth.

3. Interdisciplinary teams

Collaboration on the team and of teams of teams is vital for the holistic consideration of problem statements. Team members with varying skills and specialist knowledge (T-shaped) help in the creative process and with the reflection upon ideas.

4. Experiments and prototypes

Only reality shows whether a function or solution will last. The implementation of simple and physical prototypes helps in getting feedback from potential users.

5. Be mindful of process

For the work on the team, it is crucial that all members know where the team stands in the design cycle; which goals are currently to be attained; and which tools are to be used.

6. Visualize and show ideas

The value proposition and vision of an idea must be communicated as needed. In so doing, the needs of the user must be addressed, memorable stories be told, and pictures be used while telling a story.

7. Bias toward action

Design thinking is not based on lengthy considerations by somebody who sits alone behind closed doors. Instead, it lives from doing (e.g. building prototypes and interaction with potential users).

8. Accept complexity

Some problem statements are quite complex since we want to integrate different systems and react to events agilely and with purpose. Thinking in systems is more and more becoming a critical skill, for example, in the case of digital solutions.

9. Co-create, grow & scale with varying mental states

Design thinking helps us in solving problems. For market success, however, business ecosystems, business models, and organizations must also be designed. This is why we combine different approaches with design thinking, such as data analytics, systems thinking, and lean startup, as the situation requires.

> The mindset and the success factors are crucial because each makes us capable of acting and helps us pose the right questions. It is the small changes in our mindset that enable us to pose questions in a different way and look at problems from other points of view.

From the user's point of view

The focus on human beings and the potential users of a solution is another key element of design thinking. Then there are the questions of feasibility and economic viability. This balancing act usually accompanies us to the final prototype and often beyond it.

Successful innovations therefore evolve from the needs of the customer/user (desirability), a solution that is profitable (viability), and technical implementability (feasibility).

With design thinking, we usually want to solve complex problems, taking into account that the complexity can vary greatly from company to company and from one technology to another. The user/customer, especially if he is not technically savvy, always has a desire for a simple and elegant solution.

Thus we have developed a number of methods and tools over the years that help us to simplify, for instance, the interaction between human beings and technology.

A design team uses the design thinking process as a guide for the design of such solutions. The process is described on page 22.

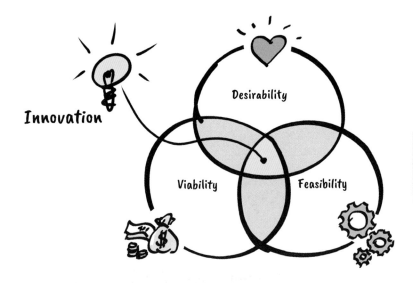

"Design thinking is a human-centered approach to innovation that draws from the designer's toolkit to integrate the needs of people, the possibilities of technology, and the requirements for business success."
—Tim Brown, president and CEO of IDEO

Why are the three dimensions important?

- They **reduce the risks** associated with the launch of new solutions.
- They help teams, organizations, and companies **learn faster**.
- They lead us to **solutions that are innovative** and **not only incremental**.

It is like working on a puzzle, only dynamically

In the context of *The Design Thinking Toolbox*, the tools can be used flexibly so that we achieve a balance between **desirability**, **feasibility**, and **economic viability**. Like with each Tetris level, the arrangement, the speed, and the sequence change with each design challenge. We need to be able to adapt the relevant tools to the given situation. In Tetris, we can also rotate the tiles at a 90-degree angle. In the same way, there are additional variants of each tool that we can use in such a way that they ultimately lead to the optimum result. If we do not agilely adapt the methods and tools in the workshop, there will be a quick "game over" for our project. What the snapshot below shows happens all the time, that is, in each micro-cycle, it will be new and adjusted to the situation. Various tools and methods are used from an initial problem definition or the formulation of a point of view all the way to the final prototype.

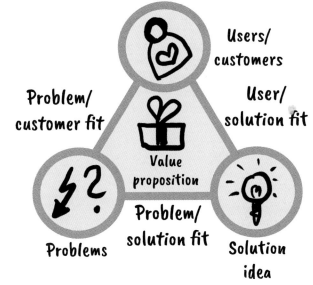

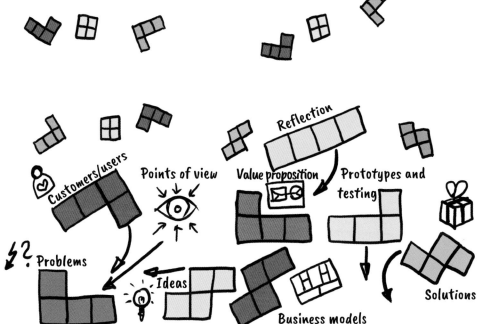

After all, we want to achieve a fit between the **problem and the customer (problem/customer fit)** as well as a fit between **the problem and the solution (problem/solution fit)**. Today, we also have the possibility of generating individual experiences and offers for customers by means of artificial intelligence and big data analytics, thus achieving an **individual user/solution fit**. The derived value proposition should optimally harmonize the three elements of problem, users/customers, and solution. In a digitized world, the complexity increases again, making it all the more important to solve the problem in iterative steps.

In general, we don't want to see the very first idea or assumption as the solution. Design thinking makes it possible for us to realize solutions that meet the wishes of the customers, solve a genuine problem, and thus provide value for the customer.

The design thinking process

In this book, we follow the six phases of the design thinking micro-cycle: understand, observe, define point of view, ideate, develop prototype, and test. In the end, we can add the phase of reflecting, which we consider to be important in order to learn from our actions. In this section, we would like to explain briefly the phases of the micro-cycle. In the double diamond model of the British Design Council, the first three phases encompass the problem space and the next three the solution space.

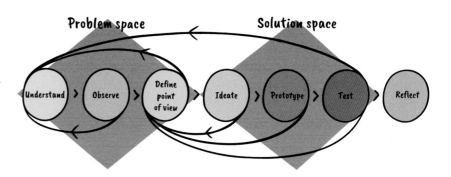

Understand

In the first phase of the micro-cycle, we want to learn more about the potential user, his/her needs, and the tasks that he/she must complete. At the same time, we define the creative framework more exactly, for which we want to design solutions. For the definition of the design challenge, we use, for example, "WHY" and "HOW" questions in order to broaden or limit the scope. Tools such as Interview for empathy (see page 57), Extreme users (see page 79), and the 5W+H questions (see page 71) support this phase. The following phases and tools help to ensure that we learn more and more about our potential users.

Observe

Only reality can show whether our assumptions, for example, presented in a persona (see page 97), will be confirmed. This is why we have to go to the place where our potential users are located.

Tools such as AEIOU (see page 107) help us with the observation of users in their real environment or in the context of the respective problem. A trend analysis (see page 119) also sheds light on technological and social trends that help us recognize developments. The findings from the "observe" phase help us in the following phase to develop or improve the persona and the point of view. When we speak to potential users in order to learn more about their needs, we should ask questions that are as open as possible, working with a question landscape, for example. A structured interview guide can also be helpful. Often, however, it just confirms your own assumptions.

Define point of view

In this phase, we focus on evaluating, interpreting, and weighting the findings we have gathered. The result eventually flows into the result synthesis (point of view). Methods such as context mapping (see page 133), storytelling (see page 129), or vision cone (see page 141) are used for the presentation of the findings. The point of view is usually formulated as a sentence (see "How might we..." question on page 125), for example, to make a statement on the basis of the findings according to the following scheme:

Name of the user/persona: (who) _____
needs: (what is needed) _____
in order to: (his/her need) _____
because: (insight/finding) _____

Ideate

Once we have defined the point of view, the ideate phase "Ideation" begins. Ideation is a step toward finding solutions for our problem. Usually, different forms of brainstorming (see page 151) and specific creativity techniques, for example, working with analogies (see page 171), are applied. Dot voting and similar tools (see page 159) help to select and cluster the ideas.

Prototype

The building of prototypes helps us to test our ideas or solutions, quickly and without risk, with our potential users. In particular, digital solutions can be prototyped with simple paper models or mock-ups. The materials are very easy: craft materials, paper, aluminum foil, cords, glue, and adhesive tape are often sufficient to make our ideas tangible and come alive. Various kinds of prototypes are presented in the Toolbox section under the heading "Prototyping" (see page 187 and what follows). The prototypes range from critical experience prototypes all the way to a final prototype. Ideation, building, and testing must each be seen as one sequence. They cover the so-called solution space.

Test

Testing should take place after each built prototype, even if individual functions, experiences, or forms were developed. When testing, the most important thing is that interaction with the potential user takes place and that we document the results. The testing sheet (see page 213) comes in handy here. In addition to a traditional test, it is possible to use digital solutions for testing, for example, online tools within the scope of A/B tests (see page 233). This way, prototypes or individual functionalities can be tested quickly and with a large number of users. The tests provide us with feedback that helps with the improvement of our prototypes. We should learn from these ideas and develop them further until we completely convince the users of the idea. Otherwise: discard or change.

Reflect

Reflection is a constant companion in design thinking since this is how we learn. Tools such as the "retrospective sailboat" (see page 243) or feedback rules based on "I like, I wish, I wonder" (see page 239), support the mindset.

The design thinking macro-cycle

In design thinking, we run through the micro-cycle several times. The aim is to create as many wild ideas and prototypes as possible in the divergent phase, which will help to sharpen our vision. In the convergent phase, our prototypes are more specific and have a higher resolution. The functional prototype helps us, for example, to review the problem/solution fit for individual elements before it matures into a final prototype. This phase is usually followed by the implementation and the market launch. These days, many products and services also need a well-thought-out business ecosystem that should be designed on the basis of a Minimum Viable Product (MVP) and Minimum Viable Ecosystem (MVE), respectively. *The Design Thinking Playbook* is the ideal supplement here. It goes one step further and shows how systems thinking and design thinking can be combined so as to apply this combined mindset to the design of business ecosystems.

In *The Design Thinking Toolbox*, the various kinds of prototypes, that is, the development stages from "first ideas" up to the finished prototype ("X is finished" prototype), are described again in detail in the "Prototyping" section (see page 187 and what follows), and are positioned, for example, in the "exploration map" tool (see page 195).

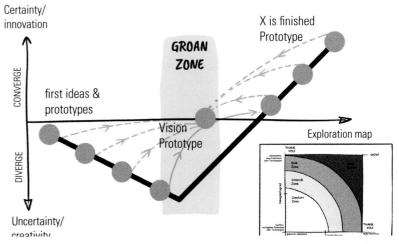

How do we apply design thinking?

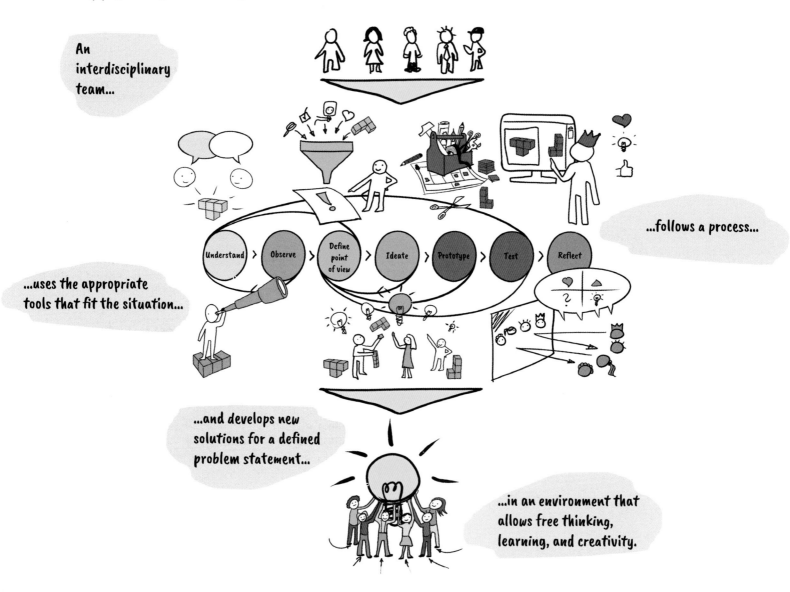

An interdisciplinary team...

...follows a process...

...uses the appropriate tools that fit the situation...

Understand > Observe > Define point of view > Ideate > Prototype > Test > Reflect

...and develops new solutions for a defined problem statement...

...in an environment that allows free thinking, learning, and creativity.

Who is Lilly?

As outlined in the introduction, we will not only describe the tools and methods but also demonstrate them in the context of the application. For this reason, we have taken a simple problem statement from Lilly. Lilly plans to establish a consultancy firm for digital transformation in Singapore.

Some of you already know Lilly. Besides Peter and Marc, Lilly is one of the three personas that accompanied us in *The Design Thinking Playbook* and presented various methods and tools. For those who do not yet know Lilly, here is a brief description:

Lilly, 28 years old, is currently working as a design thinking and start-up coach at Singapore University of Technology & Design (SUTD). The institute is one of the pioneers in design thinking and entrepreneurship for technology-oriented companies in the Asian region. Lilly organizes workshops and courses that combine design thinking and lean startup. She teaches design thinking herself and coaches student teams in their projects. In tandem with that, she is working on her doctoral thesis – in cooperation with the Massachusetts Institute of Technology – in the area of System Design Management on the subject of "Design of Powerful Business Ecosystems in a Digitized World."

To divide participants into groups, Lilly uses the HBDI (Herrmann Brain Dominance Instrument) model in her design thinking courses. Productive groups of four to five are formed this way, each one of which works on one problem statement. She has discovered that it is of vital importance to unite in a group all modes of thinking described in the brain model in order to achieve maximum success. Lilly's own preferred style of thinking is clearly located in the right half of the brain. She is experimental, creative, and likes to surround herself with other human beings.

Lilly studied Enterprise Management at the Zhejiang University School of Management. For her Master's degree, she spent a year at the École des Ponts ParisTech (d.school). As part of the ME310 program and in collaboration with Stanford University, she worked on a project there with THALES as a corporate partner, which is how she became familiar with design thinking. During that time, she visited Stanford three times. She liked the ME310 project so much that she decided to attend the University of Technology & Design in Singapore.

Through her work with different companies, Lilly sees potential for a consultancy firm for design thinking and digital transformation that she would like to found together with her friend Jonny.

What is the problem Lilly wants to solve?

As mentioned above, Lilly would like to set up a consulting firm that applies design thinking in order to support enterprises with digital transformation. What she is still looking for is the unique offer in comparison to traditional consultancies. Supporting her undertaking is a McKinsey study that had found that companies that apply design thinking have a 32% higher sales growth in a 5-year period than companies that have no skills in it. Since this is true for all industries, Lilly and Jonny don't focus on a specific segment for the time being. For them, it is more important to define a consultancy approach that also addresses cultural needs. Lilly has observed too many times how the European and American design thinking mindset failed in an Asian context. She wants to integrate local particularities in her design thinking approach: the attitude of an anthropologist, the acceptance of copying competitors, and the penchant for marketing services more quickly instead of observing the market for a long time.

> "How might we define a consultancy service for digital transformation in Asia, taking into account local cultural needs for large companies?"

Stakeholders? Target group? Business model? Scaling?

Customer experience chain? Value proposition?

What does Lilly's design team look like?

Lilly's team consists of Lilly's former students who had offered to help her with this design challenge. Over the next 14 weeks, the team wants to develop a solution. The participants certainly want to make use of the full range of methods and tools. Since Lilly is a big fan of warm-ups in order to create the right mood, she wants to use some of the most popular warm-ups for the different workshops, as needed. The comic strip of Lilly and her design team can be found on the last page of every tool and begins on page 49.

Ni hao! I am Lilly and....

... I look forward to the support of the student teams.

Quick start

- [ ] We know the expectations of the project sponsor.

- [ ] The design challenge and the problem have been sufficiently formulated.

- [ ] Design thinking is the right approach to finding a solution.

- [ ] Everybody understands the mindset in order to work iteratively and in an open and unbiased way.

- [ ] The team is interdisciplinary.

- [ ] We know the T-shaped profiles of the team members.

- [ ] There is a suitable workshop space, and we have the necessary materials.

- [ ] We have access to users, customers, and stakeholders.

- [ ] We can estimate how much time is needed for the design challenge.

- [ ] We have a rough agenda for the first design thinking workshop.

- [ ] We have a suitable and experienced workshop facilitator.

Where is the problem?

When we ask whether somebody has a good idea, we get a great number of solution proposals based on the assumption that we know the needs and problems. In design thinking, we take a step back and first explore the problem.

To gain awareness of the problem, it is helpful to formulate a problem statement, which later becomes a part of our design brief. The design brief (including problem statement) is at the same time the starting point for us as design thinkers to launch the creative process. This part is enormously important for the later course of a design challenge, because if we do not know the problem, the energy is quickly directed toward the wrong issues. This is why we have to make it clear to our teams that, in the beginning, we focus on the problem and do not search for solutions.

The exploration of problems usually takes place in the early phases of the design thinking process, namely in the "understand" and "observe" phases. Tools such as the interview for empathy (page 57) help us to get to the bottom of the causes. From actual practice, however, we know that we gather new insights on the known problem during every phase; often enough, completely new problems emerge.

A great invention or a parking problem?

You won't park this here, will you?

What makes a good problem statement?

A good problem statement must first and foremost be understood by everybody on the team. It should also be focused on human beings and their needs. Often, we tend to put other criteria in the foreground, for example, functions, sales, profits, or a specific technology. These characteristics can be a very valuable supplement to a problem statement, but they should not take center stage. A typical example is the design of a digital solution. Here it can actually make sense to provide the information that a particular problem is to be solved with the use of artificial intelligence, because it may become important for finding a solution later. The disadvantage is that the information restricts the number of possible ideas, and we might miss out on market opportunities because we were guided too much by one technology.

Two rules can be defined for the problem statement, which need to be heeded alongside the focus on people:

1) The problem statement **must be broad enough** to allow creative freedom to unfold.
2) The problem statement **must be narrow enough** for us to be able to solve it with the existing resources (team size, time, budget).

Detailed instructions on how to formulate a meaningful and actionable problem statement can be found in the "Understand" and "Define the point of view" sections. A typical problem statement that contains human beings and their needs is formulated:

How might we help [the user, customer] to achieve [a certain goal or need] applying [certain restrictions/principles]?

What does a design brief say?

As already noted, the description of the design challenge is an important instrument for the full and complete description of the task, including the problem. The formulation of the problem statement should be seen as a minimum requirement; a design brief allows for more details that may help in accelerating finding the solution. The disadvantage is that very narrow design briefs do not leave much leeway for creativity.

Thus the design brief is the translation of a problem into a structured task.

The design brief can contain the following elements and provide information on specific core questions:

▶ **Definition of design space and design scope:**
  – Which activities are to be supported and for whom?
  – Who are the users and key stakeholders?
  – What do we want to learn about the user?
▶ **Description of already existing approaches to solving the problem:**
  – What exists already, and how can elements of it help with our own solution?
  – What is missing in existing solutions?
▶ **Definition of the design principles:**
  – What are important leads for the team (e.g. at which point is more creativity demanded or that potential users should really try out a certain feature)?
  – Are there any limitations, and which core functions are absolutely indispensable?
  – Whom do we want to involve and at what point in the design process?
▶ **Definition of scenarios that are associated with the solution:**
  – What does a desirable future and vision look like?
  – Which scenarios are plausible and possible?
▶ **Definition of the next steps and milestones:**
  – By when should a solution have been worked out?
  – Are there steering committee meetings from which we can get valuable feedback?
▶ **Information on potential implementation challenges:**
  – Who must be involved at an early stage?
  – What is the culture like for dealing with radical solution proposals, and how great is the willingness to take risks?
  – Are there conditions in terms of the budget or time frame? Any restrictions?

Well, now, I don't want this shape and not in these colors. Instead, I want something like this here, only different.

When the design brief is created by clients with little expertise in design thinking, it makes sense to turn its creation also into a little design thinking project. In this case, we develop the problem statement together with the client. In this way, it is ensured that we obtain different opinions – on a multi-disciplinary basis – on the problem and work on real problems in the end, not on mere symptoms.

What makes a good design thinking workshop?

One crucial aspect in design thinking is the collaboration on the team. Therefore it is important to gather the participants in one place. Only in this way can solid understanding be created about a problem statement, ideas, and potential solutions. In addition, it enables us to make optimal use of the skills and abilities (see the "drippy T" model, page 31) of each and every team member, and exploit the positive team dynamics for our work.

We can safely set our concerns aside.

From our experience, something good comes out of most workshops, and if not, the workshop was usually poorly moderated. Perhaps the design thinking facilitator does not succeed in instructing the groups in a targeted way, for instance, or his methodological expertise leaves much to be desired.

The facilitator is crucial because he usually chooses the methods and tools and is responsible for the time boxing. He is also responsible for the planning. At the same time, he must possess enough flexibility to be responsive to the wishes and needs of the group. Also, he must be willing to implement ad-hoc changes in the sequence.

A good facilitator knows the goals of each work step, has experience regarding the time frame in which they can be attained, and generates a consistently creative atmosphere. In addition, a facilitator should be neutral, that is, it is his task to moderate, not to make active contributions in terms of content.

Preparation of a design thinking workshop

Whether we like it or not, the organization of a workshop requires planning. At the beginning, the goals and the sequence of the workshop should be defined, the participants invited, and the material organized.

As a benchmark, we can assume that the preparation takes as much time as the implementation of the workshop itself.

Participants in a design thinking workshop

We consider the following:

- Who are the participants?
- Do the participants know one another?
- How familiar are they with design thinking and the topic?
- What are their expectations? Backgrounds? Fears?

Team size and skills

A good design team consists of people with different backgrounds and varying experience. The experience and knowledge a member brings with him or her can be illustrated by the "T-shape" or the "drippy T." The horizontal axis visualizes our general experience and breadth of knowledge, while the vertical axis provides information on our expert knowledge, that is, the depth of knowledge in specific disciplines. We are seeing more and more frequently that the "T-shaped profile" is expanded to a "drippy T." In this way, other disciplines, departments, and subject fields of a team member may be highlighted.

The "drippy T" model

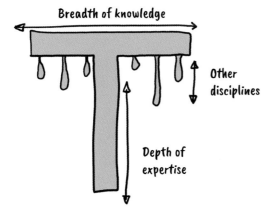

Breadth of knowledge

Other disciplines

Depth of expertise

The team size varies and is dependent on the design challenge and the available resources. It should have three to seven members. In our experience, five people are ideal. With team sizes over 10 people, coordination becomes more complex and effectiveness dwindles.

If more people want to be involved, several teams should work concurrently applying the team-of-teams technique. In our experience, it may be valuable for complicated and complex problems (so-called wicked problems) to involve an "extended team" of experts who are not part of the core team.

Prepare the room for the design thinking workshop

On the day of the workshop, we recommend you be there early in order to prepare the room. It is important that there be enough free space. If we use a projector or other technology, it is advisable to test the devices before the workshop begins. Since we need plenty of space to work, every bit of surface is used; the walls, for example, which can be turned into an excellent work surface by sticking large sheets of paper on them. Depending on the task and team size, a table island should be provided for each group.

Materials needed

Material is important for the building of prototypes and the success of the workshop (see also Materials for prototyping, page 33).

Agenda and time management

It is best to provide participants with a rough agenda so that they know where the workshop will take place, what time the workshop starts, and when breaks are scheduled. It is often underestimated how exhausting "creative work" is. It is recommended to plan sufficiently long breaks. If you are an inexperienced facilitator, it also makes sense to draw up a more detailed plan for orientation. We have good experience with warm-ups that create the right mood on the team at the beginning, after lunch, or when needed. Many facilitators make use of music, played quietly in the background, for example, during brainstorming sessions or when the teams build prototypes.

Welcome!

Agenda

Feedback on the workshop

We learn only if we regularly reflect upon what has happened so far; a round of feedback, for example, with "I like, I wish, I wonder" (see page 239) or a "mood flasher" (for example, with the question "What is going through my head right now?"), are great ways to learn and develop as a team. This retrospective can take place at two levels: 1) facilitation and team dynamics; 2) contents, goals, and problem solution.

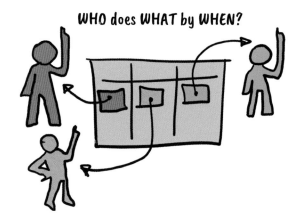

WHO does WHAT by WHEN?

Wrap-up/conclusion

The end of a workshop is just as influential as the beginning. Often the final impressions are the ones that stick with participants. An abrupt end triggers dissatisfaction, and the goal must be to ensure that people take a positive mood back with them.

Make sure that clear next steps and tasks are defined and allocated at the end.

The conclusion must be planned in just as meticulous detail as the entry point.

For most projects, countless meetings will take place in the follow-up and they are best if participants look forward to the next time and can hardly wait to continue work on their prototype or start with the implementation of their projects.

Documentation and logging

The fastest documentation of results is achieved with photos of flip charts, personas, walls with Post-its, feedback capture grids (see page 217), and completed prototypes. If extensive logging is required or desired for the design challenge, it may be useful to think about the structure and the sequence in which the results are to be presented (e.g. action items or prioritized ideas) even before the start of the workshop. Furthermore, we recommend always sending a log showing the results in a timely manner, if possible on the same day.

Photo log

Cleanup

At the end of a workshop day, we usually have one last unpleasant task: The room must be cleaned up. Enough time must be scheduled for this task, and the only tip we can give here is: It's done more quickly if everybody lends a hand. So it's best to motivate each group to take care of their work materials and results themselves. It's perfectly all right to take home good mock-ups and unusual prototypes as trophies.

Tips for the facilitator:
- Be open to dynamics and unexpected situations
- Be sensitive to the mood of the participants
- Laughter is important, especially about yourself
- Steer discussions actively in order to offer a "parking lot for ideas"
- Clear instructions and time lines for the participants
- Willingness to help with the performance of tasks
- Motivate participants to pursue the current goal, for example, substantial ideas or increased depth of findings

What materials are needed?

"Think with your hands" and "showing things is better than just talking about them" are two crucial components of design thinking. We achieve both by transforming ideas into physical prototypes. For this, we need material to be able to build simple things quickly. In addition, templates such as a lean canvas can be printed on A4 paper and used as a work surface.

Material for prototypes

It is important to have some material at hand. It doesn't have to be of high quality. Simple materials, such as aluminum foil, pipe cleaners, adhesive tape, cardboard, strings, and some Styrofoam, are totally sufficient.

Material for the groups and for moderation

We also recommend enough flip chart paper and good pens (e.g. Sharpies), paper (A4 and A3), and Post-its (in various colors and sizes). It is advisable to prepare small workshop moderation boxes for each group, so that every group is supplied with a basic set of glue pens, scissors, adhesive points, adhesive tapes, Post-its, and pens.

Technical equipment

Alongside a functioning projector, speakers, and camera, we definitely recommend bringing along a multiple sockets, extension cords, and adapters to increase flexibility in using the space.

Of course, we cannot forget water, food, coffee, tea, and arrangements for lunch for our participants.

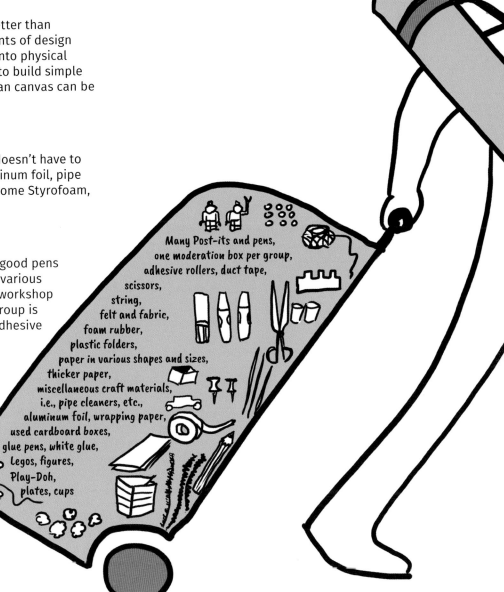

Many Post-its and pens,
one moderation box per group,
adhesive rollers, duct tape,
scissors,
string,
felt and fabric,
foam rubber,
plastic folders,
paper in various shapes and sizes,
thicker paper,
miscellaneous craft materials,
i.e., pipe cleaners, etc.,
aluminum foil, wrapping paper,
used cardboard boxes,
glue pens, white glue,
Legos, figures,
Play-Doh,
plates, cups

The workshop canvas and example agenda for a design thinking workshop

An excellent way to prepare yourself is to work with a workshop canvas. In this way, you keep an eye on the most important elements and are able to create a 3-day workshop, for instance.

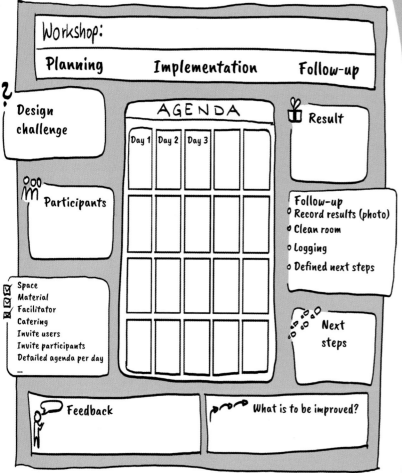

Workshop:

| Planning | Implementation | Follow-up |

Design challenge

Participants

- Space
- Material
- Facilitator
- Catering
- Invite users
- Invite participants
- Detailed agenda per day
- ...

AGENDA

| Day 1 | Day 2 | Day 3 | | |

Result

Follow-up
- Record results (photo)
- Clean room
- Logging
- Defined next steps

Next steps

Feedback

What is to be improved?

Day 1:
Kick-off & warm-up
- Introduction of the team and of the skills on the basis of T-shaped profiles
- Presentation of the design thinking mindset

Scoping
- Presentation of the design challenge
- Definition of the problem statement

Brain dump
- Brainstorming

Research
- Exploration of existing solutions; observe and understand users

Synthesis
- Exchange of observations and storytelling
- Point of view

Day 2:
Persona
- Create a persona based on observations and the point of view (POV)

Ideate
- Different types of brainstorming
- Cluster and connect ideas
- Prioritize ideas

Build and test prototypes
- Building and testing of critical experience prototypes
- Building of various prototypes
- Testing of prototypes
- Improving of prototypes

Day 3:
Build and test prototypes
- Creation of final prototype

Validation
- Testing of prototype, lean canvas, and story

Presentation
- Presentation of the solution

Wrap-up
- Next steps
- Reflection/feedback
- Clean up and say goodbye

Tool for download

AGENDA CANVAS

1 2 3

www.dt-toolbook.com/agenda-en

What should a creative space offer?

The space in which we unfold creatively has an impact on the team dynamics, the results, and on the joy in working. We have implemented design thinking workshops in a wide variety of locations and came to the conclusion that design thinking works best in a place where people feel comfortable.

A good space should stimulate, inspire creativity, be right for reflection, promote collaboration, and above all be right for the purpose. The furnishings are basically irrelevant as long as the spatial concept leaves us enough flexibility to change things so that we can work and practice design thinking. A good space allows working in various positions (e.g. sitting, standing).

Ideally, the work is done standing up. It helps get the participants actively involved and do more than just consume information. When we sit, we quickly slip into a "conference" mode – cozily drinking coffee and being lulled by endless sequences of PowerPoint slides. That is relaxing but of little help when it comes to shaping the next big market opportunity.

We also had good experience with switching locations and gathering in rooms that were not associated with memories of day-to-day business, thus impeding the creative work. If this was not possible, we tried to make the room look different.

In general, flexible furniture helps in any kind of room, since it can be adapted quickly to the requirements of the group or individual work situations. It should be large enough to allow interaction, thus at least 15 square meters for a group of four participants.

Often, there are no high tables. They can be easily created by placing a table on four chairs. Test stability before use, but normally it works amazingly well. In addition, it immediately gives the desirable impression of "being different."

All sorts of whiteboards and flip charts are welcome in order to capture and visualize work results. Another thing that has proven its value is covering large areas of the wall with paper so that participants can write or stick posters, photos, and flip charts on them. It goes without saying that in a good creativity space, the prototyping material (e.g. pens, Post-its, craft utensils) is always within reach.

Finally, as mentioned above, we make sure that enough water, coffee, juice, as well as fruit, chocolate, and cookies are provided for a little refreshment in between. A good workshop also goes through the stomach, and creative work makes you hungry.

The Toolbox

The Design Thinking Toolbox begins with announced warm-ups before the experts present various tools and methods. For better orientation, the tools follow the phases in the design thinking process in which they are most frequently applied. This is why we begin with techniques that help us have a better understanding of the problem and learn more about a potential user. This is done in the "understand" and "observe" phases. The resulting synthesis is based on these findings. We show strategies that help us to formulate a point of view. In the solution space, it's all about generating ideas, building first prototypes, and testing them. There are various resources that successfully guide us through this phase of design thinking. Finally, methods for reflection are presented in the Toolbox.

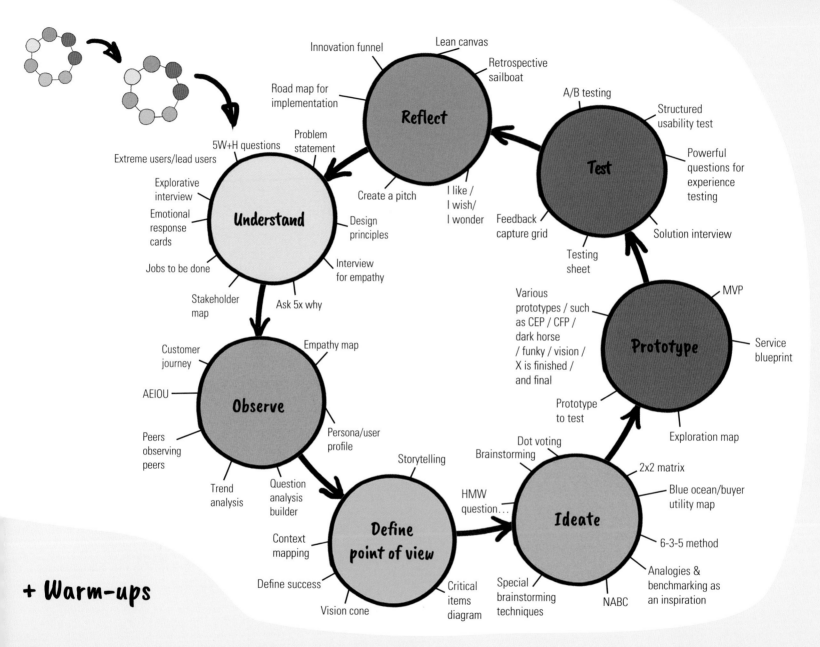

Reflect
- Innovation funnel
- Lean canvas
- Retrospective sailboat
- Road map for implementation
- Problem statement
- Create a pitch
- I like / I wish / I wonder
- Design principles

Understand
- 5W+H questions
- Extreme users/lead users
- Explorative interview
- Emotional response cards
- Jobs to be done
- Stakeholder map
- Interview for empathy
- Ask 5x why

Test
- A/B testing
- Structured usability test
- Powerful questions for experience testing
- Solution interview
- Feedback capture grid
- Testing sheet

Observe
- Customer journey
- Empathy map
- AEIOU
- Peers observing peers
- Persona/user profile
- Trend analysis
- Question analysis builder

Prototype
- MVP
- Service blueprint
- Various prototypes / such as CEP / CFP / dark horse / funky / vision / X is finished / and final
- Prototype to test
- Exploration map

Define point of view
- Storytelling
- Context mapping
- Define success
- Vision cone
- Critical items diagram

Ideate
- Dot voting
- Brainstorming
- 2x2 matrix
- Blue ocean/buyer utility map
- 6-3-5 method
- Analogies & benchmarking as an inspiration
- NABC
- Special brainstorming techniques
- HMW question...

+ Warm-ups

Warm-ups that fit the setting!

Popular warm-ups

In sports, warm-ups are used to heighten the performance of muscles. For musicians, warming up means preparing the voice for singing. In motor racing, warm-ups help to fine-tune technical details. In design thinking, we use warm-ups not only at the beginning of the workshop but also after a break or when we realize that the group is no longer working efficiently. This can take place in any phase of the collaboration and have different goals. Warm-ups can stimulate creativity, boost group dynamics, bring about relaxation, or be used as an icebreaker to get to know one another.

Warm-ups promote collaboration and strengthen a curious attitude. Well-chosen warm-ups thus support the design thinking process, serve as an energizer, and improve problem solving. But they can also have the opposite effect. If the context doesn't fit or the culture of the organization is not taken into consideration, an exercise can end up fostering nervousness and irritation. So here is our advice: If you want to perform a warm-up, make sure you have chosen it very carefully.

On the following pages, we offer warm-up suggestions.

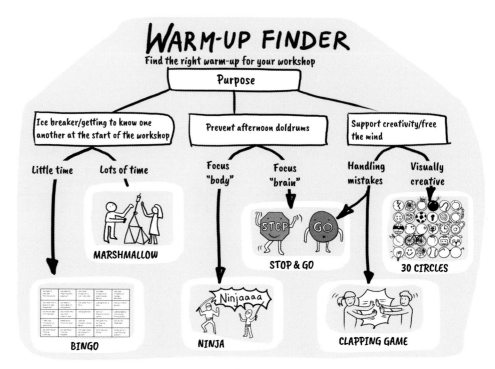

WARM-UP FINDER
Find the right warm-up for your workshop

Purpose
- Ice breaker/getting to know one another at the start of the workshop
  - Little time → BINGO
  - Lots of time → MARSHMALLOW
- Prevent afternoon doldrums
  - Focus "body" → NINJA
  - Focus "brain" → STOP & GO
- Support creativity/free the mind
  - Handling mistakes → CLAPPING GAME
  - Visually creative → 30 CIRCLES

Why do we do warm-ups?

- Create a positive group atmosphere
- Give workshop participants the chance to get to know one another
- Remove social barriers
- Reduce pressure to succeed
- Activate and release positive energy
- Distract the group a little bit so concentration is improved afterward
- Prepare the team for a certain mindset or way of working
- Have fun and share a laugh

Our tip:

If you want to do a warm-up, make sure you have chosen it very carefully! Adapt the warm-up to the participants.

Clapping game

I would like...

to generate a positive mood.

Learning objective:

Handling mistakes

1.

Each participant chooses a partner.

2.

Together they count up to "three," repeating it with increasing speed.

3.

In order to increase the complexity somewhat, the number "two" is replaced by a clap. Then you get a numberclap rhythm.

4.

In the next step, the number "one" is replaced by a finger click. The numberclap rhythm is supplemented with a finger click, and there will be lots of laughing participants.

One, two, three!

One, clap, three

Click, clap, three!

Group size	Typical duration	Materials needed
≥2	5 Min.	• No materials are necessary

Variations:

In order to put stronger emphasis on the acceptance of mistakes, a reflection on one's own mistakes and the mistakes of other players can be integrated. A cheer after every wrong clap, click, or count intensifies the feeling.

Bingo

I would like...

for the participants to get to know one another better in an entertaining and fast way.

Has read 3 English novels	Has eaten pizza prosciutto 3 times	Has been to the United States at least 3 times	Has visited at least 3 other countries	Has drunk at least 3 Red Bulls
Has been to Australia or New Zealand	Has seen 3 James Bond movies in the movie theater	Has been to Paris	Favorite color is blue	Has read Harry Potter
Speaks three or more languages	Has a parent from another country	Has siblings	Can play a musical instrument	Loves the Beatles more than the Rolling Stones
Wears sneakers rather than leather shoes	Likes to vacation at the sea	Loves hiking and the mountains	Has used car sharing	Joined the Boy Scouts
Has some design thinking experience	Owns the Design Thinking Playbook	Has bought something at Kickstarter	Knows the lean canvas	Would like to work in a start-up

1.

First, a pen and a prepared bingo card are distributed to each participant.

2.

After the start signal, the search for participants who fit in one of the categories (can answer a question with "Yes") begins.

3.

There are only two rules:

1) Each person is allowed to be used only once in order to get into a conversation with as many people as possible.
2) First the field must be offered, only then is the discussion allowed to start.

Hi, how are you?

I bet your favorite color is blue!

Yes, that's right!

BINGO !

4.

The participant who is first to write a name in each field shouts "Bingo!," and the game is over. If nobody is able to fill in the card completely, the game ends after the specified time, and the participant with the highest number of squares filled wins.

5.

A final reflection of the statements rounds out the warm-up.

Group size

 ≥16

Typical duration

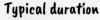 7-15 min.

Materials needed

- Pen
- One bingo card per participant

Variations:

Depending on the attitude of the workshop, the cards can be prepared for certain topics and contain specific questions, for example: has a whiteboard in his office, has already worked with design thinking. Particularly unusual questions can also be used: keeps to a vegan diet; goes skydiving regularly, etc. Depending on the group size and the time frame, the goal of the game can be varied. The aim is to fill one row (horizontal, vertical, or diagonal) and shout "Bingo!"

Stop & go

I would like...

to break through or overcome social obstacles, heighten concentration, and have fun.

Learning objective:

Handling mistakes

Work instruction

- Everybody is moving freely in the room.
- By calling "stop" or "go," the moderator gives instructions to stand still or keep walking.
- In order to heighten concentration, the meaning of the terms is switched: You keep walking at "stop" and stand still at "go."
- In the next step, two more actions are added: "name" (stating one's name) and "clap" (clapping your hands).
- The meaning of these two terms is also switched.
- "Jump" and "dance" are added as two more commands.
- And again the meaning of these terms is swapped.
- If everything is done right, "name, name, name" triggers a round of applause at the end.

Group size	Typical duration	Materials needed
>6	8 min.	• No materials are necessary

Variations

- The moderator can be replaced by participants, and the commands can be issued from the group. Depending on the context and the situation, the individual measures can be adapted; jumping can be replaced by sitting down, and clapping by high fives or something similar.
- Other words can be used; e.g. Cola = turn right, Fanta = turn left, Sprite = jump, Red Bull = ...
- Anyone who makes a mistake cheers and claps their hands.

30 Circles

I would like...

to encourage the participants to act creatively.

Learning objective:

Create confidence in one's own creativity; remove the "white sheet blockade" and direct the focus on the message, not on the beauty of the sketch.

Work instruction

- Supply each participant with a pen and sheet of paper on which circles are drawn.
- Ask the participants to transform as many circles as possible into recognizable products.
- With "Go!," the set time period begins, and the participants start to color in the circles.
- After 2 minutes, the time is stopped.
- Compare the results. Pay attention not only to the number (how many circles were colored in) but also to the individuality of the results (e.g., a volleyball, a football, and a basketball are more similar to one another than a clock, a ring, and an eye). Has somebody "broken the rules" and connected two or more rings to become one product?

Group size	Typical duration	Materials needed
>3	5-10 min.	• Pen • Paper

Variations

- State a word, for example, pot lid. Challenge the participants to write down as many alternative uses for the item as possible, for example, toboggan, frisbee, wheel cover, drums.

Ninja

I would like...

to distract the participants so they can concentrate again later.

Learning objective:

This warm-up requires quick thinking and body control and is lots of fun.

1.
Divide participants into small groups and tell them to stand in a close circle (hands can touch the shoulders of their neighbors).

2.
One person shouts "Ninjaaa!" (lengthening the word makes for a greater effect), and everybody jumps back and freezes in a Ninja pose of his or her choice.

3.
A previously appointed member of the group begins to attempt hitting another person's hand with only one movement and one step. Anyone touched must freeze in this position! The person who is attacked is allowed to pull his or her hand away.

4.
When your hand is hit, you are "out" and must leave the game.

5.
As soon as the move is completed, the next player in a clockwise direction starts to move, based on the original sequence in the circle. The game continues until only one person is left.

Group size	Typical duration	Materials needed
5-6	10 min.	• Lots of space

Marshmallow challenge

I would like...

to encourage the participants to translate ideas into practice quickly and promote teamwork.

Learning objective:

To promote thinking with your hands and recognize that iterations and tests are important.

1.

The challenge is to build, as a group, a free-standing sculpture that is as high as possible, with the marshmallow on top.

2.

Each group gets a specified range of building materials.

3.

The marshmallow is the measuring point, so it must be placed at the very top of the structure.

4.

The structure is only allowed to be connected to the floor or the table surface. It is not allowed to be fastened to the ceiling.

5.

The sculpture must be standing free at the latest when the specified building time has expired, and it must not collapse in less than 10 seconds.

6.

Each group has 15–20 minutes to complete their edifice. If a group finishes earlier, the moderator can be summoned at any time to determine the height.

Group size

Groups of 5

Typical duration

20 min.

Materials needed

- 1 marshmallow
- 20 spaghetti
- 1 m adhesive tape
- 1 m cord

Tip:

The reflection afterward is important. Talk about action prejudices, "Fail early, fail often!," the number of iterations, tests, and the teamwork. Instructions and videos for this are available online.

Phase: Understand

A good understanding of the problem is the be-all and end-all in design thinking. In the "understand" phase, we want to make ourselves familiar with the problem. In order to substantiate the design challenge, we formulate a question, also referred to as the "problem statement." Through various techniques and tools, the problem statement can be broadened or narrowed down. Tools such as the 5W+H questions or Ask 5x why are quite helpful here. The aim is to learn as much as possible about the needs of a potential user. These findings in turn help us to sharpen the problem statement iteratively and come to a common understanding of the problem on the team.

Problem statement

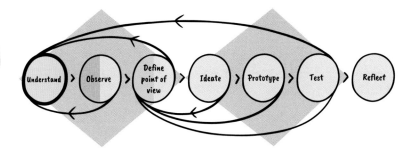

I would like...

to define the key problem statement coherently and capture it in a simple sentence.

What you can do with the tool:

- Develop common understanding of a problem with the clients and on the team.
- Formulate the collected findings from the problem analysis in a design challenge.
- Outline the direction and the framework for ideation.
- Create a basis for the formulation of targeted "How might we..." questions (HMW questions).
- Develop a reference value for the subsequent measurement of success.

More information on the tool

- In design thinking, we always start with the problem, never with a solution.
- A design challenge starts with the understanding of the problem statement.
- Before we begin to solve a problem, we must first understand it correctly.
- The problem statement is a key tool for consolidating and capturing the analysis results.
- A problem statement (see also "point of view") marks the starting point and the end of the relevant problem space and the transition to the "ideation" phase.

What tools can be used as an alternative?

- Design brief (see page 29)
- Design principles (see page 53)

Which methods support the creation of a problem statement?

- Context mapping helps to recognize contexts and patterns in the collected information (see page 133).
- Cause-effect diagrams help to differentiate the causes and the impact of problems.
- "How might we..." questions help to transfer the resulting problem definition into design opportunities (see page 125).
- 5W+H questions (see page 71)

How much time and what materials do we need?

Group size

- Ideally, in a group of 3-5 from the design team
- Optionally, 1-2 stakeholders or the client (if available)

3–5

Typical duration

- Formulating normally requires some time as well as blood, sweat, and tears.
- Short cycles of at least half an hour are useful.

30—40 min.

Materials needed

- Pens and Post-its
- Several sheets of A4 paper in portrait and A3 paper in landscape
- The structure of the question can be given as a fill-in-the-blank text

Procedure: Problem statement

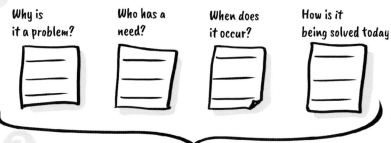

How the tool is applied...

- Sketch the structural elements yourself on the sheets of paper or use the template.
- **Step 1:** The following questions (problem/actor/context) help with the formulation of the problem statement:
  - ✓ What is the problem? Why is it a problem?
  - ✓ Who has the problem? Who has a need?
  - ✓ When and where does the problem occur?
  - ✓ How is it solved today?
- Write down the questions on several A4 sheets (portrait) and leave enough space for answers underneath.
- Use different colors for the questions and answers and write legibly and as large as possible.
- Produce at least 10 of such problem definitions.
- **Step 2:** Attach these papers to the wall and put an A3 sheet in landscape layout underneath them. Then consolidate the problem definitions or select the most appropriate, for example, through dot voting (see page 159).
- **Step 3:** Start transferring the individual problem definitions systematically into an overarching problem, for example, in the form: "How might we redesign... [what?] ...[for whom?] ...so that...[his need]...is satisfied?"

This is the favorite tool of Stefano Vannotti

Position:
Director of Studies, MAS Strategic Design, at the Zurich University of the Arts (ZHdK)

"The felicitous synthesis of all the findings from the problem analysis is the most decisive moment in every project. Without knowing the key challenge, no problem can be solved successfully."

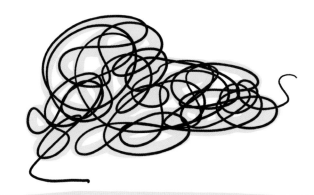

Why is it his favorite tool?

Outlining the specific design challenge clearly and comprehensibly is a prerequisite for a targeted generation of ideas. In many projects, the problem situation must first be correctly understood. The method of the problem statement can help define the right point of view and appropriate framework for the development of innovative solutions. In my opinion, here lies the true strength of good design thinking: creating a well-thought-out foundation for the successful development of creativity.

Expert tips:

Reframe the problem
- It goes without saying that a well-formulated definition does not solve the problem. Nonetheless, the clear formulation of a problem provides a solid foundation for the later phases. Reframing sometimes requires a lot of persuasion with respect to the project sponsor, but it is certainly helpful for a better understanding. Many projects deal with challenging problem statements that must be considered from more than one perspective. In certain cases, it makes sense to formulate several problem statements from different user perspectives.

Get it right
- Often, problems, causes, and effects get all muddled together. Try to create structural clarity.
- Closely linked with the correct definition of the problem is an early vision of a desirable result. In this context, it is important to realize that the problem and the solution mutually influence and change each other over the course of a project.
- Problem statements are helpful to define the basic challenge precisely and to the point. For the following steps in the projects, appropriate design opportunities should be derived in the form of HMW questions, however.

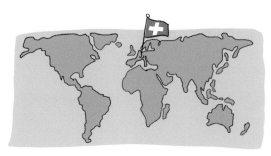

Country:
Switzerland

Affiliation:
Zurich University of the Arts (ZHdK)

Checked by: **Martin Steinert**

Company/position: Norwegian University of Science and Technology (NTNU), Professor of Engineering Design and Innovation

Description of the use case

- Lilly describes the problem. With their initial research, the teams supplement the problem. They analyze it by raising different W+H questions.
- Then the various problems are stated, and a specific actor as well as the context are described. These elements are integrated in a jointly formulated problem statement in reverse order.
- The discussion helps to develop a common language and get an understanding for the target group.

Key learnings

- The development of a clear and concise problem definition frequently requires multiple rounds.
- The joy in precise formulation and choice of words is a crucial factor here.
- Create variants and discuss them in the group.

Tool for download

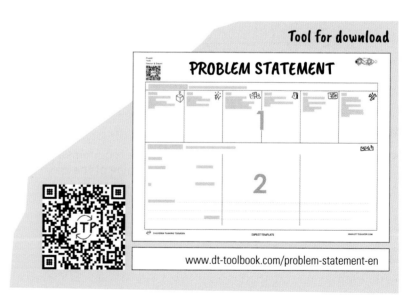

www.dt-toolbook.com/problem-statement-en

Design principles

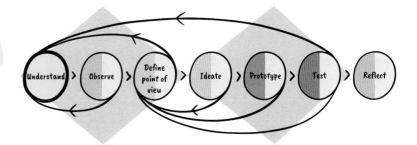

I would like...

to define guidelines that constitute the framework for the team during a design thinking project.

What you can do with the tool:

- Put a clear focus on a specific mindset or the requirements for the product/service as early as at the beginning of the project.
- Provide the team with a uniform understanding of the task so that everybody is on the same level.
- Provide guidance so that decisions of the design team can be made faster.
- Define general characteristics that should be treated with a higher priority.
- Develop a guideline that ensures that future design challenges are created on the same overarching principles.

More information on the tool

- Across the entire design thinking cycle, design teams get into situations in which decisions must be made. At these critical points, design principles can support the team.
- Design principles range from broad and overarching concepts to project-specific requirements that support the decision on the design direction in each case.
- In addition, the most important features of a product can be communicated to other interest groups by means of design principles.
- Design principles are important even beyond the design thinking cycle since they give the teams in follow-up projects a better understanding of what the guiding ideas were in the design.
- In addition, design principles are like a knowledge base for teams since the principles are based on experiences with products, services, and functions.

What tools can be used as an alternative?

- Define success (see page 137)

Which tools support working with this tool?

- Stakeholder map (see page 83)
- List of project sponsors or other relevant interest groups, for example, decision makers and the steering committee
- Mission and vision of the organization that assigned the task
- Dot voting (see page 159)

How much time and what materials do we need?

Group size

5–12

- Depending on the design challenge, between 5 and 12 participants, consisting of the design team+selected stakeholders, and the client.
- Usually led by the facilitator or project manager.

Typical duration

90–180 min.

- The design principles constitute an important basis for the project.
- It can take up to several hours to come up with a definition. A clear definition helps the team to get quick support should uncertainties crop up over the course of a project.

Materials needed

- Whiteboard, pens, Post-its,
- Colored dots for the vote (dot voting)
- History and documentation of other design challenges and experiences with design principles

Procedure: Design principles

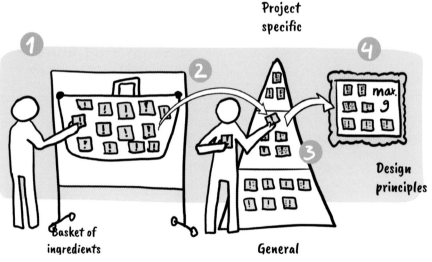

Project specific

Design principles

Basket of ingredients

General

How the tool is applied...

Invite the core team and the relevant stakeholders for a whiteboard session with the aim of defining the design principles for the task.

- **Step 1:** Sketch a "basket" and a pyramid on the whiteboard. Then invite all participants to write design principles on Post-its and place them on the "basket." Whenever a team member puts a principle on the "basket," he or she is requested to explain why it is a design principle.
- **Step 2:** As soon as the "basket" is full, sort the design principles on the pyramid, for example, by dividing them into three groups. The sorting is carried out according to the rule: the higher up on the pyramid, the more project-specific the principle is. General design principles are located at the bottom of the pyramid.
- **Step 3:** Once the assignment of the design principles is completed, a vote can be carried out (e.g. with glue dots). The aim is to reduce the design principles to a maximum of three per section, that is, a maximum of nine per pyramid.
- **Step 4:** It's best to put the selected and adopted design principles in a place where the team is often confronted with them and to which it has quick access.

- Inspirations for design principles can be found on websites such as: www.designprinciplesftw.com.

This is the favorite tool of Slavo Tuleja

Position:
Innovation Lead, ŠKODA AUTO DigiLab

"For me, design thinking is a great set of principles to follow, but ultimately we are all judged on execution. Think project launch, number of customers acquired, units sold, and lives changed."

Why is it his favorite tool?

When applying design thinking, I often see that people are unable to cope with creative freedom: Team members sit there with an empty piece of paper in front of them that they can use as they wish but don't know what to do with it. Design principles is my favorite tool because it can be used in various phases of the development of services and products. I use them mainly on teams with little design thinking experience. Design principles act as guard rails across the entire design cycle; they help, for instance, in coming to a decision.

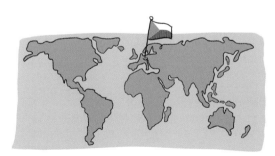

Country:
Czech Republic

Affiliation:
ŠKODA AUTO
DigiLab

Checked by: Tobias Lüpke

Company/Position: Ernst & Young | Director International Tax, Markets & BD

Expert tips:

Start with why
- Question: Why are we doing this project? Why now? Why in this scope?
- We let ourselves be inspired. Others have already taken this path or a similar one and developed design principles for various applications.
- We make sure that this activity is carried out with the entire core team and that everybody understands why it is important to define the design principles at the beginning of the project. This also applies to our stakeholders when we involve them in the definition of the design principles, and we want to maintain a good relationship with them.

Show it boldly
- We put the design principles in a place, for example, as a huge poster, where they can be seen by all team members.
- Design principles can also help us to communicate the most important characteristics of a solution.
- In addition, they are a good basis for the definition of a vision and help with the successful implementation of future projects.

Show, don't tell
- Some stakeholders (e.g. decision makers) will be happy to see the design principles in action and not only perceive empty words
- In addition, the principles help us to defend our solutions that we developed as a team during the project.
- When creating design principles, we should not be too obsessed with details, though, because in the end it is more important to do something rather than just talk about it.

55

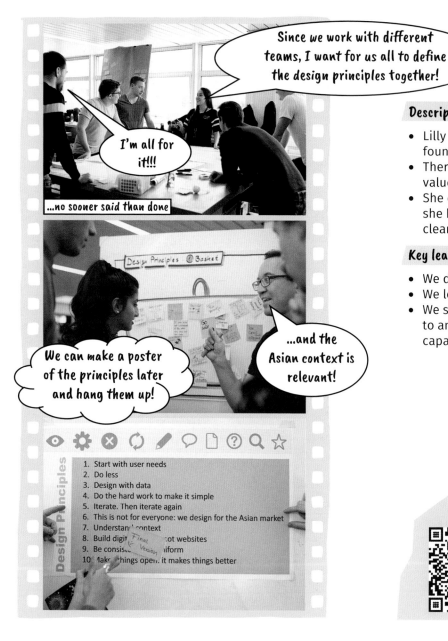

Description of use case

- Lilly has a total of 5 teams with 4 to 5 members each. She has found that the ideas of the individual groups differ greatly.
- Therefore she wants to define the key design principles and values in the project.
- She ends up with a list of 10 defined design principles, which she hangs up on a poster in the design studio where they are clearly visible.

Key learnings

- We develop the principles with the core team.
- We let ourselves be inspired by existing design principles.
- We see design principles as "instructions for use" in order to answer our questions more quickly as a team and remain capable of acting when making decisions.

Tool for download

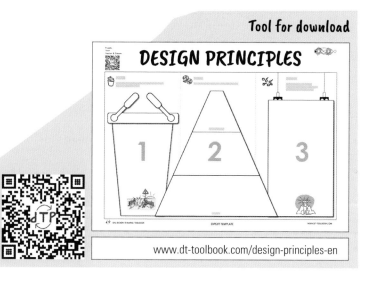

www.dt-toolbook.com/design-principles-en

56

Interview for empathy

Including variation as an in-depth interview with a question map and a journey map

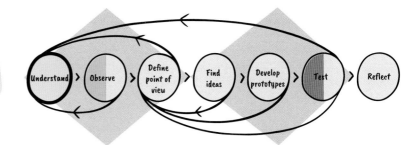

I would like...

to consider the problem from the point of view of the user and build empathy with a user.

What you can do with the tool:

- Build up a solid understanding of the user's needs, emotions, motivations, and ways of thinking.
- Gain insights that would have remained hidden in a superficial consideration (e.g. a user's frustration and deeper motives).
- Find out in the context of the usage which task flow the user prefers and what mental model he bases it on.
- Validate information already obtained and gain new insights.
- Establish a solid basis for discussions with the design thinking team.

More information on the tool

- Interview for empathy aims at looking at the world from the point of view of a user.
- The tool is normally used at an early stage in the design thinking cycle in order to understand the context in which the user acts. Only then can the development of a solution begin.
- The tool also helps to overcome existing patterns of thought. Especially if, previously, a more analytical and less human being-centered approach had been applied to problem solving.

What tools can be used as an alternative?

- Explorative interviews (see page 63)
- Peers observing peers (see page 115)

Which tools support working with this tool?

Before and during the interview:
- 5W+H questions (see page 71) or Ask 5x why (see page 67) for the clarification of ambiguities that can be addressed in a dialogue

After the interview:

- Field notes, video and photo documentation, sketch and empathy map (see page 93) to summarize, document, and pass on the findings
- Role-playing and shadowing for the validation of findings
- Storytelling to share the empathy gained with the rest of the design team (see page 129)

How much time and what materials do we need?

Group size

1-2

- Ideally, in a group of 2
- Always best with two people: One conducts the interview, and the second person takes notes on emotions and body language.

Typical duration

30–60 min.

- Together with the explanation of the problem and the confrontation with the problem, the interview usually lasts 30 to 60 minutes.
- Usually, the interviewees tell their true history and give important insights in the end, when the actual interview is over.

Materials needed

- Notepad or template and pen
- Camera or smartphone for the documentation with video or photos (ask the interviewee's permission beforehand)

Template: Interview for empathy

Existing assumptions about the persona and the problem:		
How might we build a relationship with the interviewee in order to give him/her such a good feeling that he/she shares personal stories in the context of the problem?	Key questions for the exploration of stories:	Keywords and topics in connection with the emotions shown:
Outline of the story:		

How the tool is applied...

- Start by introducing yourselves and then explaining the problem you are trying to solve via the interview.
- Emphasize to them that the interview is not about finding a solution but, rather, to learn something about their motives.
- Successful "interviews for empathy" succeed in building a relationship with the interviewee. It's most effective when the interviewee feels comfortable and is, therefore, willing to share his story with the design team in the context of the problem.
- If you succeed in having the interviewee tell his story, interrupt him as little as possible and, in general, be cautious about not influencing him with your own previously held assumptions.
- Listen sincerely and use open questions (e.g. W+H questions) if the motives are still not clear.
- Avoid questions that can be answered with yes/no or a single word.
- Ask additional questions that are not directly associated with the problem, or introduce statements that might confuse the interviewee at first but help to consider the problem from different points of view.
- Pay attention to the gestures and body language of the interviewee and, if required, note down and clarify if these signals are contradictory to the answer.
- Use the template in order to describe assumptions, write down key questions, and finally outline the story of the interviewee.

How much time and what materials do we need?

Group size

1–3

- Ideally, with a team of 2 or 3 with 1 or 2 observers and one interviewer
- The interviewer has the active part in the discussion. Together, the findings are documented and interpreted.

Typical duration

30–120 min.

- Depending on the complexity of the project, the interview may take up to one hour.
- Add up to 90 minutes for the documentation and transfer to journey stages.

Materials needed

- Paper for question map, pens
- Visualization of the journey stages on a large whiteboard
- Optionally, camera or smartphone, to document the environment

Template: In-depth interview with question map and journey stages

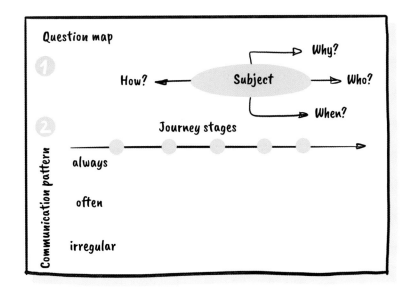

How the tool is applied...

- **Step 1:** Create a well-thought-out question map; it is crucial for an in-depth interview. Write the topic at the center of the sheet with W+H questions and explore the subject with the interviewee. Under no circumstances use a structured questionnaire. It would only serve the purpose of confirming our assumptions. Discuss the new findings with the design team.
- **Step 2:** Work with "journey stages" in addition to the question map. It helps to identify patterns at an early stage.
- Ask the interviewee to present or deepen a topic in the form of a sketch or a chronological sequence. This activity provides the interviewer with the opportunity to conduct even more in-depth discussions, even on sensitive subjects or subjects previously untapped.
- The question map and the "journey stages" aim at gathering unexpected insights that are triggered by different thought processes.
- For example, in this way, a user of an online shopping website can be questioned so as to find out:
  - All the places where a user had gathered information before
  - What information was valuable
  - When he made a decision for the purchase, and what was the decisive point for him
  - How easy the payment was

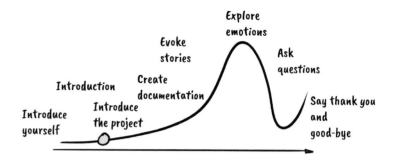

The in-depth interview and the "journey stages" can be used to produce a complete journey map. In addition to the empathy with the user and his interactions, the aim here is to show specific information on touch points that a user/customer had and discuss them with the team.

Expert tips:

Conduct an interview!
- Find out who would be a good interview partner. Think of individuals who are directly or indirectly connected with the problem.
- Start the interview with an introduction to make the goal and the larger context clear. Do not try to explain the problem to the interview partner.
- Be friendly and don't talk too much. Good listening and observing are key skills in an in-depth interview.

Ask simple questions!
- Begin with simple questions such as "How did you come across the offer?" Then expand with more open questions, for example: "Can you describe how you solved the problem?"
- In general, open questions help to identify interrelationships and dependencies.
- Where are there contradictions, and why do they exist?
- Observe non-verbal information and repeat a question to find out what the interviewee is thinking.
- Avoid closed questions that can be answered only with yes or no.

Explore the expectations at the end!
- At the end of the interview, try to summarize the expectations and needs, for example: "Was it exactly the experience you expected?"
- A final question can also be revealing and give new insights in the end, for example: "Would you like to add anything else?"

This is the favorite tool of Adharsh Dhandapani

Position:
Intrapreneur and Software Engineer, IBM

"Design thinking enables one to find the 'x' without needing an equation."

Why is it his favorite tool?

Thanks to mirror neurons in our brain, we – as humans – have a natural ability and tendency to have empathy for others. The "Interview for empathy" tool helps us to make use of this natural ability, so that we can see the world from the user's point of view. Achieving a new point of view also empowers us to identify and discredit the existing false assumptions and widely held beliefs in your problem area, which – in itself – can possibly differentiate you from the rest.

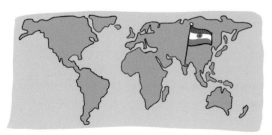

Country:
India

Affiliation:
IBM

Checked by: **Jui Kulkarni**

Company/Position: IBM iX, Application Consultant

Mirror neurons are triggered when people perform an action and also when they see other people performing the same action — with no difference between the two! It follows that mirror neurons are the reason that humans can empathize.

Expert tips:

Begin the interview by building trust
- We can begin the interview with an "ice breaker," for example. Additionally, it is important to make the interviewee feel safe by assuring him that the personal information shared during the interview will not be revealed to the public. If necessary, we also assist the interviewee with how to use the microphone and other technical equipment used in the interview.

Build a personal relationship with the interviewee
- Interviewees who know us personally will feel more secure when sharing their personal stories with us.
- Emphasize that the interview aims at the design for a better solution for him as a user.
- Generally people are averse to cold emails and cold calls from salesmen trying to sell products. Hence, right from the first contact, clearly specify that you are reaching out strictly for research purposes and would never use it as a marketing/sales opportunity.

Address as many senses as possible
- Mirror neurons require a firsthand sensory perception to work, and it is therefore important to design the interview to engage as many senses as possible. Meeting the users face-to-face in their natural environment and using a smartphone recorder for viewing and making sense of it later are useful ways to achieve this.

Validate the information from the interviews
- The authenticity of the interviewee's statements can be verified with tools such as role-playing or shadowing.

Use storytelling to share the message with the team
- Storytelling is a challenging but crucial tool for sharing the insights about users with rest of the team.

Description of use case

- The student team has planned the interview, and the team members – equipped with the prototype and the question map – ask a student about her fears concerning artificial intelligence (AI).
- The student interacts with the AI prototype, and the team records the feedback.
- Later, the design thinking team consolidates the insights in an interview journey map.

Key learnings

- You don't necessarily need to be a professionally trained ethnographer or designer to use this tool.
- It is difficult to remember all the information from an interview; hence it is always best to go there in pairs, make notes, and record the interview, if possible.
- Empathy interviews offer a unique opportunity for spending time with a user, listening to his stories, and digging deeper with W+H questions.

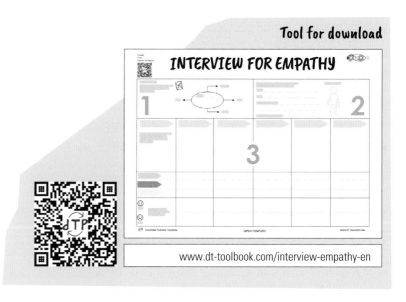

Tool for download

www.dt-toolbook.com/interview-empathy-en

Explorative interview

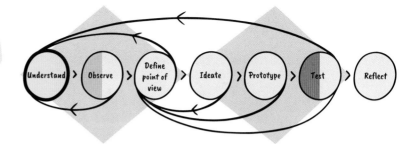

I would like...

to learn more about the user before thinking about new products or services.

Product-centered   **Human-centered**

What you can do with the tool:

- Explore the everyday life of people.
- Obtain a deep understanding of the user and his unspoken needs.
- Get a view of the basic values, beliefs, motivations, and aspirations that influence behavior.
- Create a mindset that does not put the product but the person and his or her needs in the foreground.
- Explore cultural and social aspects that might affect the satisfaction of needs.
- Minimize risks, identify opportunities, and test initial conceptual ideas at an early stage.

More information on the tool

- An "explorative interview" is usually used in the early phase of the design thinking cycle.
- With this type of interview, our main goal is to learn something about the everyday life of the people for whom we are creating a solution.
- The "explorative interview" is a good opportunity to get away from the focus on the product and show the team that our users have other needs.
- Thus it is suitable to question assumptions made and direct the development to functions and experiences that are actually relevant.

What tools can be used as an alternative?

- Observations, for example, with the AEIOU tool (see page 107) or other ethnographic methods, in order to gain a deep understanding of the lived experiences of people

Which tools support working with this tool?

- Customer journey (see page 103)
- Persona/user profile (see page 97)
- Association cards
- Walk and talk
- Visualizations of activities, such as "Day in a life"

How much time and what materials do we need?

Group size

1–2

- One interviewer is ideal to establish a deep relationship with the interviewee.
- As an alternative, one person can conduct the interview, while a second person takes notes.

Typical duration

60–120 min.

- The development of an interview guide usually takes 40 minutes; conducting the interview 60–120 minutes.
- Allow enough time for the exploration of the environment in order to gain a deep understanding for the everyday lives of the participants.

Materials needed

- Interview guide
- Pen and paper
- Camera or smartphone to capture images and videos if the interviewees allow it

Procedure: Explorative interview

Interview Guide:

1 Introduction:
Begin with general things. What are "broad" questions to open the conversation and break the ice?

- What is your profession?
- Tell me what you experienced recently.
- Tell me what annoyed you recently.

2 Get to know the entire story:
What are the questions that help you to understand the hopes, fears and motivations of the people interviewed?

- What are you saving for?
- What helps you to save money?
- What was the biggest challenge in this context?
- Wait..., what exactly do you mean by that?
- What happened before/after/during?
- Why?
- ... (pause)

3 Conclusion: Explain what happens with the answers and thank the interviewee for the discussion. Always be appreciative!

- "If you had one wish to make...."
- Thank you very much for the conversation

How the tool is applied...

- **Step 1:** First create an interview guide with the topics and questions to be dealt with. Start with broad questions and zoom in on the topic step by step.
- The interview should take place at the location of typical use or at a location where the participant feels comfortable – the most suitable place may be his or her home.
- Be prepared to depart from the interview guide if questions and topics come up that are important to the interviewee.
- **Step 2:** Ask open questions, such as "what," "why," and "how" and avoid yes/no questions.
- Make sure that the questions allow the participant to describe his behavior or his opinions from his own perspective.
- Ask about concrete examples to avoid standard answers and search for specific events, for example, "When did you last...."
- Try to dig deeper, for example, "What does this mean to you..." or "Why did you...."
- At the same time, try to speak the language of the participant and avoid technical terms. Keep in mind that the interviewee is the expert in his life.
- **Step 3:** Complete the interview with questions such as: "What would happen if you had one wish to make?"

This is the favorite tool of Rasmus Thomsen

Position:
Design Director & Partner at the strategic innovation agency IS IT A BIRD.

"I love design thinking because it has the potential to answer two fundamental questions in every innovation process: Are we designing the right thing? And are we designing the thing right? For me, the first question has always been the most important, which means we need to do the early work thoroughly by being truly explorative and curious about people and the worlds they inhabit."

Why is it his favorite tool?

Products or services will be used in our daily life. If we do not completely understand the context in which they are used, we cannot design meaningful solutions. After all, they should be designed in such a way that they really present added value for the user. The explorative interview is a good way to make sure we develop the right thing for our target group.

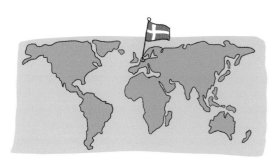

Country:
Denmark

Affiliation:
IS IT A BIRD

Checked by: Philipp Bachmann

Company/Position: The University of Applied Sciences of the Grisons, Head of Service Innovation Lab SIL, Professor of Strategy and Innovation

Expert tips:

Focus on human values
- We question our own assumptions and hypotheses.
- In doing so, we do not shy away from seemingly banal questions or from challenging things that most people take for granted. For example: If we asked a 5 year old what a radio is, we will get an answer that is completely different from the answer we get from an adult.

A picture says more than a thousand words
- With sketches and pictures, we can make even abstract topics more within grasp of the scope of the "explorative interview" and have a more concrete type of conversation.
- If it makes sense, we ask the participants to show us how they do things instead of just talking about it.
- When we are at their home, we ask participants about objects that have a personal meaning for them in order to get an additional personal component about the interviewee.

Good conversations have room for silence
- We use short lulls in the conversation so the participants can analyze the situation.
- During the evaluation of the interview, it is particularly important to watch out for new topics and questions that crop up during the interview. Surprising insights are the order of the day with such interviews.

Get help from outside if necessary
- We encounter our interviewees on an equal footing in relation to language and clothing style.
- If we need help, we take an experienced design thinker to the interview.

Description of use case

- We all tend to seek a solution first instead of getting to the bottom of things. A popular mistake is to develop an offer for a target group without having asked whether these people actually need such an offer.
- A better way is first to use the "explorative interview" in order to understand the problem before developing a solution.
- The success of a design thinking project depends on whether we solve the right problem or not.
- Lilly can be proud of her team. There will even be a follow-up meeting.

Key learnings

- Be open: People who were interviewed may have a completely different world view and value system.
- Pay attention: At the beginning of the design thinking process, the goal is to explore and understand.
- Be naive: Don't be afraid of asking "dumb" questions.

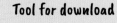

www.dt-toolbook.com/explorative-interview-en

Ask 5x why

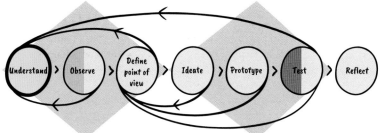

Understand > Observe > Define point of view > Ideate > Prototype > Test > Reflect

I would like...

to understand a problem in depth, not just scratch the surface.

What you can do with the tool:

- Discover the true cause of a problem.
- Develop a sustainable solution.
- Dig deeper and get to know more than just exploring the symptoms that are obvious.
- Dig deeper and deeper to gain new and surprising insights.

More information on the tool

- We ask 5x "Why?" in order to understand the situation and the true causes of a problem.
- This questioning technique can be used whenever we ask questions and observe a user and want to explore critical experiences and functions of a problem in a more in-depth way.
- The tool is mainly used in the early stages of the design cycle and in the testing of prototypes.
- Asking repeatedly also helps us to identify hidden problems that a user would not mention if only asked once. In this way, we gain insights on a different level and are better able to assess situations.
- If we use this interviewing technique in the "test" phase, it may help us to understand more exactly what functions and experiences work and which need to be adapted or should be discarded.

What tools can be used as an alternative?

- The feedback capture grid in the test phase in order to learn more about the user and the problem to be solved (see page 217)

Which tools support working with this tool?

- Explorative interview (see page 63)
- Persona/user profile (see page 97)
- 5W+H questions (see page 71)

How much time and what materials do we need?

Group size

2

- Ideal are groups of 2.
- One person conducts the conversation and the other focuses on documentation.

Typical duration

30–40 min.

- The required time is the duration of the interview, usually 30 to 40 min.
- "Ask 5x why" can be used for a specific problem or as a guide to direct the conversation toward greater depth.

Materials needed

- Notepad and pen
- Smartphone or camera, if the interview partner consents to the recording

Template: 5x why

1 Detailed description of the problem.

2

1. Why is it a problem (problem description)?	Consequence
	What is the problem? **What are its symptoms?**
2. Why?	**Direct impact**
	Why does the problem occur? **What technology is used?**
3. Why?	**Cause – effect**
	What could be another cause of the problem?
4. Why?	**Organizational hurdles**
	How could the problem be avoided?
5. Why?	**Systematic hurdles**
	The systematic approach might prevent the occurrence?

How the tool is applied...

- Use the template or write the answers on a blank sheet of paper.
- **Step 1:** Describe the problem in as much detail as possible and use photos or sketches to illustrate it.
- **Step 2:** Start with a "root cause" analysis and ask "Why?" as often as possible. Try to counter each answer with a follow-up why question.
- Stop asking "Why?" once it no longer makes sense. Then explore another problem in this way or get into an in-depth discussion with the interviewee on the answers given.
- Integrate simple prototypes and sketches into the solution discussion to obtain first reactions from the users.

Variation:

In addition to "Why?," you also ask 5x "How?" Use this interviewing technique to find a lasting solution to the "root causes" of the problem. With the "Why?" questions, design thinking teams can review the problem; with the "How?" questions, they can determine how to solve it.

Position:
Founder of Aïna, author of Le Design Thinking par la pratique, Eyrolles

"Empathy and experimentation through prototyping are the key elements of design thinking which I use for reinventing the life of the elderly. There isn't a better tool to start tackling aging than to put yourself in the shoes of our elders and understand their deep needs."

Why is it her favorite tool

Good design is based on a keen understanding of the problem. In order to develop innovative solutions, I must therefore carefully analyze the origin of the problem. Asking 5x why helps me to go deeper and not get stuck on the surface of a problem. 5x why is the simplest tool we can use when we want to achieve an interview with good results. It helps us to understand the roots of the problem, which in turn results in better solutions.

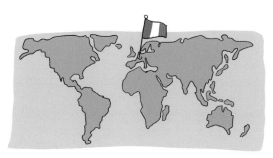

Country:
France

Affiliation:
AÏNA

Checked by: Sebastian Garn

Company/Position: B&B Markenagentur GmbH, Creative Director

Expert tips:

Don't make any assumptions
- Try not to make any assumptions about the roots of a problem.
- We let our interview partner tell his or her story, listen attentively, and ask further questions should something still be unclear.

Don't stop asking questions too soon
- There is no guarantee that five why questions are enough to get to the bottom of things.
- We keep asking until it gets uncomfortable or until the real cause is discovered.

Check the results with reverse questions
- In order to verify that we really discovered the root of the problem, reverse questions in the form of an if-then sentence are great.

Example:
- Why did you get sick?
  - Because I spent some time outside in the fresh air on the weekend.

Reverse question:
- If you hadn't spent time outside in the fresh air on the weekend, then you wouldn't be sick now?
  - The lack of a jacket was probably more of a cause than being in the fresh air. The fresh air is therefore only a part of the cause. With more why questions, the root of the problem can be further broken down.

Description of use case

- Contradictory statements were repeatedly noticed during the interview and in the subsequent discussions with the design thinking team.
- The team would like to explore these areas again. The team goes into the next interview, having resolved to ask "Why?" at least five times, this time before letting up.
- They go as far as to ask "Why?" so many times that the interviewee stops giving answers and the questions become quite philosophical.

Key learnings

- Describe the problem in as much detail as possible at the beginning.
- Involve experts and users in the problem-cause analysis.
- Ask why at least five times.
- Don't forget to document the findings.

Tool for download

www.dt-toolbook.com/5xwhy-en

70

5W+H questions

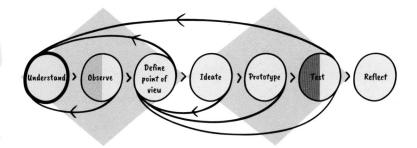

I would like...

to gain in-depth insights as well as new findings and information in order to grasp the problem or situation holistically or simply to find relevant questions for an interview.

What you can do with the tool:

- W+H questions help to gain new insights and information, thus capturing the problem or situation in a structured manner.
- Infer more abstract, potential emotions and motives from your concrete observations in a specific situation.
- Use W+H questions during the observation phase in order to observe more closely and dig deeper when you discover something new.

More information on the tool

- Intuitively, the 5W+H questions are question words starting with a W or H: Who?, What?, When?, Where?, Why?, and How?
- Investigative journalists, for instance, use the 5W+H questions as a basis for their research. They use the 5W+H questions since they are open questions that allow a wide range of answers.
- The W+H questions allow us to learn more about the wishes and opinions of the user or a customer.
- The simple structure of the W+H questions helps in the divergent phase to gain a basic overview and in-depth insights. The findings of the team and photos of observations can be analyzed with this tool and guide the team into areas where previously undiscovered needs and knowledge are unearthed.
- During the observation phase, the W+H questions help to explore "what" happens, "where" it happens, and "how" it happens.

What tools can be used as an alternative?

- Interview for empathy (see page 57)
- Explorative interview (see page 63)
- AEIOU (see page 107)

Which tools support working with this tool?

- Problem statement (see page 49)
- Design principles (see page 53)
- Ask 5x why (see page 67)

How much time and what materials do we need?

Group size

3–5

- 5W+H questions can be applied on the team or to prepare for an interview.
- This is why the team size is secondary.

Typical duration

30–60 min.

- The duration varies. 5W+H questions can be used quickly and perfunctorily as an entry point or intensively with many discussions.
- Usually, W+H questions are a profitable tool in many phases of the design cycle.

Materials needed

- Print the template or sketch the 5W+H grid on a sheet of paper
- Pens, Post-its

Template: 5W+H questions

Who	What	When	Where	Why	How
Who is involved?	What do we already know about the problem?	When did the problem start?	Where does the problem occur?	Why is the problem important?	How could this problem be an opportunity?
Who is affected by the situation?	What would we like to know?	When do people want to see results?	Where was it resolved before?	Why does it occur?	How could it be solved?
Who is the decision maker?	What are the assumptions that should be scrutinized?		Where did similar situations exist?	Why was it not yet solved?	What has already been tried to resolve the problem?

How the tool is applied...

- The 5W+H questions can be used in all sorts of situations. We would like to introduce two situations.

Situation 1: To understand the problem better

Objective: to get an initial overview of the problem as well as information about possible hypotheses and starting points

- Try to raise and answer all relevant W+H questions.
- If a W+H question does not make sense in the given context, skip it.
- Look where uncertainties exist or further questions crop up. Find out what questions should be raised in the interview.

Situation 2: Learn more about the needs

Goal: to provide a basis for an interview with users or stakeholders

- Prepare a list of possible sub-questions (e.g. in the form of a mind map).
- Vary the questions and "play" with them. Adapt them to the situation.
- Create the interview questions or a question map from all this.
- Try to get a lot of information. Ask why even in the context of other W+H questions.

This is the favorite tool of Kristine Biegman

Position:
Trainer / Coach / Facilitator human-centered design launchlabs GmbH, Berlin

"Design thinking forces us to open up, let go assumptions, experiment, embrace insecurity and 'failure' and above all: to trust the process. For me, design thinking is a powerful vehicle to make wonderful things happen in and between people while designing for people. I'm grateful to contribute to this every day!"

Why is it her favorite tool

The 5W+H questions are probably one of the most commonly used tools across the entire design thinking cycle. The questions are particularly valuable for understanding the problem statement and the associated problem area better. In addition, W+H questions help analyze and scrutinize information already gathered. W+H questions are my favorite tool because they help me dig deeper!

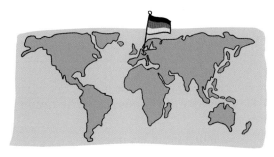

Country:
Germany

Affiliation:
launchlabs

Checked by: Moritz Avenarius

Company/Position: oose, Design Thinking Facilitator & Strategy Consultant

Expert tips:

Always ask several times for answers
- By asking and asking again, we dig deeper. Even if we think we already know the answer, we ask again. It seems strange, but use a "beginner's mind" and ask "Why?" several times in succession like a child would.
- In addition, we should try to find more than one answer to every question. Conflicting answers can be of particular interest for unearthing more information on genuine needs.
- If a W+H question from the table does not make sense in the context of the problem statement, we simply skip it.
- We try to gather as much information as possible with the 5W+H questions, and combine them with other interviewing techniques, for example, 5x why. A list of possible sub-questions can be created, for instance, which are then combined into a mind map.

Turn questions into the negative in order to create different perspectives
- Turning the questions into the negative can bring advantages and encourage creativity, for example, "When does the problem NOT occur?" or "Who is NOT affected?"
- We also found it to be very useful to use the 5W+H questions in the context of a brainstorming session or as a basis for an initial brain dump in order to find out everything the team thinks they believe or know.

No fake news – always go with the facts
- Furthermore, it is always good to underpin the answers with facts – with the help of desk research and data analytics, for instance.

Description of use case

- For the preparation of in-depth interviews with decision makers in Singapore, the team is divided up.
- W+H questions aim at a better understanding of the problem.
- In the end, the design team has collected more than 40 different W+H questions that will help them learn more about the digital transformation of companies in Southeast Asia.
- Lilly spurs the design thinking team on to use the 5W+H questions even more often in the process.

Key learnings

- Define the right W+H questions for the situation.
- Answer the team's questions in order to come up with a structured overview.
- Dig deeper in the customer interview and ask again.
- Supplement the answers with important facts.

Tool for download

www.dt-toolbook.com/wh-questions-en

Jobs to be done (JTBD)

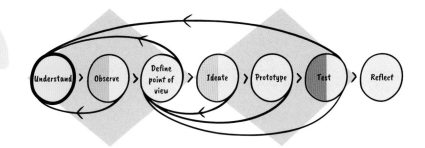

I would like...

to focus the problem solution on things that are an added value for the customer and help him accomplish his tasks.

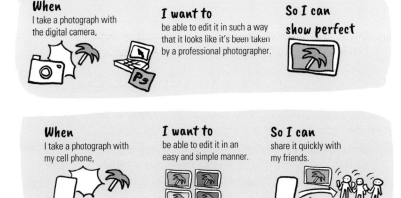

When
I take a photograph with the digital camera,

I want to
be able to edit it in such a way that it looks like it's been taken by a professional photographer.

So I can
show perfect

When
I take a photograph with my cell phone,

I want to
be able to edit it in an easy and simple manner.

So I can
share it quickly with my friends.

What you can do with the tool:

- Capture the customer tasks (jobs to be done) in a structured way and gain new insights.
- Find hidden tasks of the customer that were not mentioned before in order to derive from them customer needs later or give known needs a clearer contour.
- Optimize the entire customer experience, for example, to give a service a unique purpose.

More information on the tool

- The "jobs to be done" (JTBD) approach by Clayton Christensen helps us to focus on the customer/user and find new solutions.
- If the tasks a customer must perform are understood in great depth, the potential for success is virtually guaranteed.
- This is why JTBD has become more and more popular in the design thinking community. The alignment to the job the customer has to perform acts as a compass and makes disruptive business models possible.
- The basic idea of JTBD is that customers "scream" for a product or service whenever they have to solve a task.
- The aim is, above all, to satisfy the deeper social, emotional, or personal tasks of the customers.

What tools can be used as an alternative?

- Persona/User profile (see page 97)

Which tools support working with this tool?

- 5W+H questions (see page 71)
- Ask 5x why (see page 67)
- Interview for empathy (see page 57)
- Customer journey (see page 103)

How much time and what materials do we need?

Group size

3–5

- JTBD can be used for teams of all sizes. An efficient team size should not exceed 5 persons.
- Direct interviews with the customer are best conducted in pairs.

Typical duration

60–120 min.

- 30-60 minutes per problem statement should be estimated for each interview.
- Conduct at least two interviews.
- Basically, JTBD can be done in a couple of minutes; it may trigger further discussions, though.

Materials needed

- Post-its, pens, markers
- Flip chart, wall, or other free surface
- If fitting, templates with sample customer tasks

Template: Jobs to be done (JTBD)

When I,	I want to	so I can
————	————	————
————	————	————
————	————	————
————	————	————
————	————	————
[situation]	[motivation]	[expected result]
❶	❷	❸

How the tool is applied...

- JTBD consists of three elements: (1) description of the situation, (2) explanation of the motivation, and (3) expected result.
- Capture the indirect goals and tasks with the JTBD approach. In order to understand them, it is necessary to dig deeper with the 5W+H questions and with the "ask 5x why" method.
- The customer tasks can be captured along the customer journey (see page 103) or across the product life cycle. The tasks are best written down individually and divided into different tasks to be fulfilled.
- Ask why with each task to be fulfilled. Begin, for example, with the question: Why does the customer buy from us?
- This procedure facilitates the collection, structuring, and prioritizing of customer tasks.
- Write down the customer task in the form of "When... (situation), I want to... (motivation), so I can... (expected result)."
- Based on this, you ask "why not" next; for example, "Why does the customer not buy from us?"
- From the replies to the JTBD sentences, you generate new ideas and finally the experiences and functions that are critical to a user.

This is the favorite tool of Patrick Schüffel

Position:
Professor & Liaison Officer of the School of Management Fribourg in Singapore
Momentum Builder at STO Global-X

"Design thinking helps me develop products and services extremely quickly and on a customer-oriented basis."

Why is it his favorite tool?

Jobs to be done is my favorite tool since, for one, it is simple and intuitively understandable; secondly, it asks about deep-rooted customer needs. When used correctly, this tool can provide insights decisive for a match in situations that may seem trivial at first.

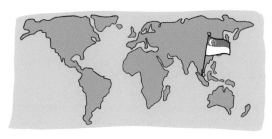

Country:
Singapore

Affiliation:
STO Global-X

Checked by: Line Gram Frøkjær

Company/Position: SODAQ, Mechanical Design Engineer

Customers don't just buy products, they hire them to do a job.
– Clayton Christensen

MORE THAN JUST ...

Expert tips:

Find the real needs
- The JTBD approach is valuable because customers/users are reluctant to talk about their needs, but they are able to talk about the tasks they have to perform and the challenges they face.
- For the JTBD approach to be beneficial, it should be used not only superficially, but a number of principles must also be observed. The focus of the value creation is on the core task to be accomplished by the customer. JTBD constitutes the basis for a market opportunity, that is, other tasks must also be considered to attain a holistic picture (i.e. adjacent and emotional tasks as well as the touch points of a customer/user across the product life cycle). Do not combine these tasks but measure them separately. In addition, each task can be measured by KPIs that are defined beforehand. The expected result is part of a market and describes precisely what the customer wants to achieve. The results are independent of solutions and should be verified and measured by quantitative survey techniques.

Also look at the pains and gains
- At the same time, try to document the pains (problems and troubles) and gains (benefits and joys) the customer has with the tasks.
- Workarounds and improvised solutions on the part of the customer can also be very illuminating. They show points where customers invest time and money to solve their problems.

Description of use case

- Lilly's team defines the tasks that the user should carry out. She uses the customer journey as a basis and complements it with further important emotional and social tasks.
- After prioritization, the most important tasks within the "jobs to be done" framework are described.
- For each sentence, the major pains and gains are determined. The individual JTBDs are a vital starting point for Lilly to redesign the customer experience.

Key learnings

- The customer tasks are written down according to the pattern: "When I ... (situation), I want to... (motivation), so I can... (expected result)."
- The hidden non-functional, social, emotional, or personal customer tasks are particularly significant and often constitute the key to the solution.
- Use the JTBD framework for all tasks along the customer journey.

Tool for download

www.dt-toolbook.com/jtbd-en

Extreme users/lead users

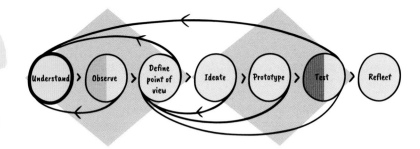

I would like...

to find new, innovative ideas and user needs (as yet) unknown to the average user.

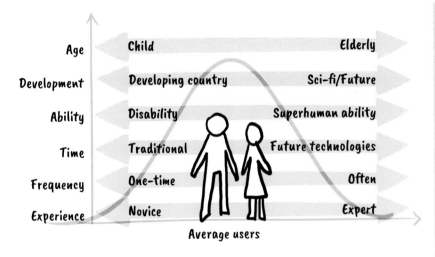

What you can do with the tool:

- Explore those user needs that average users are not able to articulate.
- Find new, innovative ideas.
- Identify early trends in user behavior or needs.
- Ideate for a more inclusive design.

More information on the tool

- Extreme/lead users (also known as power users and expert users) are based on the same basic idea. Through the interaction with them, we want to gather better information on users and their needs.
- A lead user often appears as an innovator himself. Lead users have needs that are way ahead of the mass market. A lead user is a user that has had a strong need already, no matter whether a product exists, and may even have created a solution – since they have a lot to gain from a solution. In the case of complex products, the traditional lead user methods hit their limits.
- An extreme user, however, is a user who goes beyond the usual usage limits or utilizes the product, system, or the space significantly more than an average user (e.g. taxi driver vs. normal car driver, extreme athletes vs. casual athletes).
- Extreme users experience the world differently than an average user. This means that their needs can be more prominent. The needs uncovered with groups of extreme users are frequently also latent needs in the wider population.

What tools can be used as an alternative?

- Interview for empathy (see page 57)
- Explorative interview (see page 63)
- AEIOU (see page 107)
- Empathy map (see page 93)
- Peers observing peers (see page 115)

Which tools support working with this tool?

- Ask 5x why (see page 67)
- 5W+H questions (see page 71)
- Jobs to be done (see page 75)

How much time and what materials do we need?

Group size

2

- Teams of 2 are ideal, so one person can concentrate on the conversation, the other on recording the statements.

Typical duration

30–120 min.

- The interaction with the user in her environment may vary in length.
- It usually takes a lot of time and persistence to seek out the lead user. Extreme users are easier to find.
- Ask known users about recommendations for other potential lead users.

Materials needed

- Notepad and pen
- Smartphone or camera, if the interview partner gives his/her permission, to document the findings

Procedure: "Extreme users/lead users"

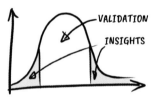

	Characteristics	Complexity	Outcome	Procedure
Lead user	Ahead of the trend Willing to invest time and resources, very experienced and well connected	Hard to find	Usually very good insights	1. Identify trend 2. Identification of lead users 3. Co-creation with lead user 4. Reflection and projection of the results onto the problem statement
Extreme users	Extremes: young /old, poor/rich Differences: regular/infrequent user, expert/amateur	Easy to find	Useful additional information	1. Identify extreme users 2. Determine observation and interaction (questioning, shadowing, or group interview) 3. Use findings for persona, sharpen problem statement, or collect initial ideas

How the tool is applied...

Lead User

- Identify the potential lead user for a market trend or a relevant problem statement area.
- Interview or co-create with the lead user. It is always advisable to ask the lead users about recommendations for other potential lead users.
- Previously unconsidered solutions or paths to a solution may arise from the interaction with lead users.

Extreme User

- Identify potential extreme users based on dimensions in which such a user could be of interest (e.g. a child or a much older person, a beginner or a super expert).
- Decide how best to learn more about them.
- Use the findings to accumulate information about the problem or a broader target group. Power users are heavy users who are characterized by a high intensity of use.

Procedure

- When interviewing and observing lead users, power users, or extreme users, we should especially look for workarounds or previously unknown solution alternatives such a user might have developed. Such findings should then be validated later by testing prototypes to ensure that the idea meets the needs of the target users as well.

This is the favorite tool of Katja Holtta-Otto

Position:
Professor of Product Development, Design Factory, Aalto University

"Design thinking is really people thinking. It is thinking about the people we develop for, also the non-obvious people."

Why is it her favorite tool?

For me, interaction with these users is as if someone handed me a magnifying glass that allows me to see their needs, which of course had been there all the time but which I had not been able to recognize before. In different design challenges, the work with extreme users helped me enormously. In one project, I gained insights about wheelchairs. In the interaction with extreme users, I became aware of the fact that these aids should not only work on the road but also on uneven surfaces such as the lawn or gravel road.

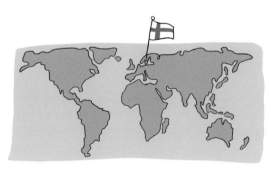

Country:
Finland

Affiliation:
Aalto University

Checked by: **Andreas Uthmann**
Company/Position: CKW, Head of New Business & Innovation

Expert tips:

Search for wild ideas
- The inspiring exchange with extreme users often leads us to wild and new ideas. We should take every opportunity to spend time with this type of user.
- Generally, we should treat every user as an expert. We respect their concerns, particularly if we are dealing with sensitive population groups.

Collaborate across boundaries
- We have had very good experience with interacting with groups (i.e. 8 to 12) of extreme users. The different opinions and the interaction within the group often yield additional insights.
- This suggests that we should always observe and interview several extreme users. As a result, the probability of recognizing needs patterns increases.
- But watch out! Not everyone who applies something in an extreme way is innovative. An extreme user is not a lead user.

Use all channels to stay in contact with lead users
- There are different possibilities for interacting and staying in touch with lead users. They include WhatsApp groups or temporary blogs. They can be geared to normal users or lead users and offer a broad range of possibilities for discussion.
- In addition, chats can be set up temporarily for which all participants can create contributions. A "letter box" for spontaneous first ideas, thoughts, and limited surveys also fuel interaction.

Description of use case

- Lilly's team determines lead users and extreme users in order to capture the needs of the majority.
- A gamer is an extreme user. He is at home only in his virtual world and no longer notices many things in the real world. But he has very specific ideas about what should be well-designed virtual worlds.
- Lilly's team wants to focus on such extreme users in order to refine further their understanding of the problem.
- Images of the identified lead and extreme users help the team to build empathy with them.

Key learnings

- Take all extreme user needs into consideration, even if they don't seem relevant at first glance. Often, we don't properly perceive things (e.g. we cannot hear properly in a loud environment).

- Test the requirements later with all types of users and not only with the extreme and lead users.

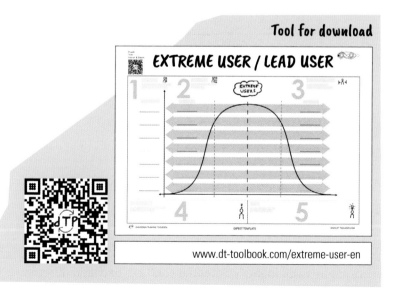

www.dt-toolbook.com/extreme-user-en

Stakeholder map

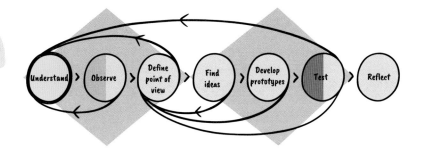

I would like...

to get an overview of all stakeholders, that is, organizations and people who have a claim or interest in the problem and a potential solution.

What you can do with the tool:

- Obtain valuable information for strategic and communicative planning as well as future activities.
- Make assumptions about the influence of certain actors in the project.
- Identify clues that suggest a lack of information regarding actors, for example, which actors have not been sufficiently taken into consideration so far (white spots).
- Draw first conclusions with respect to alliances or power structures and identify potential conflicts between different stakeholders.

More information on the tool

- The stakeholder map is a visualization that helps to clarify the positions of the various stakeholders. This tool is part of the stakeholder analysis that aims at identifying the interests, the inhibitory and supporting factors, as well as power structures within the system.
- The stakeholder map and the analysis yield information on the characteristics of all interest groups and the relationships among them, and serves the purpose of communicating effectively with all relevant stakeholders.
- Understanding the interest groups and building a relationship with them is an essential part of the process.
- Knowledge about stakeholders is vital, since they are the ones who decide on the "top or flop" of a project; in addition, they are crucial for the implementation of solutions.

What tools can be used as an alternative?

- Power-interest matrix

Which tools support working with this tool?

- 5W+H questions (see page 71)
- AEIOU (see page 107)
- Brainstorming (see page 151)

83

Group size

3–6

- Ideally, the team is complemented by a representative of the respective stakeholder.
- Often, the design team develops a first map and then validates the results in follow-up discussions with the stakeholders.

Typical duration

60–240 min.

- The creation of a stakeholder map takes from 60 to 240 minutes, depending on the complexity.
- Often it takes some time before all parties involved speak openly about stakeholders and their needs.

Materials needed

- Large sheet of paper and pens
- Large square table or whiteboard
- Using Legos or Playmobil figurines, you can assign a character to the individual actors

Procedure and template: Stakeholder map

1 Define use case
2 Stakeholder brainstorming

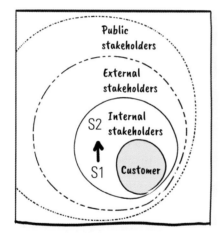

Public stakeholders

External stakeholders

S2   Internal stakeholders

S1   Customer

 Draw in connections.

_____ Close relationship (frequent contact, exchange of information, coordination, mutual trust, common interests).
_?_ Weak or informal relationship. Question mark shows unclear relationship.

===== Institutionally established alliances and cooperative projects.

——▷ The arrow indicates the flow direction, for instance, of information and values.

—⚡— The lightning sign shows tensions, conflicts, or dangers between stakeholders, broken or injured relationships.

How the tool is applied...

- **Step 1:** Start by defining the use case. It can be a product, project, or the collaboration of different departments.
- **Step 2:** List all stakeholders involved.
- In addition, deepen the understanding of the various stakeholders by asking questions. The questions are defined in accordance with the use case:
  - Who will benefit from the success? Who has an interest in it being a success?
  - Who do we collaborate with? Who provides us with valuable ideas?
  - How can sales and marketing make a mark?
  - Who is blocking the idea, and for what reasons? Who benefits from a failure?
- **Step 3:** First create a stakeholder map and enter the various stakeholders on the map. Then enter the connections of the stakeholders to one another.
- Define and use different symbols for the connections, for example, broken lines for more complex relationships.
- Reflect on the stakeholder map and determine the next steps, actions, and possible consequences from working with the stakeholder map.

Position:
Co-founder of THES - TauscHaus - EduSpace

"I live according to the principle: Only when you are able to visualize 'it' have you really understood 'it.'"

Why is it her favorite tool?

The dynamics within the team, department, organization, and other interest groups are often hugely exciting, complex, and crucial. It is very important to understand these interactions, and for that the creation of the stakeholder map is essential. Then the relationships identified must be dealt with in a constructive way, which requires a great deal of sensitivity, clarity, and transparency.

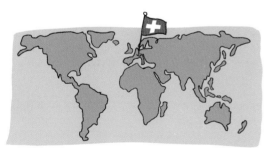

Country:
Switzerland

Affiliation:
THES

Checked by:　　　**Remo Gander**

Company/Position:　　Bossard Group, Group Project Manager

Expert tips:

Bring together the right people for the job
- For the creation of a stakeholder map and the analysis of the stakeholders, it is important to select the participants carefully. For one, we need expert knowledge; secondly, we need participants who bring along a fresh perspective. Frequently, it makes sense to create the stakeholder map on the project team and later interview the most important actors, at the same time questioning our assumptions.

Work efficiently and effectively
- Generally, when defining stakeholders, it is important to get away from general profiles and be as specific as possible.
- Enough time should be scheduled for brainstorming, the positioning, and the evaluation of the stakeholders. A common symbolic language helps with interpretation. We have had very good experience with using different figures for stakeholder maps (e.g. the animals from Lego Fabuland). Cords and pipe cleaners in different colors can be used for the connections.

Identify key stakeholders for implementation
- Communicating the results and regular updating during the entire project is recommended. A stakeholder map for the implementation of a project can be instrumental for its success. Applying stakeholder analyses when preparing the implementation of solutions has proven its worth many times over.

Description of use case

- Lilly first does a brainstorming session with her team. Subsequently, they pick the most important stakeholders together. For a better identification with the stakeholders, the team uses symbolic figures that describe or symbolize the personality.
- They are then arranged in such a way that they represent the relationships among one another and determine who are the most important ones and who, in what way, will be involved.
- This way, communication measures can be defined at an early stage, and nobody will be forgotten. Based on this, Lilly can now involve the key stakeholders and, for instance, test the prototype with them.

Key learnings

- Define a specific use case.
- Compile a list with all relevant stakeholders.
- Ask specific key questions, for example, "Who will benefit from the success?"
- Enter the stakeholders on a stakeholder map and visualize the relationships to one another.
- Reflect on the result and infer from it specific steps to be taken.

www.dt-toolbook.com/stakeholder-map-en

Emotional response cards

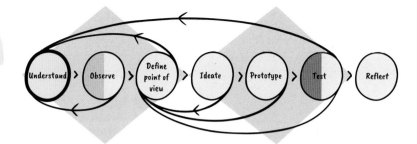

I would like...

to learn more about the a user's feelings when interacting with him to obtain better interview results and insights.

What you can do with the tool:

- Test existing products for their attractiveness before redesigning them and compare them to new ideas.
- Learn more about competitive products, brands, and experiences.
- Collect statements on strategy, information architecture, interaction, aesthetics, and speed.
- Vision: Find out from the client as early as in the kick-off how he wants his product to be characterized by the user.
- In the case of new products, find out what the user experienced, thought, and felt (e.g. after a usability test).
- Compare prototypes across various iterations.

More information on the tool

- The emotional response cards are a qualitative tool for empathetic target group analysis. The cards provide the target group with a simple aid that enables them to talk about a situation in a targeted and deeper way.
- As a result, members of the target group are encouraged to speak about their emotions, beliefs, and perceptions. People can remember well what something felt like but they usually need a trigger to start talking about it.
- The emotional response cards are normally used in the early stages of the design thinking cycle to gain understanding and determine the direction of the development.
- The "Microsoft reaction cards" were mentioned for the first time by Joey Benedeck and Trish Miner in 2002 in their publication "Measuring Desirability" – at that time, still on the basis of 118 cards. Fifty emotional response cards have proven useful to us.

What tools can be used as an alternative?

- Interview for empathy (see page 57)
- Empathy map (see page 93)

Which tools support working with this tool?

- Persona/user profile (see page 97)
- Structured usability test (see page 229)
- Solution interview (see page 225)
- 5x why (see page 67)
- 5W+H questions (see page 71)

How much time and what materials do we need?

Group size

1–2

- Teams of 2 are ideal. One person observes the conversation, while the other person poses the questions.
- But it also works with one interviewer.

Typical duration

15–20 min.

- You need about 5 minutes for the preparation of the emotional response cards.
- Depending on the follow-up questions, 10-15 minutes should be planned for one run.

Materials needed

- 50 emotional response cards
- Notepad and pen

Template and procedure: Emotional response cards

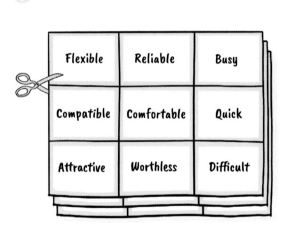

Flexible	Reliable	Busy
Compatible	Comfortable	Quick
Attractive	Worthless	Difficult

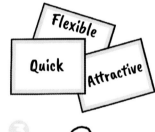

Flexible
Quick
Attractive

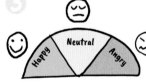

Happy   Neutral   Angry

Why?

Note: based on Microsoft Desirability Toolkit

How the tool is applied...

- **Step 1:** Print the 50 cards and glue them on thin cardboard.
- **Step 2:** Lay the cards on the separate table in any order.
- **Step 3:** Ask the users after the test to select 3 cards from the set that best describe their experience with the product. Add that it is not important for the adjective to be absolutely exact and that it is also allowed to be negative! It serves only as a trigger for an emotion. The person is also allowed to show emotions during the selection and talk to himself/herself. Write down anything conspicuous! As soon as the test person picks up a card, put it aside on the table and write down the adjective. Leave a little space with your notes for later insights.
- **Step 4:** As soon as the user has selected the 3 cards, explore (through questions) the adjective for the respective situation in which the user felt like that and deepen the insight by asking "why" questions. Other question techniques yield supplementary information, for example, "What did you expect instead?," and so on.
- **Step 5:** Also write down the statements as direct quotes. Take a photo of the map situation or record the stories on video.

88

This is the favorite tool of Armin Egli

Position:
UX consultant and lecturer for User Experience and Innovation

"Design thinking is my magical toolbox with which I can create the right product together with the customer."

Why is it his favorite tool?

I think the way to a good product is not obvious. The solution often suggests itself (in the problem) but is invisible. It is my job to grasp the core of the project and of the problem. The most important question in this context is WHY. I discover connections and original problems when I get a really close look at the people involved. This requires trust. When I have trust, I can research for personal stories. The response cards provide a simple entry point for it. Then I dig deeper.

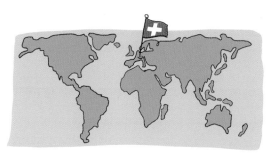

Country:
Switzerland

Affiliation:
Zühlke

Checked by: **Philip Hassler**

Company/Position: Venturelab | Co-Managing Director

Expert tips:

Emotional response cards can also be used to clarify a vision or in the context of a prototype test.

Describe the bigger vision
- The cards are used to raise the client's awareness of his later product and its properties even before the beginning of the project.
- The duration: 5 minutes for considerations of the product (not final) and 5 minutes for the "why" questions. When interviewing the CEO and the product manager, for instance, it is intriguing to see on which level the interviewees answer (strategy, function, interaction, aesthetics). This can already result in eureka moments, which in turn provide important information for the design principles.

Explore the response to a prototype
- The cards are used for the in-depth analysis of the user's point of view, for example, after testing a prototype.
- The typical duration: approx. 3 minutes for selecting the 3 cards and approx. 10 minutes for the stories ("why" questions) the user tells for each card.

Keep in mind
- If current situations are queried (possibly with several tools) and afterward the desired future situation is also to be asked about: First pose questions about the current situation with all tools. Only then, find out what the user thinks about the target situation. Otherwise, we run the risk that the questions about the current situation are influenced.

Description of use case

- Within the framework of "Future of Work," the design teams have designed various floor layouts for agile collaboration.
- After a typical walk-through in a 3-D model, the team uses the "emotional response cards" to test the relationship to the space concept regardless of the room size.
- The test person selects the adjective "difficult" and says to it: "If I have to imagine working in this room...ouch.... They are not directly conducive to working together effectively, and it is difficult, for example, to hold a stand-up meeting in the narrow corridors."

Key learnings

- People remember emotions!
- People find it easier to remember if they are given a trigger, such as an emotional response card.
- Users and customers normally want to be polite. The cards help to lower inhibitions.

Tool for download

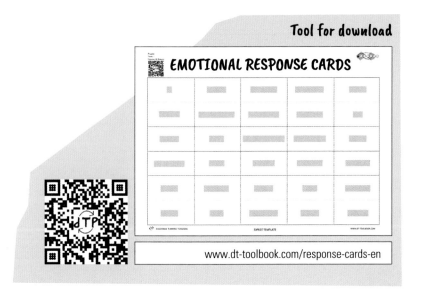

www.dt-toolbook.com/response-cards-en

Phase: Observe

After we have defined a problem, the next phase in the design thinking process is observation. In this phase, we want to learn as much as possible about a user and his/her needs. This is why we use with customer experience chains, personas, and explorative interviews, and simple tools such as the AEIOU framework. These tools help us to collect and document insights.

Empathy map

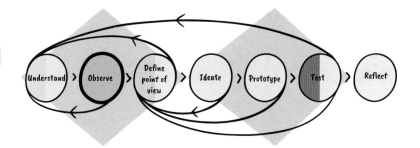

I would like...

to understand the customer/user better, perceive his/her feelings, and empathize with his/her actions.

What you can do with the tool:

- Document the insights from observation or testing with users and capture the user from different perspectives in order to build empathy.
- Understand better where the user has problems (pains) or potential benefits (gains) and infer his tasks (so-called jobs to be done).
- Collect findings to create a persona.
- Summarize observations concisely and record unexpected insights.

Some information on the tool:

- An empathy map is a tool for empathetic target group analysis. It is used to identify feelings, thoughts, and attitudes of existing or potential users and customers and understand their needs.
- The aim is to obtain in-depth insights on the potential user by means of W+H questions.
- In comparison to a customer journey map or a persona, the empathy map focuses more on the emotional state of potential customers.
- We use the empathy map mainly in the "understand," "observe," "define point of view," and "test" phases.
- We also suggest speaking to experts who know the user/customer well and, of course, being active yourself and doing what the user is doing. "Walk in the shoes of the user!"

What tools might be used as an alternative?

- Interview for empathy (see page 57)
- Feedback capture grid (in the "test" phase, see page 217)
- Value proposition canvas

Which tools support working with the empathy map?

- Customer journey (see page 103)
- Persona/user profile (see page 97)
- Jobs to be done (see page 75)

How much time and what materials do we need?

Group size

2–3

- A team of 2 per interview is ideal.
- One person documents and records, while the other person poses the questions.

Typical duration

20–30 min.

- Usually 20-30 minutes or as long as the interview or conversation lasts.
- The inference of a task to be performed can take some additional time since the "job to be done" is often not obvious.

Materials needed

- Print several empathy map templates in A4 or A3
- Pens and Post-its in order to write the essential points on the empathy map

Template: Empathy map

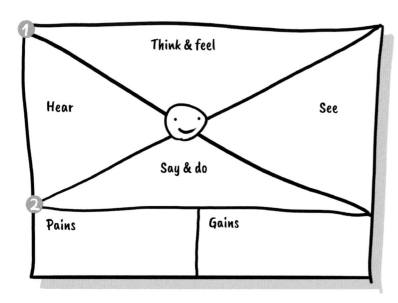

How the tool is applied...

- In the empathy map, we explore "needs." We think in terms of verbs (activities) for which the user needs help, not in nouns (solutions).
- Outline the layout on paper or use the empathy map template.
- **Step 1:** Fill in the fields in the template during (or just after) the interview.
  1. WHAT DOES THE CUSTOMER/USER SEE?
     - What does his environment look like?
     - Where is the customer? What does he see?
  2. WHAT DOES THE CUSTOMER/USER HEAR?
     - What does the user/customer hear?
     - Who influences him? Who speaks with him?
  3. WHAT DOES THE CUSTOMER/USER THINK & FEEL?
     - What emotions drives the customer/user?
     - What do the customers/users think?
     - What does it say about them and their attitudes?
  4. WHAT DOES THE CUSTOMER/USER SAY & DO?
     - What does the customer/user say?
     - What are all the things the customer/user must do?
     - Where does the user behave in a contradictory way?

- **Step 2:** Also fill in the fields PAINS AND GAINS
  - What are his/her biggest problems and challenges?
  - What are the opportunities and benefits he/she might have?

94

This is the favorite tool of Laurène Racine

Position:
Product Manager at Ava

"Ambiguity surrounds us in every aspect of life. Design thinking not only provides a mindset to solve problems in an ambiguous world but also to thoroughly enjoy them."

Why is it her favorite tool?

Good design is based on a deep understanding of the person for whom you design. Designers have many methods to develop this kind of empathy. The empathy map helps us to navigate the situation with curiosity, like a beginner. Consciously and with all our senses, we undergo the experience the user is undergoing! The map is an excellent supplement. It helps to understand the persona and the situation of a customer, for example. But it works best if we put ourselves in the same situation.

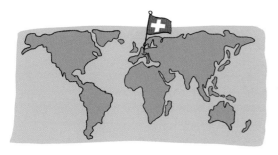

Country:
Switzerland

Affiliation:
Ava

Checked by: Jessika Weber-Sabil

Company/Position: Breda University of Applied Sciences, Sr. Researcher and Lecturer

---

There are other templates for the empathy map. If necessary, adapt them to the situation.

QUOTES AND THINGS SAID (SAY)	THOUGHTS & ATTITUDES (THINK)	
INFLUENCERS (HEAR)	JOBS TO BE DONE (DO)	FEELINGS & EMOTIONS (FEEL)
PAINS	GAINS	

Expert tips:

Create a basis for the value proposition
- Complete the PAINS AND GAINS later in the discussion with the team. This way, a review of the statements in the empathy map and reflecting on them takes place at the same time.
- Infer from the DO the customer tasks (jobs to be done).
- This way, you get a solid basis for the creation of the persona and the value proposition canvas.

Document the findings
- The findings from the interaction must be well documented. Using photographs and videos is useful here because it is easy to share them with the design team.
- Write down the most surprising and most important quotes and statements verbatim.

Focus on human values
- Thoughts, opinions, feelings, and emotions cannot be observed directly. Instead, they are inferred from a wide range of clues. Also, pay attention to body language, tone, and word selection; they usually say more than the spoken words. Capture them with a video camera.

Focus on the key aspects
- Focus on the most important points, that is, only the three major PAINS and GAINS.

Look for contradictions
- Pay attention to contradictions and think about their significance. Often, we can identify something new from contradictions between two characteristics or statements – for example, a contradiction between what the user/customer is saying and how he ultimately acts.

Description of the use case

- After the interview, all participants summarize their key findings and enter them on the empathy map.
- Since Lilly's team has recorded the entire interview with the extreme user on video, key passages can be viewed again.
- In the end, the pains and gains as well as the customer tasks (jobs to be done) are determined. Then the team transfers these findings to the user profile, later to a persona that conforms to these findings.

Key learnings

- Empathy is the ability to understand other people, their lives, their situation, their work, and solve problems from their perspective. Building empathy means meeting the user.
- Use verbs, not nouns. Needs are verbs (activities with which the user needs help). Nouns are usually solutions.
- Review and question assumptions and derive insights from it.

Tool for download

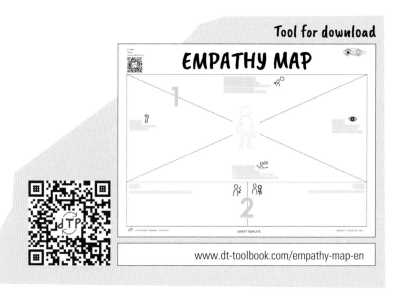

www.dt-toolbook.com/empathy-map-en

Persona/User profile
including variations as freestyle persona and future user

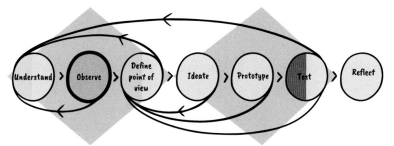

I would like...

to learn more about the user/customer and a possible solution.

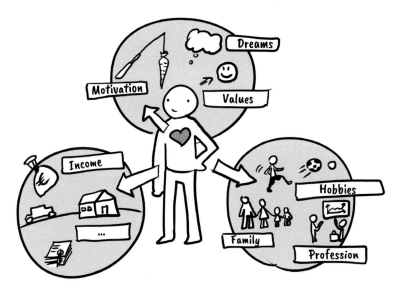

What you can do with the tool:

- Create a fictional character who is a potential user/customer of a solution.
- Create a picture of the user/customer that is shared by everybody on the team.
- Visualize the goals, desires, and needs of a typical user/customer and share them with the design team.
- Come to a consistent understanding of a target group.
- Document stories and pictures that a typical user/customer experiences.

Some information on the tool:

- A persona (often referred to as user persona, customer persona, or buyer persona) is a fictitious character created to represent a user or customer type.
- The persona puts a potential new solution (e.g. a website, a brand, a product, or a service) into the context of the respective needs and the jobs to be done.
- This can refer to individual functions, interactions, or the visual design of a website.
- A persona should be described as accurately as possible. This means it has a name, gender, and the basic demographic data (e.g. age, profession, hobbies). Information on the personality and characteristics of the persona are also recorded. Goals, needs, and fears are inferred from it. Similarly, the biography of a persona may help to draw conclusions about the purchasing behavior from the social milieu.
- The team should be able to meet the persona like a real person.

What tools might be used as an alternative?

- Persona from the Internet
- Freestyle persona (see variation on page 99)
- Future user persona (see page 100)

Which tools support working with the user profile or the persona?

- Interview for empathy (see page 57)
- Empathy map (see page 93)
- 5W+H questions (see page 71)

How much time and what materials do we need?

Group size

2–5

- The entire design team (2-5 members) takes part actively in the discussion and contributes observations and insights.
- The user profile can also be filled in separately.

Typical duration

20–40 min.

- For the mere creation of a customer profile, 20-40 minutes are usually enough. For more details (e.g. based on photos), more time must be planned
- A separate customer profile or persona should be created for each problem statement.
- In addition, two or more people can make up a target group.

Materials needed

- Template or flip chart with a structure drawn in
- Pens and Post-its
- Photos from the observation of potential customers in their natural environment

Procedure and template: Persona/user profile canvas

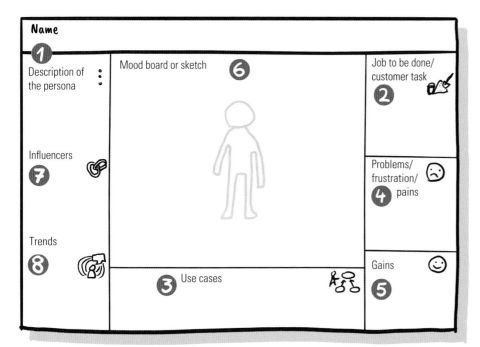

How the tool is applied...

- Collect information on a potential user and discuss with the team which type of persona might be representative for the problem statement.
- **Step 1:** Describe the persona. Give the persona a name, gender, and age. Add additional attributes such as social milieu, family, hobbies, and so on.
- **Step 2:** What is the task (job) the user does? Where can he be helped?
- **Step 3:** Describe all use cases in the context of the problem statement (where? what? how?). Where does the user make use of our proposal? What happens before and after? How does he do it?
- **Step 4:** What are the biggest difficulties and problems the user has? They can be unsolved problems or difficulties the user has with existing products and offers.
- **Step 5:** Determine the gains (possibilities, benefits) and pains (problems, challenges) the user has or might have.
- **Step 6:** Draw a sketch that visualizes the customer (optional); or supplement the user profile with photos or clippings from magazines, similar to a mood board like the ones designers use for inspiration.
- **Step 7:** Think about who has an influence on the persona (family, children, stakeholders, etc.) and what general trends (e.g. megatrends, market trends, technology trends, etc.) influence the persona (**Step 8**).

How much time and what materials do we need?

Group size

2–5

- The entire design team (2-5 members) takes an active part in the discussion and contributes observations and findings.

Typical duration

20–60 min.

- 20-60 minutes are needed for the creation of a persona.
- In addition, enough time must be scheduled to gather information on the persona and for verifying the persona.

Materials needed

- Sheet of paper 2×1 meters
- Pens, Post-its, marker
- Magazines, newspapers
- Adhesive tape, glue
- Pictures from the Internet
- Photos

Procedure: Freestyle persona

How the tool is applied...

- The freestyle persona emerges ad hoc and is based on the memories of a user we encountered.
- **Step 1:** Create a life-size model of the user.
  Tip: Spread the sheet of paper on the floor. One person lies down on it in the desired position, and another team member draws the outline.
- **Step 2:** Depict the user in the context of the problem or of his actions. Complete the drawing with typical elements.
- **Step 3:** Complete the freestyle persona with demographic information; define age and gender.
- **Step 4:** Give the persona a name.
- **Step 5:** Use elements from the customer profile (e.g. pains, gains, jobs to be done, use cases) and add behaviors, habits, emotions, and social relationships of the persona.
- **Step 6:** Complete the persona. Fit out the persona with pictures from magazines and newspapers and discuss which brands he/she likes wearing, by whom he/she is influenced. Be specific when it comes to values, morality, and environmental factors.

How much time and what materials do we need?

Group size

2–5

• The entire design team (ideally, 2-5 members) takes an active part in the discussion and contributes observations and findings.

Typical duration

45–60 min.

• 15-30 minutes are needed for the creation of a future user.
• Additional time (15-30 minutes) must be planned for the collection of information.
• Allow for time devoted to interpretation.

Materials needed

• Sheet of paper 2×1 meters
• Pens
• Magazines, newspapers
• Adhesive tape, glue
• Pictures from the Internet
• Photos

Procedure: Future user persona

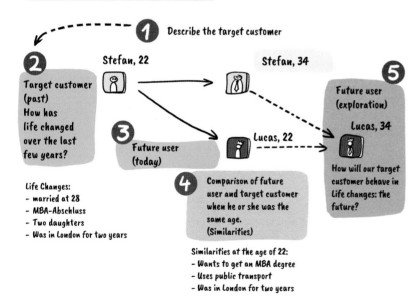

① Describe the target customer

② Target customer (past) How has life changed over the last few years?

Life Changes:
– married at 28
– MBA-Abschluss
– Two daughters
– Was in London for two years

Stefan, 22

Stefan, 34

③ Future user (today)

④ Comparison of future user and target customer when he or she was the same age. (Similarities)

Similarities at the age of 22:
– Wants to get an MBA degree
– Uses public transport
– Was in London for two years

Lucas, 22

⑤ Future user (exploration)

Lucas, 34

How will our target customer behave in Life changes: the future?

Note: Based on the *Playbook for Strategic Foresight and Innovation* by Tamara Carleton and William Cockayne, 2013, available at www.innovation.io/playbook

How the tool is applied...

The design team tries to extrapolate the persona into the future. Particularly in the case of innovation projects with a long time line (>5 years), such considerations make sense.

• **Step 1:** Describe the target customer.
• **Step 2:** Think about and discuss on the team what lifestyle and values this customer had 12 years ago and the decisions he made then.
  – How has all this changed over the course of time? (Changes due to marriage at 28, MBA degree, father of two daughters, stay abroad in London for 2 years)
• **Step 3:** On the basis of this generational research, describe the future user in the here and now.
• **Step 4:** Compare the two persons (Stefan and Lucas) when they were 22 years old and try to understand what has changed in their lives and what has stayed the same until they reached the age of 34.
  – Similarities at the age of 22: both want to possess an MBA degree; both use public transport; both are single.
• **Step 5:** Extrapolate the future target customer. Our future user is the same age as our current target customer.
• **Step 6:** What insights do you gain from this? What will be more important in the future?

This is the favorite tool of Carina Teichmann

Position:
Agile Digitization Consultant, Mimacom AG

"Personas represent the core of design thinking. With the persona concept, we investigate the user's education, life style, interests, values, goals, needs, desires, attitudes, and actions to build radical innovation."

Why is it her favorite tool?

I find it exciting to imagine the person I want to develop a product for – lots of roles and characters pop into my head. A freestyle persona makes working with a potential user more vivid; this way, I can understand the needs and wishes of the customer better. A life-size persona helps to imagine the potential customer or user better.

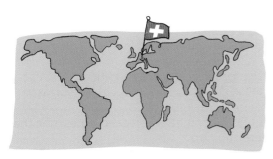

Country:
Switzerland

Affiliation:
Mimacom AG

Checked by: **Florian Baumgartner**

Company/Position: Innoveto by Crowdinnovation AG | Innovation Enabler and Partner

Expert tips:

Be as realistic as possible
- With certain problem statements, we have come to see so-called persona twins as rather useful; for example, a married couple or other systems that interact with one another (e.g. Robona in human/robot interaction).
- General and gender-neutral personas that are relevant across all age categories should be avoided. This is why we recommend describing the persona in as much detail and as realistically as possible.

Continuously improve the persona
- In general, we tend to make quick assumptions about certain target groups. As a result, stereotypes emerge that are based on false assumptions. If we feel uncertain, we should go out to find somebody who is like our persona. If we don't find anybody, our assumptions were wrong.
- Develop personas across the entire design cycle. With every interaction, when testing prototypes and when making observations, insights are added that we then share with our design team and stick on the persona.

Use quotations where appropriate
- We also achieved good results by enriching the persona with meaningful quotes from customers and users. This way, the persona is even more authentic and alive.
- With respect to the number of personas per problem statement, we should only create as many personas as we, on the team, can remember, including their characteristics.

Description of the use case

- In this project, Lilly's team works with a user profile canvas for several types of customer. The team likes the structure, because it makes key findings visible quickly.
- They describe the background of the persona, his/her information, behavior, pains, gains, and so on, and enrich the persona with quotes.
- The team would also like to work with future personas. The human/robot relationship is becoming more and more important in the future, and Lilly's team would like to see how people integrate that fact into their teams.

Key learnings

- A persona is a fictitious character, which is created to represent a user or customer type.
- The persona is based on facts from interviews and observations.
- Complete the persona with pictures from newspapers and magazines.
- The aim is to learn more about the pains, gains, and the tasks to be fulfilled (jobs to be done) of the persona in the context of the problem statement.

Tool for download

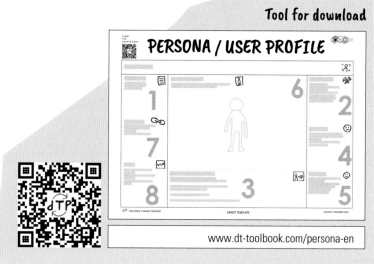

www.dt-toolbook.com/persona-en

Customer journey map

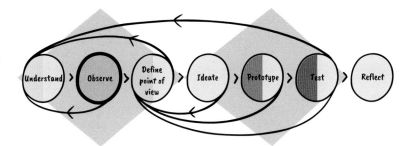

I would like...

to walk in the shoes of my customers to understand in great detail what they experience when they interact with our company, our products, or services.

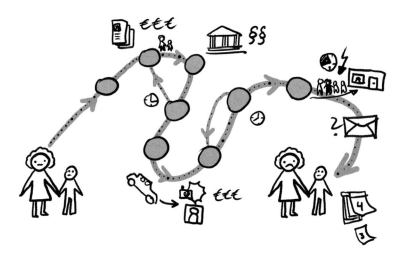

What you can do with the tool:

- Establish a common understanding on the team about the experiences of customers with a company, product, or service.
- Identify "moments of misery" that negatively affect the customer experience.
- Achieve a solid understanding of all the customer's touch points.
- Close problematic points and gaps in the customer interaction and realize a unique experience.
- Design a new and improved customer experience.
- Develop new products and services continuously on a customer-oriented basis.

Some information on the tool:

- A customer journey map allows us to build empathy with the customer by visualizing his actions, thoughts, emotions, and feelings that emerge in an interaction.
- In contrast to a process map, which can usually only map the internal processes of a company, a customer journey map is geared to the human being and his/her needs.
- In addition, a customer journey map looks at the actions that are not directly associated with the product or service (e.g. informing, waiting, ordering, delivery, installing, customer service, disposing of).
- The customer journey map is usually developed and used in the "understand," "observe," and "prototype" phases.
- The customer journey also provides a good base for the creation of a service blueprint.

What tools might be used as an alternative?

- Service blueprint (see page 203)

Which tools support working with the customer journey map?

- Interview for empathy (see page 57)
- Persona/user profiles (see page 97)
- Jobs to be done (see page 75)

How much time and what materials do we need?

Group size

4–6

- Mixed teams of experts and people with little experience in the respective process.
- Ideally, 4-6 members in each group.

Typical duration

120–240 min.

- The duration depends on the complexity. An initial draft can emerge after 120 minutes.
- Often, variations are needed for specific customer groups and events on the customer journey map.

Materials needed

- Post-its, pens, markers
- Large whiteboard
- Plenty of space on the wall for hanging up pictures of customers, locations, activities, and for visualizing the journey

Procedure and template: Customer journey map

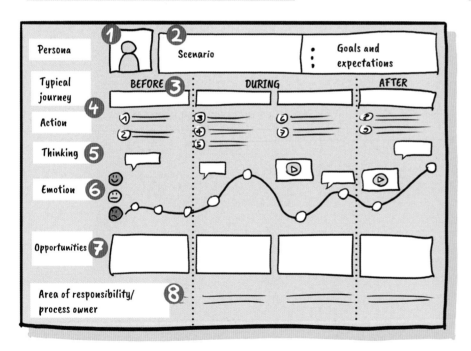

How the tool is applied...

- **Step 1:** Choose a persona to be used in the customer journey map and share the story of the persona with the design team.
- **Step 2:** Then choose a scenario or job to be done. What does the persona do and what is the context? It may be an end-to-end experience or a part of it.
- **Step 3:** Define what happens BEFORE, DURING, and AFTER the actual experience to make sure that the most important steps are included. Mark all experience steps (e.g. using Post-its). It is easier to compile an overview on the meta-level before expanding and elaborating.
- **Step 4:** Decide which interactions should be assigned where and how. The template gives us space for the typical journey and the respective actions.
- **Steps 5 & 6:** Supplement what the persona thinks (Step 5) and the emotion he/she feels (Step 6). Capture the emotional status (positive and negative) of each step with colored glue dots or emoticons.
- **Steps 7 & 8:** Define potential areas of improvement (Step 7) and the people responsible for the action/process within the organization (Step 8). Once a clear picture of the experience emerges, the design team automatically comes up with questions, new insights, and potential improvements.

Position:
Customer experience designer and innovation consultant for new way of working, including customer experience, design thinking, lean startup, and innovation.

"Design thinking, as with many other methodologies, should be approached from a principles point of view. The tools should be applied in a 'fit for-purpose' manner in line with these principles rather than in a dogmatic, prescribed sequence."

Why is it her favorite tool?

Companies and innovation teams are good at improving an existing process or at pondering and creating new ideas in an isolated manner behind closed doors. They focus too rarely on the customer and his experience with a company across all interactions. Customer journey maps trigger "EUREKA" moments for innovation teams because the process is looked at from a different perspective.

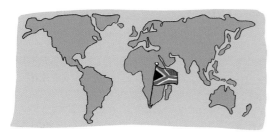

Country:
South Africa

Affiliation:
Independent Consultant

Checked by: **Bryan Richards**

Company/Position: Design innovator at Aspen Impact and professor at Indiana University

Expert tips:

Think creatively
- Think like an investigative journalist, ask questions to deepen the emotional customer journey substantially.
- The context (person and scenario) is important. The purchase of a house is an entirely different journey for newlyweds who buy their first home than the purchase of a holiday home is for a millionaire.
- "Journeys" that are useful for the understanding of an existing experience are, for instance, all actions a customer undertakes; the context of the activity; thinking about a decision; the feeling after the purchase; and all possibilities for improving the interaction.

Create actions and goals
- Actions, goals, customer expectations, and failures are "journeys" that we can use for the design of a future experience, for an existing process, or for a new product. Also for situations that exceed expectations.
- Measures that exceed expectations.
- We can map a possible customer journey in such a way that it can be used as a first prototype. We can test the initial contact of a customer interaction, for example.
- There are many ways to improve a customer journey, for example, removing emotions or offering solutions earlier on the journey. In addition, interfaces between the physical and digital world can be designed, positive experiences can be intensified, negative experiences removed, or the sequence can be changed.

Description of the use case

- Lilly's team divides the customer journey map into main phases and looks at each phase separately. This way, the design thinking team is better able to focus on each phase.
- The team makes sure that all consider the same use case and agree on the goals.
- On the basis of the customer journey map and the emotion curve, the team determines the major problem areas that should be considered.
- New insights emerge from the discussion, for example, that the scaling via franchising has not been optimally set up.

Key learnings

- The customer journey map helps the team to come to a shared common understanding of the customer and his problems by capturing the emotions along a journey.
- The touch points show the points of contact the user has with a company. They can be selectively optimized in order to offer the user the desired experience.

Tool for download

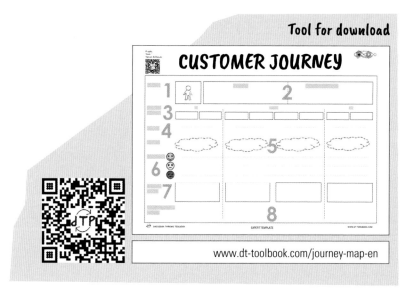

www.dt-toolbook.com/journey-map-en

AEIOU

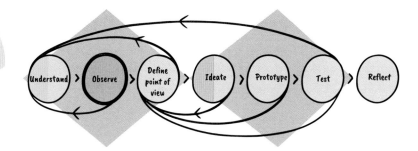

I would like...

to learn more about the problem, the user/customer, and his environment.

What you can do with the tool:

- Bring structure to an observation and ask the right W+H questions that are decisive for gaining knowledge.
- Facilitate the evaluation of many findings by larger design teams performing parallel observations.
- Relate the user to the activity, the space, and to an object.
- Collect insights that are not out in the public.
- Have inexperienced design teams also collect insights, because the AEIOU tool provides structure and guidance.

Some information on the tool:

- The AEIOU framework was developed by Rick Robinson, Ilya Prokopoff, John Cain, and Julie Pokorny in 1991.
- In design thinking, AEIOU is used in field observation and as a visualization technique for new insights.
- The aim is to obtain in-depth insights on the potential users by means of W+H questions.
- AEIOU is mainly used in the "understand" and "observe" phases. It can also be a source of inspiration for new ideas.

What tools can be used as an alternative?

- Spradley's 9 dimensions: space, actors, activities, objectives, acts, events, time, goals, feelings
- A (x 4): atmosphere, actors, activities, artifacts
- Sotirin: territory, people, stuff, talk
- POSTA: person, objects, situation, time, activity

Which tools support working with the AEIOU framework?

- Explorative interview (see page 63)
- Persona/user profile (see page 97)
- 5W+H questions (see page 71)
- Ask 5x why (see page 67)

How much time and what materials do we need?

Group size

1–2

- 1-2 people per observation are ideal.
- Depending on the situation, all those involved make observations and do the documentation; or one person interacts with the user, while the other person does the documentation.

Typical duration

60 min.– 24 hrs.

- An observation can take from 1 hour to one whole day.
- The duration and frequency depend on the problem statement and on how fast insights can be collected.

Materials needed

- Print the AEIOU questionnaire in A4 size, glue to a piece of firm cardboard or fasten to a clipboard, so it's easy to write on it
- Pens

Procedure and template: AEIOU

 ① Research

  ② Observation

 ③ + ④

Activities	What happens? What are the persons doing? What is their task? What activities do they carry out? What happens before and after?
Environment	What does the environment look like? What is the nature and function of the space?
Interaction	How do the individual systems interact with one another? Are there any interfaces? How do the users interact among one another? How does the operation work?
Objects	What objects and devices are used? Who uses the objects and in which environment?
Users	Who are the users? What role do the users play? Who influences them?

How the tool is applied...

- **Step 1:** Start with the research and find out where the user can be found, at what times, and how to contact him.
- **Step 2:** Be where the user/customer currently is in the context of the problem statement.
- **Step 3:** Work with the AEIOU template that provides questions and instructions in the individual areas to be observed.
- Each team member is handed a questionnaire for the observation, so everybody can take notes. A smartphone makes it possible to take photos and make videos.
- Collect impressions in the form of notes, photos, videos, interviews, and field observations.
- Especially in the field observation, the AEIOU framework can be used as an entry point for observing the user in his/her environment.
- Lend structure to the records after the observation. It's best to operate within the structure of the corresponding headings.
- Supplement the direct observations with photos or short videos.
- After completion of the field observation with the AEIOU framework, cluster and sort the findings in thematic blocks with summarizing headings so you can identify a pattern.

Position:
Design Thinking Coach & Design Strategist at relevate

"Design thinking is not just a method or process, it's a mindset of how you approach challenges. It helps us to create products and services that bring real value to people and gives us creative confidence to navigate the landscape of an ever-changing world."

Why is it her favorite tool?

Working with the AEIOU tool is a little like a treasure hunt: You never know what great things you'll discover. After all, discoveries are at the heart of innovation. It is also a fairly humbling experience that reminds us of how little we basically know about our users, their environment, and their interaction with things.

Expert tips:

Adapt the AEIOU framework to your needs
- The AEIOU framework is a good starting point for an observation.
- The questions in AEIOU should be adapted to the specific needs.
- AEIOU is not a rigid framework – it simply provides categories that have proved to be useful. Among other things, AEIOU is used as a method within the framework of "Design your future" (see page 289), where it serves as a reflection on records from an energy journal. The "activities" area in this example contains questions about yourself, for example, "What activities do I enjoy?"

Tailor the structure to the problem at hand
- For more complex problem statements, it is advisable to work with sub-categories. This is recommended when events happen in a chronological sequence.
- In general, the individual AEIOU categories are strongly connected to one another, and it is advisable to establish a mental link in this respect.

Show, don't tell
- Drawings of a sequence and storytelling allow us to describe the bigger picture and share it effectively with our team.

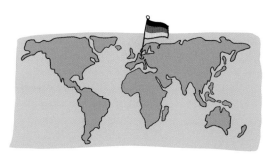

Country:
Germany

Affiliation:
relevate

Company/Position: SIX, Innovation Manager

Description of the use case

- The AEIOU framework gives Lilly's team a simple structure for observations. The results of different observations can later be easily consolidated.
- In addition, this procedure already contains the most important W+H questions.
- Ad-hoc observations can be made without much preparation.

Key learnings

- AEIOU helps in intensive research and field observation for inspiration, and gaining basic knowledge of a problem.
- It is particularly suitable for inexperienced design teams because it provides structure and a framework, and the results can be quickly consolidated later.

Tool for download

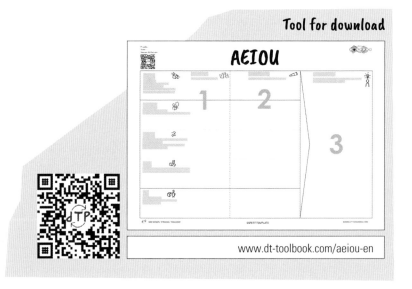

www.dt-toolbook.com/aeiou-en

Analysis questions builder

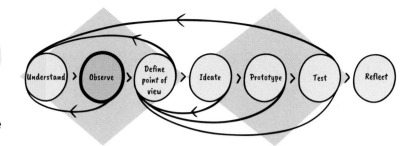

I would like...

to make it possible to gain insights from big data analysis that are useful in various phases of the design thinking process.

What you can do with the tool:

- Identify relevant factors of influence that constitute the basis for a new or improved product or offer; then analyze it in a targeted manner.
- Make sure that you are sufficiently creative in the analysis process, because the focus is on technical "details."
- Boost the efficiency of the analysis process by avoiding empty runs.
- Make use of a standardized procedure in order to examine the problem and solution space again with the help of data.

Some information on the tool:

- Data yields many answers, provided the right questions are asked. The analysis questions builder helps us to ask the right questions in order to gain good insights.
- A structured procedure creates freedom for the necessary creativity to identify the relevant factors of influence, because diversion by creativity killers is avoided.
- When we are aware of the factors of influence and then work systematically with the W+H questions, we will develop appropriate questions for the analysis within a short time and quickly gain insights into the actual analysis process afterward.
- We use the analysis questions builder mainly in the "understand" and "observe" phases.

What tools can be used as an alternative?

- Extreme users/lead users (see page 79)
- Context mapping (see page 133)

Which tools support working with the analysis questions builder?

- 5W+H questions (see page 71)
- Ask 5x why (see page 67)
- Jobs to be done (see page 75)

How much time and what materials do we need?

Group size

- An interdisciplinary team of 2-5 is ideal.
- Prior knowledge in the field of data analytics is not necessary.

2–5

Typical duration

- The duration and frequency depend strongly on the problem statement. Usually 30-60 minutes per question.

30–60
min.

Materials needed

- Multiple large sheets of paper (e.g. flip chart sheets) and a whiteboard to write down the questions that have been developed
- Pens

Procedure: Analysis questions builder

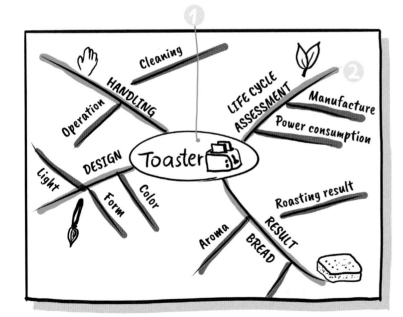

Ask WH questions

Select WH questions and analyze data

How the tool is applied...

- **Step 1:** Define the center of the analysis questions builder. It can be a new product, offer, or a new process. The needs the product must meet, that is, what it must be able to do, are defined as relevant factors of influence; for example, life cycle assessment (power consumption, resources for production). These ramifications are made so often until it can be ensured that really everything that is relevant is listed. With this procedure, we can often dig up new insights.
- **Step 2:** Next, define the most relevant factors of influence. Either relevant data is already on hand, or ask a focus group and explore whether the design thinking team already has the knowledge.
- **Step 3:** In the next step, the questions are determined. Use the W+H questions for the three to five most relevant factors of influence. Example: the aroma of toast: Who likes toasted bread? How dark is the bread allowed to be so it doesn't taste burned? What constitutes the flavor of toast? When does it have to taste especially good? Where can you buy the best toasted bread?
- **Step 4:** In the last step, go through the recorded W+H questions and think about where data could help in answering them. Only then should you think about where the data comes from. The data is usually available in the company, on the Internet, or it must be collected.

This is the favorite tool of Esther Cahn

Position:
Co-Founder and CEO of Signifikant Solutions AG

"Design thinking is a valuable instrument to bring structured creativity to an analysis process."

Why is it her favorite tool?

In the numerous workshops in which this tool was used, we discovered time and again how all of a sudden aspects and factors of influence cropped up that nobody had on their radar. Once the questions are defined, the subsequent analysis process is considerably more efficient.

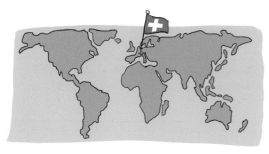

Country:
Switzerland

Affiliation:
Signifikant
Solutions AG

Checked by: Amanda Mota

Company/Position: Docway Co., UX designer

Expert tips:

Use all the elements of the design thinking mindset
- Drawing up a map is an important creative process. We should take time for it, so the work is well prepared with data.
- The use of this tool has been of great value to us, especially on interdisciplinary teams, so that no factors of influence are forgotten.
- We should not be put off by the fact that it may be difficult to obtain certain data. Once we know what data we actually need and do a little research, we'll unearth more data than we initially thought possible.

The hybrid model combines design thinking and data analytics
- Our experience with the application of the hybrid model (combination of big data analytics and design thinking) was generally quite good. The model pushes us to use data insights and human insights as the situation requires it throughout the entire design thinking cycle.

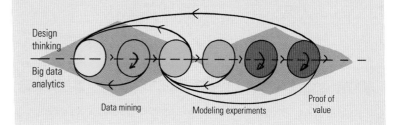

113

Description of the use case

- Lilly recommends that if her teams work with big data analytics in a design project, they should refrain from applying the analytics tool directly; instead, they should first think about the structure and the questions to be answered with the data analysis.
- In the example of a virtual assistant, one of Lilly's design teams considered what features make a good assistant, which attributes are really important, and finally how these questions can be answered with data analytics.

Key learnings

- Starting with specific questions in a data analysis process makes it far more efficient.
- Data and tools are usually not the real problem.
- Be creative, even when it comes to big data analytics.

Tool for download

Analysis Questions Builder

www.dt-toolbook.com/analyse-builder-en

Peers observing peers

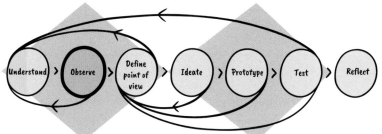

I would like...

to understand at eye level what is really going on.

What you can do with the tool:

- Explore the behavior and the needs of a user in a "natural" and inconspicuous way.
- Obtain a better understanding of the problem or the defined design challenge.
- Obtain new insights on how the problem is solved today, what workarounds are used, and how the process is lived in the real world.

Some general information on the tool:

- The observation of peers helps us to understand how users behave in a "natural" environment.
- Peers observing peers is especially helpful in cases where interviews are not possible, or if no direct interviews are to be conducted in an initial phase.
- This procedure can also provide far more profound insights in the "test" phase, for example, of prototypes or minimum viable products (so called MVPs).
- Peers observing peers is mainly used in the "understand" and "observe" phases.

What tools can be used as an alternative?

- AEIOU (see page 107)
- Interview for empathy (see page 57)
- Persona/user profile (see page 97)
- Solution interview (e.g. in the test phase, see page 225)

Which tools support working with peers observing peers?

- Empathy map (see page 93)
- Ask 5x why (see page 67)
- 5W+H questions (see page 71)

How much time and what materials do we need?

Group size

3–7

- Depending on the situation and the design challenge, no more than 3 people should carry out a single observation.
- Optimally, one peer observes another.

Typical duration

60–240 min.

- The duration depends very much on what we want to observe. Usually 60-240 min.
- After the observation, the documentation and the exchange with other observers may take some time as well.

Materials needed

- Notepad and pen
- Cell phone or video camera, if the observed people agree to it
- Sketches or photos

Procedure and template: Peers observing peers

How the tool is applied...

Always make a distinction between observation and interpretation. Peers observing peers is about what we see, not about what we think. This is why we use the template and only describe what we really see.

- **Step 1:** Describe what is seen, for example, how something is done. If we already have knowledge about the context and want to find out the frequency of a certain behavior, additional categories can be defined to determine how often something happens, for instance.
- **Step 2:** Write down all of the steps the "peer" makes. It is necessary to ensure that the subjects behave as normally as possible during the observation.
- **Step 3:** In addition to collecting insights, it is advisable to discuss with other observers how they perceived the process. Typical questions are: What came as a surprise to you? What have you learned?

This way, we often gather more information that goes beyond the documented observation.

- **Step 4:** Interpret the behavior.
- **Step 5:** Infer relevant conclusions from it.

This is the favorite tool of Ina Goller

Position:
Professor of Innovation Management at Bern University of Applied Science Founder of Skillsgarden AG

"Design thinking is by far the most fun approach to generate and validate ideas so that sustainable solutions can be generated."

Why is it her favorite tool?

With peers observing peers, we can learn a lot. Not only does it enable us to talk about problems or solutions, it also allows us to gain profound insights into routines, for example. It is my favorite tool because I have complete confidence in the approach and the significance of the findings. It gives us information on reality and on how processes are actually lived. It shows how informal organizational paths are taken in order to accomplish a task.

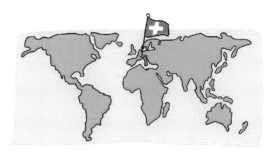

Country:
Switzerland

Affiliation:
Skillsgarden

Checked by: **Jean Michel Chardon**

Company/Position: Logitech AG | Head of AI, CTO Office

Expert tips:

Define a clear focus
What is to be observed? Who is to be observed? What is to be learned?

Training is essential
Observation without interpretation can be learned; likewise, how the findings of the observers should be handled.

It's not just about observation
The process of data collection is also very important. The same is true for interviewing the observers after the observation.

Separate observation from interpretation
Pay heed to shortcuts and workarounds that were not intended in this way and for which the user uses homemade aids or uses things for purposes they were not made for.

Pay attention to routines and details
Also provide quantifiable information, for example, how long something takes. Quantitative analyses can be easily visualized with charts and graphs.

If possible, do it yourself
Slip into the shoes of other people and imitate their actions. Say out loud what is being done, while the other people on the team take notes.

Description of the use case

- Lilly's teams want to learn more about the processes in large companies.
- In many observations that they had made themselves, they came away with the impression that the people did not behave authentically.
- With peers observing peers, they want to choose a different approach. They instruct employees in which way they should observe their environment and their colleagues. The team gets a completely new perspective!

Key learnings

- Define what is to be observed.
- Find motivated observers. Make sure they know what the difference is between observation and interpretation.
- Take advantage of the interaction between the observers for gaining knowledge.

www.dt-toolbook.com/observing-peers-en

Trend analysis

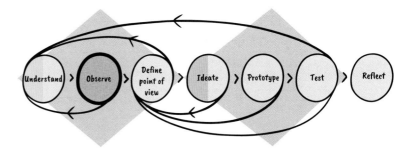

I would like...

to recognize trends at an early stage and integrate them in the problem definition and find a solution.

What you can do with the tool:

- Explore megatrends, trends, and their points of contact.
- Visualize the greater correlations between trends and discuss with the design thinking team or clients whether and how the trends interact.
- Avoid a viewpoint that is too simplistic, subjective, and possibly monocausal and find a holistic approach.
- Identify and present overlaps and causal relationships between trends and draw conclusions about the possible significance of a trend.
- Gather valuable context information about the problem statement or an idea.

Some information on the tool:

- The goal of trend analysis is to identify and quantify trends. In addition, the causes and the influence on the project are explored. On this basis, opportunities and risks are identified and options for action are inferred.
- The trend analysis tool helps with the collection of valuable context information revolving around societal, economic, and technological developments.
- It serves as a starting point for further steps, for example, the preparation of product or service concepts.
- The understanding of trends that are dependent on one another lends depth and quality to the design process.
- When looking for individual phenomenological characteristics and overlaps of the trends, we proceed in small iterative steps, which then continually lead to new findings.

What tools can be used as an alternative?

- Context mapping (see page 133)
- Phenomenology
- Scenario techniques
- Prognostic crowd sourcing

Which tools support working with the trend analysis?

- Explorative interview (see page 63)
- Ask 5x why (see page 67)
- Vision cone (see page 141)

How much time and what materials do we need?

Group size

2–5

- Ideally on teams with 2-5 members.
- Depending on the focus in terms of the subject and on the complexity, more people can be involved concurrently or one after the other.

Typical duration

120–240 min.

- The time period depends on how complex the question is and how much research had been done in the run-up.
- A first trend analysis with a matching affinity chart can be done in 2 hours.

Materials needed

- Large piece of paper or cardboard
- Colored cords (subway lines)
- Pins, small clothespins
- Pens
- Post-its (in different colors)

Procedure: Trend analysis

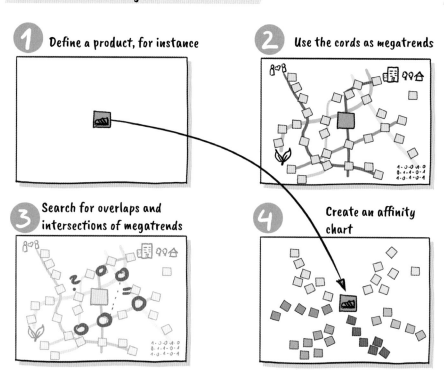

1 Define a product, for instance

2 Use the cords as megatrends

3 Search for overlaps and intersections of megatrends

4 Create an affinity chart

How the tool is applied...

Use the trend tube mapping (megatrends) for the trend analysis

- **Step 1:** The focus is on a product, service, or a development to be considered, which is written on a Post-it.
- **Step 2:** The cords in different colors represent the megatrends such as urbanization, digitization, and sustainability. The phenomena or manifestations of the megatrends are hung from the cords. They have been determined beforehand in a workshop or a focus group.
- **Step 3:** Subsequently, connections and any overlaps are searched for, just as they can be seen on a subway line map. Then the team investigates where the product or service is located (ideally at the intersection of several megatrends).

Expand the trend analysis with an affinity chart (trend topics)

- **Step 4:** An affinity chart is a grouping of matching elements and visualizes typical patterns. It is used for the structured output of the trend analysis. For example, the elements at the crossing points are examined more closely and possible characteristics and directions are searched for (e.g. hiking → city hiking). The picture is completed by small cards matching industry, consumer, marketing, and technology trends.
Note: Cards can be used in multiple ways by simply duplicating them.

This is the favorite tool of Thomas Duschlbauer

Position:
CEO KompeTrend

"Even though the work with trends and megatrends has certain limitations, it opens up new perspectives and kicks off the discussion on the design team."

Why is it his favorite tool?

I like working with the physical trend analysis because when dealing with the trends directly in a small group, new viewpoints emerge, can be revised, and reformulated. It is a struggle for insights, and the visualizations help to get a grip on the complexity.

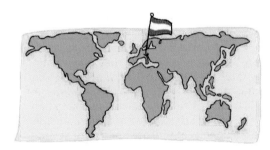

Country:
Austria

Affiliation:
KompeTrend

Checked by: Yves Karcher

Company/Position: InnoExec Sàrl | Workshop Facilitator for Innovation and Organisations design

Expert tips:

Validate the findings with statistical data
- Since, for starters, the application of the trend analysis provides only a purely qualitative perspective, it is advisable to substantiate and verify these assumptions with statistical data.

Visualizations help to reduce complexity
- It is necessary for the visualization to have the megatrends at hand in a documented and up-to-date form.
- The more megatrends (trend tube mapping) we identify, the more complex the process and the more space we need for implementation.
- If we want to locate an already developed product or service in the context of trends (e.g. for a business plan), then a smaller selection of trends and their manifestations (e.g. digitization → IOT, Big Data, AI, VR, AR, etc.) is sufficient.

Use the insights gained to their full extent
- We have found it very helpful to use the trends for new business models, products, or services. A manifold consideration of trends and their manifestations can, in combination, be the key for disruptive innovations (e.g. combination of artificial intelligence and blockchain).
- The 4th step (affinity chart) is especially valuable in our experience when we have specific questions about target group behavior or about the use of new technologies.
- The trend analysis also helps detect niches or identify opposing trends.

Description of the use case

- The design team has discovered a lot of vital issues by means of desk research. The statistical data and trends found help to understand the problem better.
- The quantitative trends as well as qualitative trend analyses with pictures show that Lilly's team relies on the right elements, which will become even more important in the future.

Key learnings

- With the trend analysis, the design team gets better guidance with regard to a problem statement or an idea.
- The discussion in the group helps to create a common image of megatrends, trends, and developments.
- Trends are constantly evolving, and continual reflection and analysis help to follow these changes.
- Use trend reports as well as Google Trends, an important (and free) online tool, for the detection and visualization of trends.

Tool for download

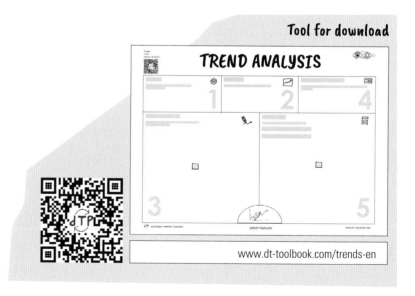

www.dt-toolbook.com/trends-en

122

Phase: Define point of view

At the end of the problem analysis, the results are summarized, clustered, discussed, and evaluated. The team view of the problem is formulated as a point of view. It is used later as a starting point in the search for a solution. Various methods, such as storytelling and "How might we..." as a questioning technique, support this process.

"How might we..." question

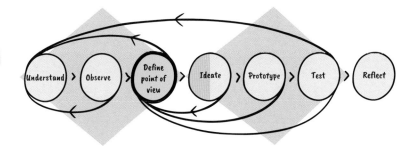

I would like...

to formulate a question that makes it possible later, in the "ideate" phase, to work in a targeted manner.

What you can do with the tool:

- Transform the needs identified into a real design challenge.
- Write down the goal of the later ideation and the goal of the design thinking team in a concrete sentence.
- Define the extent and scope of the ideation process.

Some information on the tool:

- The "How might we..." (HMW) question is an elementary component in *The Design Thinking Toolbox*.
- The HMW question uses a special language that helps to switch to a different way of thinking.
- "How" implies that there are more possible ways to solve the question. "Might" creates a safe space in which we know that a potential idea might work. "We" reminds us that we solve the problem as a team.

What tool can be used instead?

- Devil's advocate – "What would happen if people could not remember things?"
- By contrast – "What would happen if the pain is transformed into a gain?"
- Vice versa – "What would happen if, for example, the patient diagnosed the doctor?"
- Time frame – "What will/did the situation look like in 20 years/20 years ago?"
- Provocation – Photo/fabric/quote/sound/smell – "How do we design a solution when nobody wants to use anything else?"
- Analogy – Finding an analogy in order to solve the problem on this basis – "What can we learn from the pit stop at Formula One on the subject of time?"
- Miracle – "If we were magicians, how would we solve it?"

Which tools support working with this tool?

- Most of the tools from the "understand" and "observe" phases (see page 49–122)
- Storytelling (see page 129)

125

How much time and what materials do we need?

Group size

- Develop each HMW question in groups of 3-5.

3–5

Typical duration

5–15 min.

- The HMW question can be formulated quickly if good findings have been identified.
- The definition of an HMW question usually takes no longer than 15 minutes.

Materials needed

- Whiteboards or movable walls
- Post-its, pens, paper

Template: "How might we ..." question

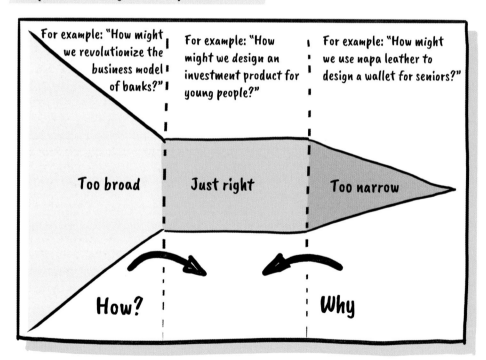

For example: "How might we revolutionize the business model of banks?"

For example: "How might we design an investment product for young people?"

For example: "How might we use napa leather to design a wallet for seniors?"

Too broad | Just right | Too narrow

How? | Why

How the tool is applied...

- Reflect upon the findings from the previous phases of "understand" and "observe." The result is a synthesis of the insights.
- Determine what needs the team should address and what qualifying additional information is relevant in this context.
- Motivate the design thinking team to come up with several "How might we..." questions that address the identified needs or opportunity field.
- Each question should adhere to the logic of "How might we..." followed by a verb (e.g. design), a noun (e.g. investment product), and the type of user (e.g. name of persona).
- Read the HMW question aloud and ask if the team is inspired by the question to find many solutions. If not, the question might be too narrow (e.g. it already anticipates a solution or does not allow for further exploration). Or the HMW question is too broad, that is, the question tries to improve the world, and the team feels lost when confronted with the task.
- In order to counteract this dilemma, there are two question techniques: "WHY," in order to expand the focus and "HOW," in order to narrow down the focus of consideration.
- Once the HMW question is rolled out, the ideation phase can begin. Start, for example, with an open brainstorming session that generates initial ideas.

This is the favorite tool of Andrés Bedoya

Position:
Innovation Project Manager, d.school Paris at École des Ponts

"Design thinking is more than a process, it's a culture that has the tremendous power of facilitating the transformation of reality into something that makes sense for humans."

Why is it his favorite tool?

As an engineer, I am a huge fan of different ideas, and the HMW question for me is the interface between the in-depth understanding of the users and an infinite number of possibilities that we can explore in the "ideate" phase, ultimately to realize a good solution for the user or customer.

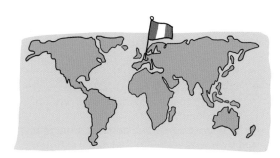

Country:
France

Affiliation:
d.School Paris

Checked by: Bettina Maisch

Company/Position: Siemens Corporate Technology, Senior Key Expert Consultant

How might we...

KNOW	UNDERSTAND	APPLY	EVALUATE	CREATE
define	predict	solve	frame	create
identify	reflect	apply for	compare	develop
describe	demonstrate	construct	experiment	change
match	differentiate	choose	ask	paraphrase
recognize	discover	prepare	check	develop
select	research	produce	correlate	imagine
investigate	transform	show	separate	negotiate
tell	describe	judge	analyze	design
visualize	compare	transfer	compare	structure

Expert tips:

There is no right and no wrong in the definition of questions
- When it comes to an HMW question, there is no right or wrong. We recommend relying on your gut feeling to decide whether the HMW question fits the problem statement.
- If the HMW question fits, we feel the urge to search for ideas to answer it. If the question is not appropriate, we usually cannot think of any ideas.
- From our experience, it is more effective to prepare several HMW questions for a given subject area or subject cluster than to start a long discussion about the right cruising altitude of a specific question. Each HMW question can be understood as a prototype and tested in a short brainstorming session. The most appropriate one will then be pursued.

Be aware for whom a solution is sought
- In addition to the description of the problem, a target customer must be defined for the project. In so doing, we try to highlight the user and his/her needs as soon as the problem has been identified.

Be bold with your statements
- We've always fared well with using a thick marker in order to highlight the relevant needs.
- A large sheet of A5 paper and Post-its help to formulate the question so it can be seen by everybody.

Description of the use case

- The right "How might we..." question helps us use the time for the next "prototype & test" phase efficiently.
- Everyone on the team has prepared some questions. Together, they discuss the positioning or formulate the HMW question by means of "how" and "why" questions until there is consensus on the team, and everybody is convinced the right question has been found.
- Lilly allows enough time to find the HMW question. Especially in large groups, enough time must be allowed for the important discussion and interaction, so a good HMW question is formulated in the end. With the right question, we reach our goal faster.

Key learnings

- Do not discuss an HMW question for too long. Time pressure helps in staying agile and not getting bogged down with the final phrasing.
- It is essential to be optimistic and close to the needs of the users in order to come up with several good HMWs.

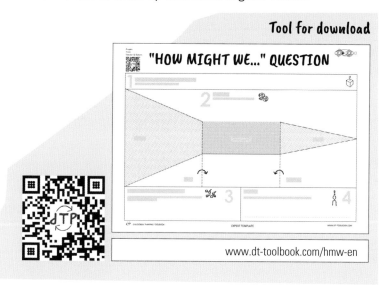

www.dt-toolbook.com/hmw-en

Storytelling

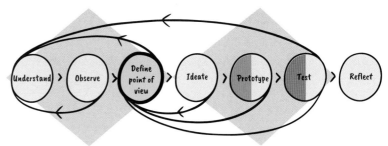

I would like...

to present my insights, ideas, and solutions to the members of my team and other stakeholders.

What you can do with the tool:

- Do research, talk with people, and have empathy to formulate profound stories.
- Summarize the results from the "understand" and "observe" phases and discuss with the team.
- Highlight unexpected results and generate new perspectives.
- In general, share insights, ideas, and results (solutions) with others.

Some information on the tool:

- Stories help us to share knowledge in a powerful way.
- Storytelling is a helpful tool that can be used in many phases across the design thinking cycle.
- For thousands and thousands of years, storytelling has helped mankind to share knowledge across generations. In the context of design thinking, it helps us to connect to the team, to focus, arouse motivation, and generate incentives for creativity and empathy!
- You can also tell stories about data. The animated visualization of data can create Wow! effects.

What tool can be used instead?

- Empathy map (see page 93)
- I like, I wish, I wonder (see page 239)
- Context mapping (see page 133)
- NABC (see page 177)
- Scenario analyses

Which other tools support working with this tool?

- Customer journey (see page 103)
- Service blueprint (see page 203)
- Feedback capture grid (see page 217)
- Interview for empathy (see page 57)
- Stakeholder map (see page 83)
- Scenario analyses
- Trend analysis (see page 119)

How much time and what materials do we need?

Group size

2–5

- A team size of 2-5 is ideal for using storytelling.
- For the discussion of the findings, each team member recounts the story he/she has observed.

Typical duration

10–30 min.

- Summarizing the findings and turning them into a story varies according to the design challenge and the number of findings (approx. 30 minutes).
- The story per user should be no longer than 5-10 minutes.

Materials needed

- Large whiteboard, flip chart or printed/painted template
- Post-its, pens, markers

Approach and template: Storytelling

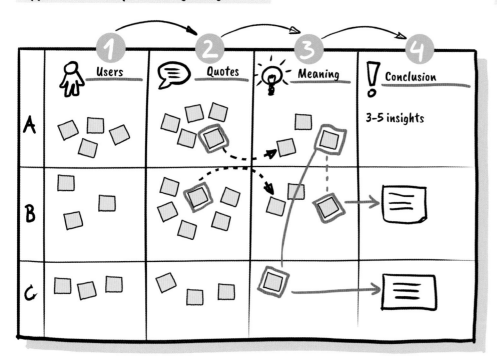

How the tool is applied...

- **Step 1:** Print the template or draw the structure on a flip chart or whiteboard. For the use of storytelling in the communication of results from the "understand" and "observe" phases, the following procedure is especially useful.
- **Step 2:** Encourage every member of the team to complete one line (e.g. per interviewed person), and then summarize the highlights and special features of the person or user (column 1). Add important quotes from the person.
- **Step 3:** Interpret the results on the team and define the meaning.
- **Step 4:** Draw a conclusion together with the team and summarize the key findings from the interview. This way, you have created a basis and are one step further toward sharing the results of the story with the team and the stakeholders. Formulate the draft of a story in bullet points, create a storyboard, or produce a short video that enacts the story.

This is the favorite tool of Jessica Dominquez

Position:
Entrepreneur and Freelance Designer

"In the highly globalized world we live, there is a need for new ideas that can help to improve our lives, and that is the precise reason innovation is important. Design thinking is the best way to materialize those ideas through an interdisciplinary team with a user-centered goal."

Why is it her favorite tool?

Storytelling is the best tool to share the findings from the interviews with others. In this way, feelings and emotions of the users or their feedback to our ideas or prototypes come alive.

Telling stories requires some courage and practice, but since there are no limits to our mind and our voice, storytelling is a very effective tool.

Expert tips:

Important hints for being successful
- Don't only write keywords on the Post-its but also draw sketches or other visualizations.
- Hang up photos or other artifacts! In this way, the storytelling board can be expanded like a mood board.
- Give the people/users names so that we know who we are talking about. Include specific identifying features, for example, "the funny guy with the blue hat" or "the Chanel lady for whom it's very important to look good."

A multi-purpose tool!
- Storytelling can also be used as a prototyping tool and helps to summarize the findings from the test.
- Storytelling supports learning, promotes innovations, and imparts knowledge and information.

Experiment with different types of stories
- Telling a very exciting story or a cliff-hanger story makes people concentrate. On the other hand, stories with an emotional background arouse a feeling of trust and establish a connection with the audience.

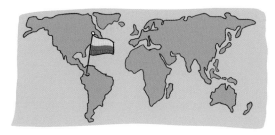

Country:
Colombia

Affiliation:
Pick-a-Box

Checked by: Jeremias Schmitt

Company/Position: 5Wx new ventures GmbH,
Co-Founder | Managing Partner

Description of the use case

- Lilly motivates the team to switch from the divergent phase to the convergent phase again and again and to summarize and structure the findings while doing so.
- It is not always easy to pool the relevant statements. Often, the team is unable to see the forest for the trees and gets lost in details.
- Lilly has achieved good results with this storyboard. It helps identify the key points, determine their meaning, and infer from it the key findings on the team.

Key learnings

- Storytelling can be used to summarize the findings from the interaction with the user. It can also serve as a prototyping and test method.
- Stories are valuable if they are true, so they must always be substantiated with real events.

Tool for download

www.dt-toolbook.com/storytelling-en

Context mapping

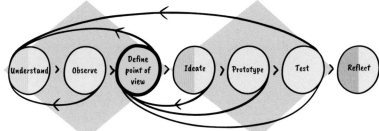

I would like...

to deal with the context, for example, of a problem.

What you can do with the tool:

- Learn from an "expert": namely the user who imparts unexpected insights into what he goes through in his life.
- Get a better picture of a particular situation. What are these experiences like for others? When do they undergo this experience? With whom and in what context?
- Follow the principle: "Knowledge is information with additional context." To have true knowledge, the context must be known, and this tool helps to create this kind of awareness.

Some information on the tool:

- The method of context mapping gives us as designers unexpected insights into a system and sub-system.
- It allows us to observe the user/customer in his/her everyday experience.
- The use of this tool makes explicit what's implicit.
- The point of context mapping is not to gain many insights. The goal is to find out more about how the respective experience is perceived.
- The mapping helps to give structure to the findings from the observation and thus understand the user better.

What tool can be used instead?

- Customer journey (see page 103)
- Analysis questions builder (see page 111)

Which other tools support working with this tool?

- Interview for empathy (see page 57)
- Empathy map (see page 93)
- 5W+H questions (see page 71)
- Ask 5x why (see page 67)

How much time and what materials do we need?

Group size

2–4

- Depending on the complexity of the design challenge, 2-4 people can work on a context map.
- If the groups are too large, the momentum is often lost.

Typical duration

40–60 min.

- Usually, 40-60 minutes are needed for a well-thought-out context map.
- The time may vary depending on the design challenge.
- Findings that have already been developed with other tools accelerate the procedure.

Materials needed

- Paper, pens, camera
- Movable walls or whiteboard

Template: Context mapping

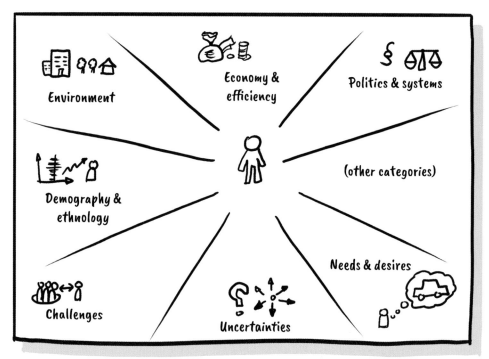

How the tool is applied...

- Many findings are necessary to get a good context map, so you should go outside as often as possible in order to observe and understand. There is no substitute for seeing reality from the point of view of the user, seeing it as he sees it. It is important to understand for whom a solution is sought.
- Observe the user and his environment. Typical questions: What does he do? Where does he do it? With whom does he do it? What is the impact of his activities on the environment? Which individuals lend support? Are there shared tools or resources?
- Take pictures of the environment and the user.
- Define areas on which the focus should be. Use your imagination for extensive context or for limited context.
- Determine categories of the respective context, for example, trends, the economy, location, or technology fields.
- If necessary, rearrange these categories in order to find new connections and gain new insights.
- Fill in the categories on the template with the insights.
- Deliberately leave one or two fields empty so the team feels encouraged to add new categories that seem important.

This is the favorite tool of Denise Pereira De Carvalho

Position:
Brazil Innovation Leader – DuPont Do Brasil

"Design thinking has changed the way I look into people, life, and experiences. It has given me a pause to ask myself what is underneath people's behavior and understand them better."

Why is it her favorite tool?

Context mapping is my favorite tool because the context is important; it changes our perspective on the situation. By using this tool, we are able to gain unexpected insights, understand the overall picture, and unlock parts of the process that are important to the user/customer.

Country:
Brazil

Affiliation:
DuPont

Checked by: Patrick Labud

Company/Position: bbv Software, User Experience Expert

Expert tips:

Walk in your user's shoes
- We have an awareness of our own perspective and for a certain situation. What is far more important, though, is to accept that the user may see things differently.
- We are open to surprises, to things that we did not have in mind at all.
- The users are the true experts of their routine and their experience.

The context changes the perception of the experience
- We keep in mind that people are not always aware of their everyday experience. They are used to it and often overlook the details that are important in a design process.
- We should not underestimate the importance of making explicit what's implicit, since it can yield valuable insights.
- We try to liberate our mind, free it from assumptions and to learn.

Any hypothesis can have its usefulness
- We liberate ourselves from expectations that something is right or wrong. We appreciate every new insight even if it doesn't match our view of the world.
- It has proven useful in our work to acquire a "beginner's mind" of "not knowing." It makes room for the new.

Variation: Context map without prelabeled elements

- Often, the great number of elements are prioritized and put on a list. The element that tops the list is seen as the most important one.
- For the visualization of various elements, a context map that is not predefined can be used (e.g. in the form of a daisy map). All eight petals of the daisy are equal, so to speak; none is visually seen as more important.
- The team determines which things are important or critical and enters them on the context map.

Description of the use case

- It is important that the team has a shared common image. The context map helps the team to understand and visualize what they already know and where there is still a lack of clarity.
- The topic of being afraid of AI and digital transformation in particular is of interest here, since the differences between Asia and Europe are quite substantial. The context map helps the team to discern these differences and understand the focus of the next iteration.

Key learnings

- Understand where the user comes from.
- The context and the experience change in different situations.
- Initial thoughts about the situation are usually wrong. Only through the exploration of insights will we be able to design good solutions.

Tool for download

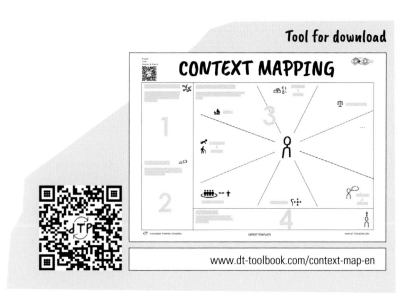

www.dt-toolbook.com/context-map-en

Define success

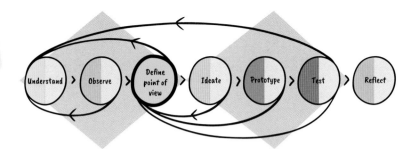

I would like...

to provide support to the team across the entire design cycle, especially in relation to the range of options.

Define success?

Success is to possess many handbags.

Success is to have no goals and plans and to be happy nonetheless.

Success is to have more money than your wife can spend.

Success is to own a Mercedes tractor that is already paid for.

What you can do with the tool:

- Vote and come to a consensus on the team as to what success is to be achieved.
- Ensure that requirements of the organization/management/ users and other stakeholders are understood; that makes it easier later to get a buy-in from the decision makers.
- Simplify the list and prioritization of options during the entire project.
- Create a basis for the measurement of KPIs if they are wanted for the project.

Some information on the tool:

- Define success can be used in different phases in the design thinking cycle for one, as part of the definition of the point of view; second, in the later implementation of the project.
- The questions are similar, but each one refers to a different time line. What do we want to have achieved in one month? Where do we stand with the business model in 5 years?
- "Define success" determines milestones for the solution of the problem and its later implementation.

What tool can be used instead?

- Storytelling in the interpretation of a vision (see page 129)
- Design principles (see page 53)

Which tools support working with define success?

- Measure and evaluate
- Stakeholder map (see page 83)
- Vision cone (see page 141)
- Scenario analyses
- Trend analysis (see page 119)

How much time and what materials do we need?

Group size

4–10

- Ideally, together with the members of the design team and if possible with the decision makers who will have to approve the project later.

Typical duration

60—90 min.

- Time: usually 60-90 minutes.
- Reflect on results on a regular basis; adjust if there are any external and internal changes.
- Always use prior to the selection of solutions for the prototype (about 5 minutes).

Materials needed

- Large whiteboard or movable walls
- Flip chart, Post-its, pens, and markers

Template: Define Success

Define questions:	Answers	Evaluate & select
How great might the financial success be (e.g. sales, revenue or market share, requirements of lenders or partners)?		
What is the value the project will have for the company or the users/stakeholders?		
What might the success for our users look like? (This means: solving a problem; better than the current solution; offering an answer to a specific new goal.)		
What might be the success for our key partners and stakeholders?		
How important might the success be for each team member and the team?		
How important would the success be for the management?		
What is the business case for my major stakeholders?		
What might be the most important milestones?		

How the tool is applied...

- Use Post-its for the "define success" tool, so each team member has the possibility of sharing his or her thoughts.
- Prepare a list of relevant issues (e.g. what does internal and external success mean), in order to ensure that a 360° vision emerges.
- Encourage all participants to write the answers to the questions on Post-its. Then collect all thoughts at once or else individually from the participants.
- It is best to have everybody share their thoughts first; subsequently, discuss and narrow down the elements of success. Then the core elements of success are selected (e.g. by forming clusters). Based on this, conduct a vote on the main areas, for example, with dot voting (see page 159).
- Ideally, involve important decision makers (e.g. management, founders, and partners), so you ensure already in the run-up that no time and no money will be wasted. Even more important is that no frustration accumulates during the design cycle or at the end of the project.

This is the favorite tool of Helene Cahen

Position:
Innovation Consultant and Founder at Strategic Insights

"Design thinking is a powerful process that helps teams work better on innovation projects with a user-centered perspective."

Why is it her favorite tool?

From my experience in working with many design teams, it is important to eliminate assumptions at the outset and align a team to what the success might look like. You can save a lot of time and money this way since the expectations are clearly defined at an early stage. With the aid of regular reflection sessions, changes in the project can be discussed early on; activities can be adjusted and budgets allocated differently.

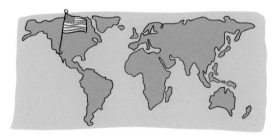

Country:
USA

Affiliation:
Strategic Insights

Checked by: Mike Pinder

Company/Position: Senior Innovation Consultant

Expert tips:

Be mindful in defining success
- When we define the factors of success, everybody writes down the answers so that we achieve a neutral view of the wishes.
- When the opinion that was written down on the Post-it is shared, we simply listen and stick the answer to the wall. We don't comment, and we don't yet judge the respective statement.
- We plan enough time for the assessment and selection. As a general rule, we need twice as much time for this than for the collection of the factors of success.

Search for success stories
- Search for known success stories in and outside of the organization so as to get a sense of what is possible.
  Examples:
  Braun: Designing a simplified IOT electric toothbrush
  PepsiCo: Design thinking as part of the strategy
  Procter & Gamble: Using design thinking for product development
  Bank of America: Keep the change program
  Deutsche Bank: Evolution of design thinking in IT
  GE Health: Building a better MRI scanner for children
  IDEO & Cambodia: Using design thinking to bring sanitation
  Nike: Design thinking infuses everything Nike does
  Airbnb: Applying design thinking in avoiding bankruptcy
  Apple: Think differently about innovation through design thinking
  IBM: Cultural change with design thinking at IBM
  Google: How to brainstorm like a Googler

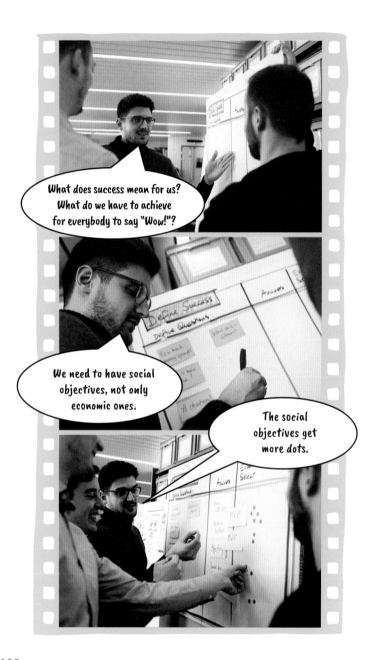

Description of the use case

- Lilly's team defines at an early stage of the project what success means for them and which components need to be fulfilled for everybody on the team to say: "Wow! That was a great project!"
- What turns out is that not only the primary economic factors are of vital importance but also the collaboration on the team and the benefits for society as a whole.
- Hence the team will pay more attention to the social and emotional aspects in the next iterations.

Key learnings

- It is advisable to come to a definition as early as possible.
- Invite key people in the project, that is, team members and decision makers.
- New information and external influences make it necessary to reflect on the definition of success constantly.

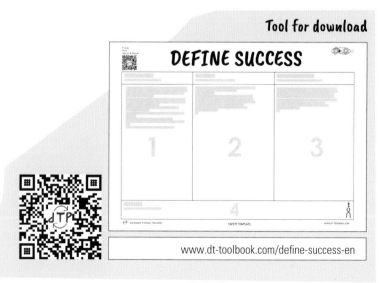

www.dt-toolbook.com/define-success-en

Vision cone

"Past - present - future"

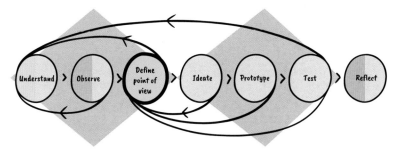

I would like...

to design a desirable future and explore what has to be done now to attain this goal over time.

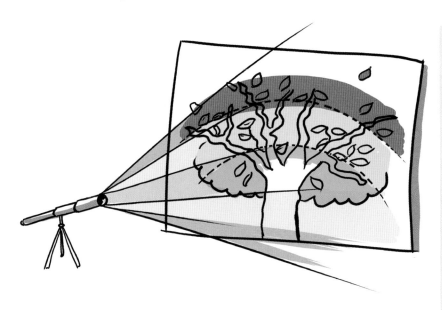

What you can do with the tool:

- Get a feeling for changes over time.
- Think in periods and time segments (e.g. from the past into the future), by mapping different results over time.
- Outline projected, plausible, possible, preferred, or absurd futures.
- Link the visions to specific next steps.
- Point out the potential of all possibilities, for example, in terms of technological and sociological developments.

Some information on the tool:

- The vision cone is a tool that connects current innovative developments with the past and the future.
- It helps to substantiate the overall vision and break it down it into actionable steps.
- The vision cone transforms daring uncertainties into positive aspects of innovation projects, for example, reinterpreting a problem as a possibility or market opportunity.
- The tool invites the design team to create this uncertain future actively.
- The tool allows the mapping of technological and societal developments and linking them to the current project.

What tool can be used instead?

- Context mapping (see page 133)
- Scenario planning tools

Which other tools support working with this tool?

- Storytelling (see page 129)
- Define success (see page 137)
- Future user (see page 100)
- Trend analysis (see page 119)
- Progression curves (see *The Design Thinking Playbook*, page 207)

How much time and what materials do we need?

Group size

2–5

- In the best case, the entire design team works on one vision cone.
- As an alternative, the team members work individually on vision cones and later consolidate them.

Typical duration

90–120 min.

- Time: 90-120 minutes
- 30 minutes for defining the status quo; 30 minutes for depicting the past; 30 minutes for creating an initial draft of possible future perspectives; the rest of the time is for reverse engineering of the required steps.

Materials needed

- Paper, pens, Post-its
- Cords and pins (optional: to create the vision cone outlines)

Approach and template: Vision Cone

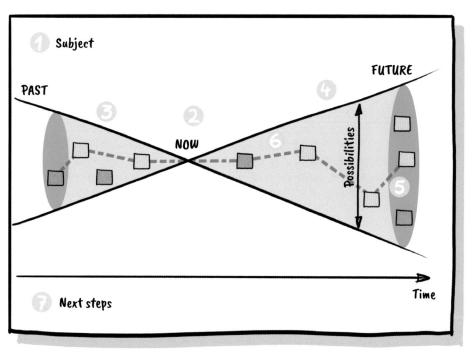

How the tool is applied...

- **Step 1:** Define a topic that matches the current challenge (e.g. mobility, health). Use the template or draw two connected cones and label them with PAST, NOW, and FUTURE.
- **Step 2:** Start with the NOW and describe the status quo of the project, the state of the art, and the current perception in society (e.g. semi-autonomous driving).
- **Step 3:** Focus on the PAST. Add the findings of research done to date as well as important technological and sociological changes. Try to be as accurate as possible when it comes to dates and link related events (e.g. 1960s, cars piloted by magnetic strips in the United States).
- **Step 4: Focus on the FUTURE.** Write down all of the findings relating to a fictitious future. Nobody knows the probability with which they arrive (e.g. autonomously flying cars).
- **Step 5:** Identify possible scenarios for the future from the findings and give them memorable names for better storytelling.
- **Step 6:** Select a future that is "desirable" in the context of the project. Work back from the identified future and reverse engineer the required steps selected that would have to happen NOW to achieve the desired future.
- **Step 7:** Infer specific next steps from it.

This is the favorite tool of Samuel Huber

Position:
Strategy & Development Lead at Goodpatch

"With design thinking, I no longer need to give presentations about the design mindset but can dive straight into conversations with a diverse set of interesting people."

Why is it his favorite tool?

When we develop something new, it is the vision that focuses all our activities on a common goal. Using a vision cone, we can place this vision in a temporal context from the past to the future. We learn where something came from, where it is now and where it might go. One of the strengths of vision cones is the way in which the possibilities are visualized, in other words: the uncertainty. There is never just one but, instead, a multitude of possible futures. Some of these futures are desirable, others we want to avoid. What they all have in common is that we need to tackle and create them actively.

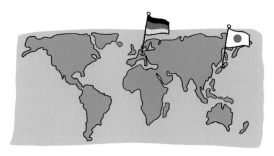

Country:
Germany & Japan

Affiliation:
Goodpatch

Checked by: Andy Tonazzi

Company/Position: Konplan AG | Chief Excitement Officer

The future is based on our imagination!
- Vision cones revolve around inspiration and imagination, and that works best when our team can work freely. Therefore "park" any fears and restrictions right at the beginning.
- It is important to understand the past and the future as a multitude of possibilities.
- The vision cone is not about predictions but about opportunities. It is up to us to decide what future we want to design. What does it mean for my company? What are the implications?

Everything is related and integrated into one system!
- There are different types of "futures": planned, plausible (based on the latest knowledge), possible (based on specific future technologies), and absurd (will never happen). The absurd future yields the best results since we only hit the limits of what is possible when we think the unthinkable.
- We let the past pass in review. This is usually quite inspiring. We should be careful, though, not to fall in love with the past, which then influences the future. We should be careful not to derive the future linearly from the past.

Design fiction is the best story of the future!
- The use of vision prototypes (see page 191) served us well for telling our story about the future. The same applies to artifacts from the past.

Description of the use case

- In the vision cone, Lilly's team also considers the social aspects of AI and digital transformation.
- The team discusses whether there might be a global tax soon on the work of robots. This would have a great impact on the distribution of income and on the way we work.
- Alongside social topics, the technologies are scrutinized. The Gartner Hype Cycle helps the team classify what constitutes a hype and what has already reached a certain maturity in the market.

Key learnings

- Start in the NOW, let the past pass in review, and build imaginary future scenarios.
- Take a desirable future as the starting point and define what would have to happen today for this future to come true.
- Use storytelling to share the vision prototype with others.

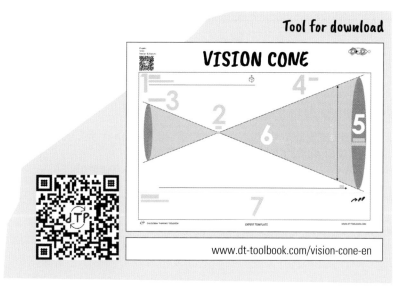

www.dt-toolbook.com/vision-cone-en

Critical items diagram

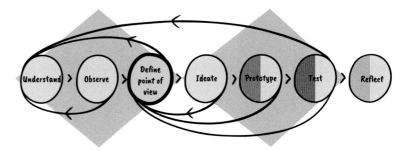

I would like...

to structure the findings from the early phases and prepare for ideating and experimenting.

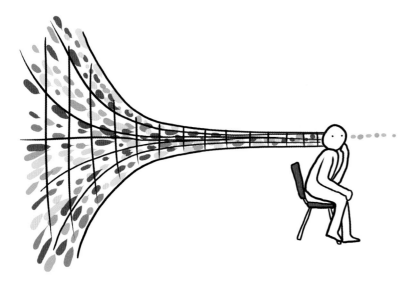

What you can do with the tool:

- Appraise the results from the "understand" and "observe" phases and filter out the critical elements.
- Prepare the "ideate" and "prototype" phases to establish a good starting position.
- Help the team to figure out the things essential for the project and to agree on them.
- Infer various "How might we" questions.

Some information on the tool:

- The critical items diagram helps the team to agree on the critical success elements for the target group based on the initial findings, the definition of a POV, or building a persona. These elements are the ones that must be solved later with the final prototype.
- The described elements in the critical items diagram can either describe the experience a user expects the solution to provide or present an expected function.
- The elements of the diagram should be questioned after each iteration. However, some will necessarily have relevance to a critical experience or critical function up to the final prototype.

What tool can be used instead?

- Context mapping (see page 133)
- Vision cone (see page 141)

Which other tools support working with this tool?

- HMW question (see page 125)
- Persona/user profile (see page 97)
- Empathy map (see page 93)
- Explorative interview (see page 63)
- Ask 5x why (see page 67)

145

How much time and what materials do we need?

Group size

2–5

- Ideally, the entire design team contributes to the critical items diagram.
- The presentation also helps in the discussion with clients for defining the problem statement more precisely.

Typical duration

30–60 min.

- The clearer the situation and the less uncertainty, the faster the main topics are defined.
- The critical items diagram lends structure and facilitates the preparation of an HMW question.

Materials needed

- Large sheet of paper.
- Post-its and pens
- Movable walls or whiteboard

Template and procedure: Critical items diagram

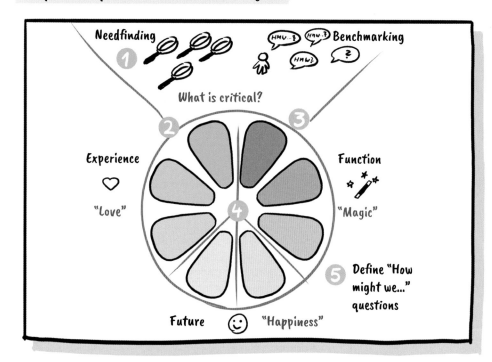

Note: Daisy map adapted from *Playbook for Strategic Foresight and Innovation* by Tamara Carleton and William Cockayne, 2013, available at www.innovation.io/playbook

How the tool is applied...

Define the critical elements of the problem together with the team and determine from them various "How might we..." questions.

- **Step 1:** At the beginning of this step, ponder the question: "What is critical for a successful solution to the problem?" This is based on the findings from the "understand" and "observe" phases.
- **Step 2:** Sketch a "critical items diagram" on the whiteboard or a large piece of paper and discuss on the team which experiences the user must have/which functions are critical for the user.
- **Step 3:** Each team member writes the eight elements that are critical to them on Post-its.
- **Step 4:** Each member names four experiences and four functions, one of which focuses on completely new or future expectations.
- **Step 5:** Consolidate the results and agree on the team on eight critical elements. On this basis, define "How might we..." questions that are interesting enough to launch the "ideate" phase successfully.

This is the favorite tool of Christian Hohmann

Position:
Lecturer for Product Innovation, Lucerne University of Applied Sciences and Arts

"Design thinking is important to me because it consistently puts the needs of all stakeholders in the forefront and helps to avoid products that are overloaded with functions."

Why is it his favorite tool?

I have always found that teams have a hard time during the process of registering the elements or criteria that are important for the problem and decisive for a successful implementation later. For this reason, I'm a big fan of the critical items diagram, because it is a very simple way of becoming aware of what is actually important at the moment. It helps the teams to agree on a common line.

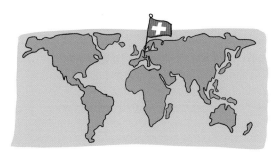

Country:
Switzerland

Affiliation:
Hochschule Luzern

Checked by: Marius Kienzler

Company/Position: Adidas AG | Senior Manager Brand Communication

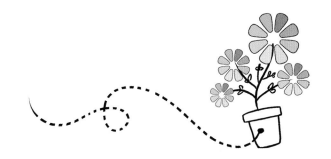

Expert tips:

As usual in design thinking, we work in iterations here as well.
- We make sure that this activity is carried out with the entire core team and that a common understanding of the critical elements emerges.
- Like many steps in design thinking, the work on these eight elements is an iterative process. So it is impossible to describe them perfectly the first time you try. After each experiment, the elements should be checked for whether they are still valid.

Don't get lost in long discussions.
- It is not advisable, however, to work too long with this tool. There is a risk that you get lost in discussions. If we cannot come to an agreement, we simply include more elements and check their importance by means of little experiments.
- Ideally, the creation of the diagram does not take longer than 60 minutes at the most. The shorter, the better.
- We put the currently valid critical items diagram on display (e.g. as a huge poster), where they can be seen by all team members.

Again: Show, don't tell.
- Visualizations and quotations from the interviews or the testing can enrich the individual elements and lead to a better understanding of the element in question.

Description of the use case

- Lilly's team summarizes all crucial factors in the critical items diagram.
- First, Lilly uses the tool to prioritize the hypotheses that the team has gained from the various interviews, inquiries, and analyses. These assumptions are then checked in the critical experience and critical function prototype.
- Lilly then uses the tool to summarize the findings from the iterations and really capture the critical factors and needs.

Key learnings

- The "critical items diagram" describes the key elements that are important in a potential solution.
- Accept that these elements can change over time when new insights crop up or other needs are discovered.

Tool for download

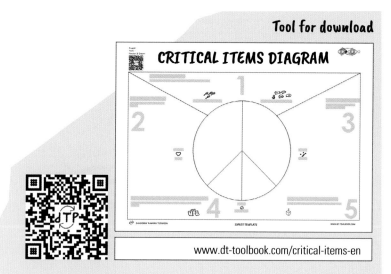

www.dt-toolbook.com/critical-items-en

Phase: Ideate

The classic way of ideating is brainstorming. Brainstorming is applied in the "ideate" phase in a variety of ways. It is primarily about generating as many ideas (ideation) as possible before they are sorted, combined, or clustered. The selection of preferred ideas usually takes place within the framework of an evaluation and vote on the team. For this, tools such as dot voting and the decision matrix are used. The selection of ideas is one of the most difficult elements in the design cycle, since the earlier phases are characterized by a high level of uncertainty.

Brainstorming

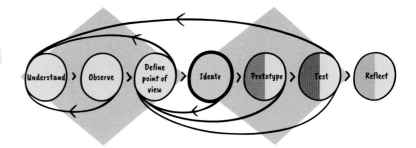

Understand > Observe > Define point of view > Ideate > Prototype > Test > Reflect

I would like...

to ideate quickly – quantity is more important than quality.

What you can do with the tool:

- Generate many ideas that the team spontaneously comes up with.
- Use the entire creativity potential of the design thinking team.
- Have a high number of variants at hand in a short period of time.
- Obtain an interdisciplinary perspective on a problem that represents different skills and knowledge.
- Collect ideas and viewpoints from a heterogeneous group.
- Inspire enthusiasm and generate momentum.

Some information on the tool:

- Brainstorming is an ideation technique in which all participants can contribute their knowledge.
- Very often, brainstorming is used in the "ideate" phase in many different ways and with changing focus.
- Good brainstorming sessions stimulate creativity and allow all participants, regardless of their hierarchical level, to contribute their ideas.
- Before the actual ideation, brainstorming is frequently used as a "brain dump" so that everybody on the team has a chance to make their ideas and solutions known. This procedure helps people clear their heads. In later brainstorming sessions, you can then focus on the respective problem statement or task.
- Brainstorming has no limits – all ideas are welcome!

What tool can be used instead?

- Brainwriting/6-3-5 method (see page 163)
- Special brainstorming (see page 167)
- Analogies & benchmarking as an inspiration (see page 171)

Which other tools support working with this tool?

- "How might we ..." question (see page 125)
- Parking lot for ideas (A parking lot for ideas serves the purpose of parking ideas that sound exciting but do not contribute at present anything toward solving the problem.)

How much time and what materials do we need?

Group size

4–6

- Brainstorming sessions are most effective in groups of 4-6.
- For large groups or groups with hierarchical differences, make sure that everybody contributes.

Typical duration

5–15 min.

- Usually a few minutes (5-15 minutes)
- After a certain amount of time, creativity declines and must be rekindled by new incentives (e.g. other methods and questions).

Materials needed

- Post-its
- Pens
- Wall or whiteboard

Brainstorming rules

#1 Creative confidence

#2 Quantity before quality

#3 Visual ideas

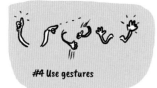

#4 Use gestures

#5 Build on the ideas of others

#6 Only one person speaks at a time always

#7 No prejudices

#8 Continue to brainstorm

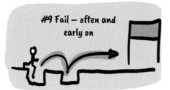

#9 Fail – often and early on

How the tool is applied...

- **Step 1:** Prepare a clear HMW question for the brainstorming session, for example, in the form of "How might we…" or "What possibilities are there…" (see page 125).
- **Step 2:** Repeat the brainstorming rules before the brainstorming session. Try to motivate the group to give more ideas during the session and build upon the ideas of others. Make sure that all are heard and all ideas are written down. Point out that only one idea is to be written per Post-it and that it should be clear and legible. Instead of words, small sketches may be drawn on the Post-its.
- **Step 3:** Cluster and assess the ideas together with the team at regular intervals.
- **Step 4:** Make a judgment as to whether even more creativity is needed (e.g. to obtain even wilder ideas); or start a brainstorming session in areas where more ideas are sought in general.

Variant: Structured brainstorming

- All participants write their ideas on a Post-it.
- After a certain period of time, one person begins to stick his own ideas on a flip chart and explain them. If there is already a similar Post-it, another one is glued next to it.
- During the explanations of the other team members, new ideas are generated (ideation) and written on new Post-its.
- The result is a clustered collection of ideas, which can be later evaluated.

Position:
Assistant Professor at the Faculty of Management, Warsaw University of Technology, and active member of the Warsaw Design Factory Crew.

"Nowadays, where the world is going faster and faster, technologies are changing in the twinkling of an eye and the young generation loves changes, so design thinking techniques are getting more and more important."

Why is it her favorite tool?

I like brainstorming because it shows, firstly, the efficiency of the entire design team and, secondly, the potential of each individual team member. It allows us have an insight into the different points of view existing on the team that vary according to discipline, age, professional experience, and life experience. The important thing is that there won't be any criticism of ideas and that even the craziest ideas can be shared. It happens frequently that over the course of the design thinking cycle, we come back to ideas that seemed not doable before. That is something that deeply impresses me time and again!

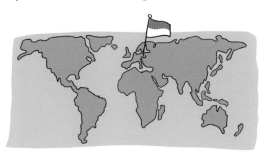

Country:
Poland

Affiliation:
Warsaw University of Technology

Checked by: **Adrian Sulzer**

Company/Position: SATW, Head of Communications and Marketing

Expert tips:

The goal isn't a perfect idea, it's lots of ideas
- We never criticize an idea, because we might need it again later!
- A brainstorming session is a good way to learn more about the other teams, how they think, and how they work under time pressure.
- We have come to appreciate the use of brainstorming not only in the "ideate" phase but also at the beginning of the project, prior to a sprint, or in the redefinition of the problem.
- A great many ideas emerge in a series of brainstorming sessions with varying questions, so it is advisable to take pictures of the walls with the Post-its, since they easily get lost in the heat of the moment.

Collaborate across boundaries
- It is best to select the preferred ideas together with the team.
- The linking of ideas often results in very good solutions; therefore it is imperative to look at the ideas quite carefully.
- Conducting a brainstorming session when the day starts has proven conducive to our work. If it's not possible, start one after a break or a warm-up.
- Brainstorming is also a good tool for improving business models and when working with the lean canvas (see page 251).
- Not having general introductions before the brainstorming session, which would include announcing who plays which role, has also proven useful.

Description of the use case

- Lilly's team is proficient in holding brainstorming sessions.
- Usually, the team uses structure. They find it more efficient than normal brainstorming – in addition, everybody gets an equal chance. Everybody writes his/her ideas on Post-its. Then the ideas are collected.
- The team sets itself a time period. They no longer need a moderator for this; nor do they need anybody to keep an eye on adherence to the brainstorming rules.
- The team works together with mutual respect and builds on the ideas of the others.

Key learnings

- Conduct the brainstorming session in a calm and relaxed atmosphere.
- Accept all ideas from everybody – never criticize them!
- Use brainstorming at various phases in the design thinking cycle. It is useful for an initial "brain dump" in the "ideate" phase as well as for the improvement of business models, for instance.

Tool for download

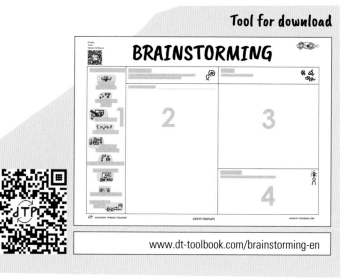

www.dt-toolbook.com/brainstorming-en

2x2 Matrix

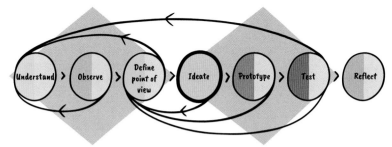

I would like...

to categorize and prioritize ideas or identify strategic opportunities and patterns.

What you can do with the tool:

- Determine quickly which ideas should be pursued and which ideas should be rejected.
- Obtain a first overview of ideas that already have a certain maturity.
- Carry out the prioritization of ideas according to strategic innovations, market opportunities, and many other categories.
- Use it wherever decisions have to be made.

Some information on the tool:

- The 2x2 matrix is a visual way of categorizing ideas.
- The matrix is highly modifiable, because any type of meaningful axis attribute may be used.
- The 2x2 matrix can also be used to change the way of thinking from a 100% idea orientation toward the recognition of unfulfilled user needs and strategic opportunities.
- The 2x2 matrix is not only used predominantly in the context of prioritizing ideas but in all other phases as well.

What tool might be used instead?

- Dot voting (see page 159)
- Kano classification into enthusiasm, performance, and basic requirements

Which other tools support working with this tool?

- Venn diagrams for feasibility, economic viability, and desirability (see page 20)
- Design principles (see page 53)
- Define success (see page 137)
- Dot voting (see page 159) for the prioritization within a quadrant

How much time and what materials do we need?

Group size

2–8

- The smaller the group, the shorter the discussion. This allows for quick evaluation.
- For groups of more than 8 people, dot voting procedures can also be helpful.

Typical duration

15–45 min.

- Depending on the number of ideas, it takes about 30-60 seconds per idea, including a short discussion.
- Open discussion and evaluation usually requires more time (e.g. 45 minutes).

Materials needed

- Whiteboard or a large sheet of paper as a template
- Flip chart, Post-its, pens, and markers
- Post-its already written on from a brainstorming session or the clustering of ideas

Example of axes in a 2x2 matrix

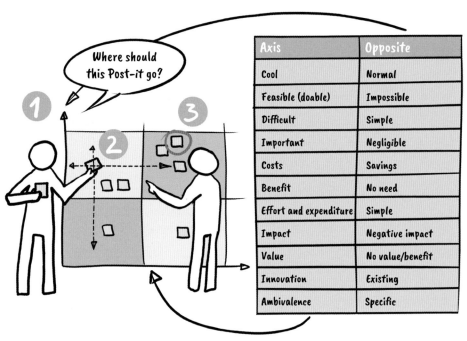

Where should this Post-it go?

Axis	Opposite
Cool	Normal
Feasible (doable)	Impossible
Difficult	Simple
Important	Negligible
Costs	Savings
Benefit	No need
Effort and expenditure	Simple
Impact	Negative impact
Value	No value/benefit
Innovation	Existing
Ambivalence	Specific

How the tool is applied...

- **Step 1:** Draw the template and designate the axes according to the requirements wanted. See table on the left as a reference. Use "high" and "low" or opposite attributes. Tip: When evaluating ideas, focus more on the benefits for the user and the feasibility and use measurable and tangible criteria for the opportunity analysis.
- **Step 2:** Start with the positioning by reading the ideas aloud on the team:
  - Start with a broad classification and the question in which quadrant the idea should be placed.
  - Place the idea in relation to the other ideas. Pay attention to the opinions on the team and try to find a consensus.
  - Alternatively, first one axis and then the second axis can be evaluated.
  - Repeat until all the ideas are positioned on the matrix.
- **Step 3:** Select ideas for further processing.
  - If there are several ideas in the field at the top right, select the top 3 for discussion.
  - If there are fewer than 3 ideas in the quarter at the top right, check the development fields for ideas that can be implemented.
  - Also check whether there are empty quadrants; they signify potential for further opportunities and unfulfilled needs.

Position:
Independent consultant

"Design thinking has been my go-to treasure box of tools for the past 8 years. I feel that design thinking is applicable everywhere, even when my colleagues and the teams I've worked with have not been introduced to design thinking as an entity. I have found it a very approachable and easy-to-convey philosophy to introduce to even the most basic everyday situations."

Why is it his favorite tool?

I am totally fascinated by the fact that the 2x2 matrix is a tool whose use is as versatile as a Swiss Army knife. With the infinite possibilities of axes, we can map the most varied use cases. The spectrum ranges from basic technical decisions to solution-oriented business models up to conceptual considerations. The pure simplicity in connection with a high visual effect makes it my absolutely favorite tool.

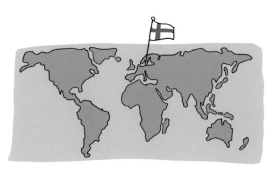

Country:
Finland

Affiliation:
Freelancer

Checked by: **Ingunn Aursnes**

Company/Position: Sopra Steria, Senior Manager, Business Design

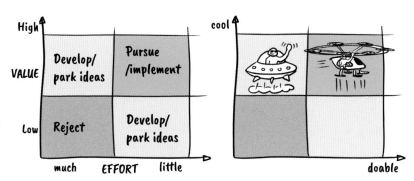

Expert tips:

Very valuable in strategic planning
- The 2x2 matrix can also be used as a tool for strategic planning: Instead of concentrating on new ideas, we focus on current uses and opportunities. This way, we can identify areas not yet covered by ideas, for example.
- Generally, it is recommended to make the axes SMART, that is, specific, measurable, achievable, realistic, and timely. As a result, the 2x2 matrix is also a valuable tool in the "prototype" phase.
- When defining limiting factors for an attribute, we ought to bear in mind that these factors can have an effect on different levels, for example, technology, the project scope, the time frame, or the resources.

Use the thinking of systems
- In the case of complex problem statements, it helps to reduce the complexity of the idea. This is done by breaking down the idea into its individual components.
- For the quick evaluation of an idea – especially in the early phases – our favorite, namely with a "cool" axis and a "doable" axis, has proven useful. The coolest idea might not yet be doable, but the two axes help with the discussion and provide us with the question: "Is there any way that this cool idea might be realized?"
- In later phases, quantification in the form of a cost/yield chart can be of help. Investors are happy to use such a chart as a basis for decision making.

Description of the use case

- In the very early phases, Lilly likes using the "cool" and "doable" axes. But because they are already on the brink of the problem/solution fit, they'd rather use the "impact" and "expenditure" axes.
- The team discusses the positioning of the individual ideas and then pursues the most interesting ones.
- The ideas in the orange area are put in the parking lot for ideas.
- If the team does not make good headway, the parking lot is a good place to get inspiration.

Key learnings

- Keep the ideas as simple as possible – complexity means confusion on the matrix.
- Rewrite a Post-it or split the idea into several ideas if it helps to clarify the positioning.
- Not all combinations of axes yield target-oriented results. Experiment with different possibilities and adapt the axes to the problem statement and the objectives.

Tool for download

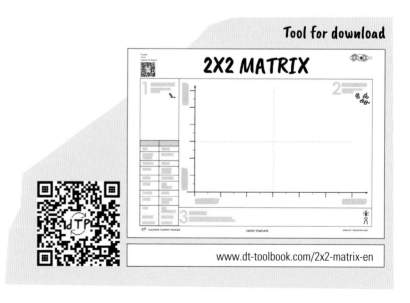

www.dt-toolbook.com/2x2-matrix-en

Dot voting

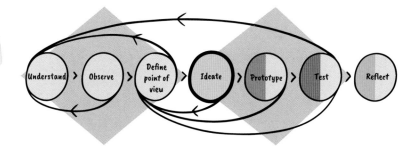

I would like...

to make a clear decision on what options should be pursued in the form of ideas or concepts.

What you can do with the tool:

- Make joint decisions as a team.
- Limit the selection, that is, simplify and prioritize.
- Make quicker decisions and avoid lengthy "analysis paralysis."
- Resolve disagreements on teams and avoid power games.
- Integrate the opinion of all participants in the decision-making process.
- Finally, focus on the best ideas and market opportunities.

Some information on the tool:

- In addition to a large number of ideas to be developed in a brainstorming session, for example, the selection of ideas is a crucial step.
- There are various possibilities for the evaluation and clustering of ideas. The use of glue dots placed on the ideas by the participants is a simple way to do it. The vote is quick and democratic.
- This tool makes it possible for decisions to be heard and made on the basis of reflection, the difficulty of the design challenge, and how well it meets objectives (and NOT on the basis of power, position, or how extroverted somebody is).
- Dot voting bestows personal responsibility and a clear understanding of the decision-making process on the participants.
- Dot voting is visual, flexible, fast, simple, and thus fits the design thinking mindset perfectly.
- We use it throughout the entire design thinking cycle.

What tool can be used instead?

- 2x2 matrix (see page 155)
- Surveys (within the team and/or external)
- Discussion of the various alternatives and consensus building

Which tools support working with the tool?

- Brainstorming (see page 151)
- Design principles (see page 53)

How much time and what materials do we need?

Group size

- Ideal for teams of 5-10.
- If the group is larger, it should be split into several smaller groups.

5–10

Typical duration

5–20 min.

- Generally speaking, 5-20 minutes are needed or as long as the participants need to look at alternatives and vote.
- Dot voting is one of the fastest procedures for capturing the mood and coming to a decision.

Materials needed

- Dots or thick color markings (monochromatic)
- A large surface with the ideas, for example, on Post-its or in idea clusters

Template and procedure: Dot voting

Define new criteria or call to mind the design principles

How the tool is applied...

Initial situation: The participants have already collected ideas on Post-its (e.g. in the context of a brainstorming session).

Step 1: Clarify the criteria before the vote. Example of criteria:
- best suitability for long-term goals
- will delight the customer/user
- supports the vision
- biggest opportunity for competitive advantages
- adherence to deadlines
- greatest impact on customer satisfaction

Step 2: Place the Post-its with ideas on the wall or whiteboard, so that everybody can see them.
- Give each participant a certain number of votes (usually between 3-5 dots) and prompt them to make a choice. In private, each participant casts his vote via dot voting on the Post-it that best meets the criteria in his opinion.
- Have the participants select whether they want to put several votes on one Post-it or distribute their votes to different ideas.

Step 3: Rearrange and regroup the ideas with the most dots. Make a transparent decision that is based on these priorities, then determine the next steps.

This is the favorite tool of Ingunn Aursnes

Position:
Senior Manager, Business Design. Sopra Steria

"For me, design thinking connects my heart and mind in a creative way. It's a powerful combo of mindset, process, and tools enabling you to empathize deeply with the users and explore new strategic business opportunities. I love how it challenges both my left and right brain hemisphere."

Why is it her favorite tool?

Dot voting is a very versatile tool. It can be integrated in a discussion, for example, and it helps us to expedite decisions and render them transparent. What fascinates me about dot voting is the speed, clarity, and positive energy emerging during the activity. The tool helps us to make lucid and quick decisions. It is especially useful when we must make decisions in the context of complex problem statements and with multidisciplinary teams, in which strenuous discussions take place frequently.

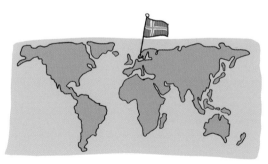

Country:
Norway

Affiliation:
Sopra Steria

Checked by: Vesa Lindroos

Company/Position: Independent consultant

Tips:

- **Let the participants present their ideas before the vote**
  A brief explanation ensures more in-depth understanding before the dot voting is carried out.
- **Equal amount of dots, what now?**
  Carry out a second vote on the winners or make use of the 2x2 matrix presented on page 155.
- **Use color markings as an alternative to glue dots**
  Each participant receives a pen and is prompted to draw small circles/dots to vote.
- **Limit the number of choices**
  Combine similar ideas or concepts.
  Bundle topics and first vote on the main topics, then on individual ideas.
- **Avoid the bandwagon effect**
  Request that participants make their decision in private and vote all at the same time. If there is a risk that an individual is too heavily influenced by one person (e.g. the boss), this person should turn in his/her assessment last.
- **Parking lot for ideas**
  It can be valuable to save ideas for future projects.
- **Crowd voting**
  Involve customers or colleagues to set priorities.
- **Color code**
  If there are different groups who evaluate the ideas (e.g. users/customers and internal people), different colors can be used.
- **Heat map**
  Dot voting can also be used to highlight parts of an idea or concept. The participants are instructed to highlight individual parts of ideas.
- **Detailed evaluation**
  Dot voting can also be done by having participants rate the ideas on a scale, for example, from 0 (do not implement the idea) to 10 (definitely implement the idea).

Description of the use case

- The idea evaluation is always exciting. Is everybody on the team of the same opinion? Does everybody have the same favorite? Or is there a broad range of opinions?
- Everybody on the team ponders where he/she wants to put the dots. Then all team members glue the dots on the ideas at the same time. They make sure that Lilly places her dots after everybody else, so nobody is influenced by her decision.
- There is one idea that everybody seems to like. The other dots are distributed all over. Now the team discusses once more the ideas that have dots, combines a number of ideas, and goes into another evaluation round to get an alternative to the first idea.

Key learnings

- Plan the dot voting and select the number of dots.
- Explain the criteria for the vote prior to the voting process.
- Separate the ideation (the generation of ideas) from the evaluation of the ideas.
- "Park" ideas that might be of relevance later.

Tool for download

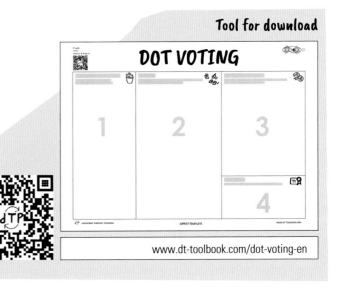

www.dt-toolbook.com/dot-voting-en

6-3-5 Method

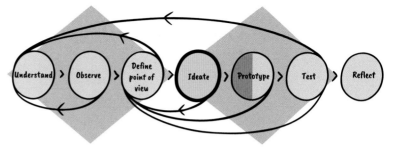

I would like...

to generate many ideas quickly and in a structured way in the group.

What you can do with the tool:

- Generate new ideas or further develop existing ideas and document them in a simple manner.
- In a structured way, familiarize inexperienced workshop participants with an easy-to-learn approach to brainwriting and the rules of brainstorming.
- Capture the creative potential of people who are more reserved in open group situations by allowing them to work quietly in private.
- Foster the generation of offbeat ideas through the explicit separation of ideation and the evaluation of ideas.

Some information on the tool:

- Brainwriting with the 6-3-5 method allows for structured ideation and further development of ideas in all iterations and across the entire design cycle.
- The name "6-3-5" is derived from an optimal team size of 6 participants who each produce 3 ideas for a problem in the first round. Each of these ideas will then be further developed by the other participants in the next 5 rounds. The technique is particularly suitable for the ideation based on specific problem statements and points of view.
- In a group of 6 participants, up to 108 ideas are collected with this tool within a very short period of time (under 30 minutes).

What tool can be used instead?

- Brainstorming (see page 151)
- Special brainstorming (see page 167)
- Analogies & benchmarking as an inspiration (see page 171)
- Other creativity techniques

Which other tools support working with this tool?

- "How might we..." question (see page 125)
- 2x2 matrix (see page 155)
- Dot voting (see page 159)
- Brainstorming rules (see page 151)

How much time and what materials do we need?

Group size

4–6

- Groups of 6 are ideal. With adaptations to the template and to the sequence, a different group size also works.
- In the case of large groups, split them into smaller ones.

Typical duration

30–40 min.

- Depending on the complexity of the question and the experience of the participants, 3 to 5 minutes for each round should be allocated for 6 rounds of ideation.
- Time should be allowed for the subsequent selection of ideas.

Materials needed

- Sheets of paper (or printed form)
- Pens, Post-its
- Glue dots for the evaluation if the selection is to be done by dot voting

Template and procedure: 6-3-5 method

	Problem	
1.1 Idea 1	**1.2** Idea 2	**1.3** Idea 3
2.1	2.2	2.3
3.1	3.2	3.3
4.1	4.2	4.3
5.1	5.2	5.3
6.1	6.2	6.3

➐ Cluster ideas

How the tool is applied...

- **Step 1:** Form groups of 6 persons each and explain the problem.
- **Step 2:** Give each participant a sheet of paper with a grid consisting of three columns and six rows (18 boxes in total) or have the participants draw the grid themselves.
  Variant: Take a sheet of 6 columns, so that 6 ideas can be developed, and 6 rows (36 boxes in total); this arrangement allows for the development of completely new ideas.
- **Step 3:** The participants write three ideas in the first row of the sheet within a defined period of time (3-5 minutes). The whole thing is done without speaking.
  Variant: Ideas can also be written on Post-its instead of on the sheet.
- **Step 4:** When the set time is over, the sheet is passed clockwise to the next group member.
- **Step 5:** Give participants some time to look at the ideas already written down. Then ask the participants to complete the next row on the sheet with more ideas, again within the defined time period. Ideally, the existing ideas are developed further. The ideas may (but need not) build on or supplement the ideas of other participants.
- **Step 6:** The process of passing on and completing the sheet is repeated until all rows, or boxes, have been filled.
- **Step 7:** Cluster and evaluate the ideas with the team and agree on the next steps.

Position:
Business Design Consultant at mm1 and lecturer

"By now, I use design thinking not only professionally, for the development of new products and business models. The mindset has gained great importance in my private life as well, for example, when we planned our wedding – a complex project full of ambiguity. Design thinking helped to keep the focus on human needs without losing sight of feasibility and economic viability. It was a very beautiful celebration."

Why is it his favorite tool?

In my design sprints, I like to use the 6-3-5 method in order to work with larger groups in a structured way and generate or develop ideas at high speed. I include groups that have little experience with design thinking or people who are rather reserved in "oral" group situations and have a tendency to defer to others.

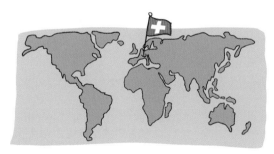

Country:
Switzerland

Affiliation:
mm1

Checked by: **Maurice Codourey**

Company/Position: UNIT X, CEO and Partner | xperts on demand

Expert tips:

Develop powerful questions
"How might we …" is good for formulating a question that has a unique and specific perspective, or point of view (e.g. a persona in his/her context). The question has a great impact on the ideation (ideas to be generated).

Keep your focus
The question must be understood by all participants in order to ideate in a focused way. It might make sense to discuss the problem statement in the group before applying the method, hang it up in the room, and then ask the participants to write it down on a sheet of paper.

Show, don't tell!
Depending on the question, it is useful to sketch ideas instead of laboriously describing them. If you want people to sketch the ideas anyway, it is advisable to use larger paper formats, for example, A3.

Develop ideas
Motivate groups to build upon previous ideas, add to them, or develop them further. Ideas already written down or sketched on the sheets of paper have the aim of inspiring the participants again in each round, so the ideas are developed further.

Select ideas
Evaluate the existing ideas on every sheet of paper, intuitively or based on criteria, then select and highlight a defined number of ideas via dot voting (see page 159). As an alternative, the ideas can be cut out and stuck to matrices (e.g. 2x2 matrix) to illustrate the idea space (see page 155).

Description of the use case

- A sub-team of Lilly's team, consisting of 6 people, wants to generate many initial ideas.
- To do so, all team members draw a 3x6 grid on a sheet of paper and write down/sketch the first 3 ideas on Post-its within 4 minutes, working in private, and put them into the grid.
- Then they pass the sheet on to the next person and write down 3 more ideas, some of which build upon the previous ones, until the sheet is full.
- In this way, up to 108 ideas are collected in less than half an hour. Again in six rounds, the ideas are then evaluated in the groups according to previously defined criteria and subsequently presented.

Key learnings

- 6-3-5 method in a nutshell: 6 people each write down 3 ideas on a sheet of paper and pass it on 5 times, so eventually it's completely filled in.
- The tool makes it possible to generate many ideas in a relatively short period of time and has the advantage that the ideas are not talked to death because people work silently.
- The method encourages the further development of ideas and separates idea generation from idea evaluation.

Tool for download

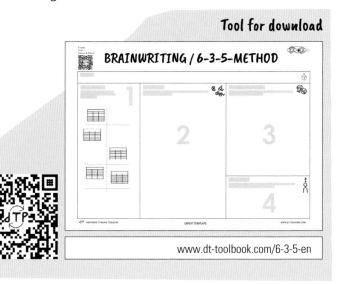

www.dt-toolbook.com/6-3-5-en

Special brainstorming

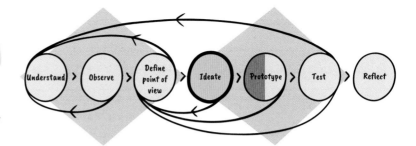

I would like...

to generate a large number of unusual ideas in a limited period of time.

What you can do with the tool:

- Generate a large number of ideas in a limited period of time.
- Promote mutual exchange and active listening between group members in order to build upon ideas already gathered.
- Adopt different perspectives and look at a problem from different angles with the aid of varying approaches.
- Boost creativity in different ways, for example, through negative brainstorming, figuring storming, or bodystorming.

Some information on the tool:

- Special brainstorming techniques can be used as an alternative to the traditional brainstorming approach.
- They are especially useful when a group gets stuck during ideation or when similar ideas are repeatedly generated.
- The special brainstorming techniques include tools such as negative brainstorming, figuring storming, and bodystorming.
- Which type of brainstorming is to be used depends heavily on the problem statement, the participants, and the goals.
- Special brainstorming techniques are predominantly used in the "ideation" phase in order to boost creativity once more or reach defined goals.

What tool can be used instead?

- Brainstorming (see page 151)
- 6-3-5 method (see page 163)
- Analogies & benchmarking as an inspiration (see page 171)
- "I like, I wish, I wonder" (see page 239)

Which other tools support working with this tool?

- Persona/user profile (see page 97)
- Empathy map (see page 93)
- "How might we..." question (see page 125)

How much time and what materials do we need?

Group size

2–10

- Typically, a brainstorming group consists of at least two to three up to a maximum of 10 persons.
- Smaller groups are particularly suitable if the group members are very diverse or practiced in adopting different perspectives.
- Larger groups can be divided into smaller sub-groups that work in tandem.

Typical duration

10–20 min.

- For each of the brainstorming techniques described, 10 to 20 minutes are needed (depending on the applied method and the size of the team).

Materials needed

- Post-its, pens
- Selection of pictures of luminaries (e.g. for figuring storming)

Presentation of 3 different special brainstorming techniques:

1 Negative brainstorming

Negative brainstorming combines the traditional brainstorming approach with the so-called reversal method. Instead of finding a solution, participants focus on anything that might make the problem worse. For example: Instead of finding approaches for improving a traffic situation, the group concentrates on maximizing the traffic jam on the respective road.

The results from this brainstorming exercise are subsequently evaluated and reviewed as to whether new starting points arise from it or whether certain aspects, which usually exacerbate a problem, can be eliminated.

2 Figuring storming

It is often easier to empathize with a certain person and look at the situation from his/her point of view in order to solve a problem. This approach follows the figuring storming method, that is, the brainstorming is done from the point of view of a third party. It involves asking the question: How would "X" solve the problem?

For example, Albert Einstein or the president of the United States can serve as celebrities, along with people from our everyday life (e.g. partners, family members, or the boss), and personas that were defined within the scope of the design thinking process.

3 Bodystorming

Bodystorming goes one step further by placing test persons physically in a particular situation. In this case, the scenario is imitated as correctly as possible by means of a relevant environment, artifacts, and persons, so as to have the test persons experience it as closely as possible. In this way, the subjects can infer new ideas by means of physical trial and error and testing.

Example: A team that develops products for elderly people can apply Vaseline on the lenses of glasses in order to perceive the world through the eyes of seniors.

One variant consists of being constantly in motion and writing down ideas while walking.

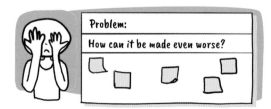

This is the favorite tool of Miriam Hartmann

Position:
Lecturer for Design Thinking at The University of Applied Sciences of the Grisons; Design Thinking Facilitator at F. Hoffmann – La Roche

"One of the greatest challenges consists of breaking away from our 'thinking in solutions' and understanding the problem holistically before we begin to develop solutions. Design thinking helps us stimulate our natural curiosity, question assumptions, and meet our customers with an open mindset."

Why is it her favorite tool?

Often, the focus of participants is quite broad in traditional brainstorming, which results in a great number of ideas that are no longer directly associated with the actual problem. Particularly in the case of abstract or complex issues, brainstorming groups frequently reach their limits. Special brainstorming techniques can help to look at a problem from a different angle and, by means of alternative approaches, reduce the pressure on the participants to come up with a good idea.

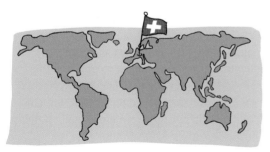

Country:
Switzerland

Affiliation:
F. Hoffmann – La Roche

Checked by: Kristine Biegman

Company/Position: launchlabs GmbH, Berlin, Trainer | Coach | Facilitator human-centered design

Expert tips:

Be in a creative environment
Brainstorming works best when the participants are relaxed. Comfortable chairs and cushions can create a "feel-good atmosphere"; large and flexible writing surfaces help to foster the group's creativity.

Time boxing
As in traditional brainstorming, a certain time pressure helps generate as many different ideas as possible and write them down unfiltered, that is, giving free rein to creativity. It is therefore advisable to do short brainstorming sequences (10 minutes) and clock them with a timer.

Avoid all types of judgment during a brainstorming session
There are no "bad" ideas because any idea, and be it ever so outlandish an idea, may lead to a good solution when further developed. This is why it is imperative to avoid any rating of ideas during the brainstorming process.

How to tackle complex or abstract problems
Special brainstorming techniques are useful for complex or abstract problems for which participants have difficulties in identifying an immediate solution. Experiment with them and collect experience in their application.

Negative brainstorming

Figuring storming

Bodystorming

Description of the use case

- In the ideation phase, Lilly's teams tried to generate many ideas for the solution of the defined problem. Brainstorming helped to identify possible starting points. However, some teams felt relatively early on that they were going in circles and couldn't move forward.
- Other techniques, for example, negative brainstorming, helped the team to broaden their mental horizon and identify new connecting factors. In the subsequent figuring storming, well-known enterprises such as Apple and Google and people like Elon Musk were used. This way, more potential approaches to a solution could be identified.

Key learnings

- Special brainstorming techniques are useful for complex or abstract problems.
- Otherwise, the following applies again: Quantity before quality; all members of the group are given the chance to speak; there are no "bad" ideas.
- Only afterward are the results clustered, rated, and documented.

Tool for download

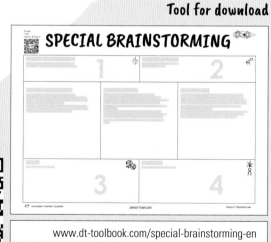

www.dt-toolbook.com/special-brainstorming-en

Analogies & benchmarking as inspiration

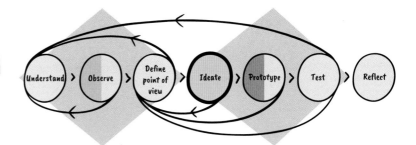

I would like...

to find inspiration for ideas and approaches by exploring "worlds" that seem to exist separately in the context of the problem statement.

How would an elephant solve the problem?

What you can do with the tool:

- Generate ideas that lead to a Wow! effect.
- Explain ideas and complex facts in an understandable way using analogies.
- Find inspiration by comparing problems and their solutions from another area with our problem.
- Integrate supporting cognitive thought processes that are necessary with open and poorly structured problems (so-called ill-defined and wicked problems).
- Unfold full creativity in combination with sketch notes.

Some information on the tool:

- Analogies and benchmarks help to change the approach to the problem in order to generate new ideas and stimulate ideation. Another industry, animals, persons, or organizations can serve as a benchmark or analogy.
- Analogies and benchmarking can be applied in the early phases of the design cycle, for example, during the definition of the problem. It's normally used in the "ideation" phase, though.

What tool can be used instead?

- Brainstorming (see page 151)
- Special brainstorming (see page 167)
- Brainwriting/6-3-5 method (see page 163)

Which other tools support working with this tool?

- "How might we..." question (see page 125)
- AEIOU (see page 107)

How much time and what materials do we need?

Group size

3–8

- Optimally in a group of 3-6 persons.
- Larger groups of more than 8 persons can be divided into smaller groups.

Typical duration

30–120 min.

- Working with analogies can be time-consuming.
- Especially the research entailed in it and the identification of characteristics and attributes as well as discussions with experts often require several hours.

Materials needed

- Whiteboard or flip charts
- Post-its, pens, markers
- Internet and printer (if analogies with people or industries are made)

Procedure: Analogies and benchmarking

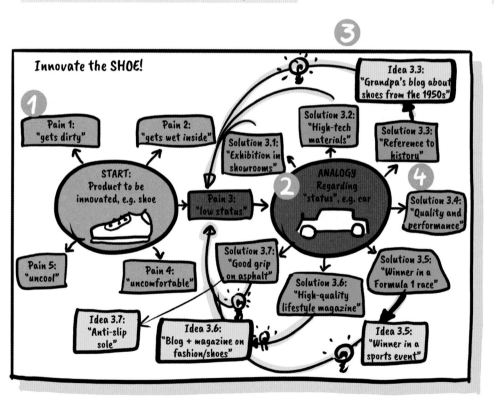

How the tool is applied...

Step 1: List the critical experiences or the biggest PAINS of the problem statement, for example, in the case of shoes, the PAIN: "low status."

Step 2: Use brainstorming or brainwriting methods to search for scenarios, systems, places, or objects that also entail PAINS but seem to have been solved. In the example (left), the PAIN of "status" was successfully solved in the automotive industry and the PAIN of "uncomfortable" in the case of a sofa, and so on. To search for analogies, ask questions like the following:

- What do other industries do?
- How does nature solve the problem?
- Why is it not a problem in other countries?

Step 3: Conduct interviews with experts who know the comparable areas, scenarios, systems, places, or objects well. Create an "analogies inspiration board" and show new insights.

Step 4: List solutions, for example, how the "status" in the automotive industry was solved by "high-quality lifestyle magazine."

Step 5: Then transfer the solution of the analogy to the original problem. Some solutions from the analogy can be transferred almost 1:1; others require a bit more creativity when applied.

How much time and what materials do we need?

Group size

1–12

- Working individually or in a group of up to 12 persons or more.
- The group size is almost scalable at will.

Typical duration

30–60 min.

- There can be several rounds.
- Each round takes about 30 minutes.

Materials needed

- One flip chart per person
- A DIN A4 or DIN A3 sheet of paper for participants working in private. In the case of group work, DIN A2 or DIN A1
- Pens and Post-its
- Optional: Internet to search for images

Template: Analogies with sketch notes

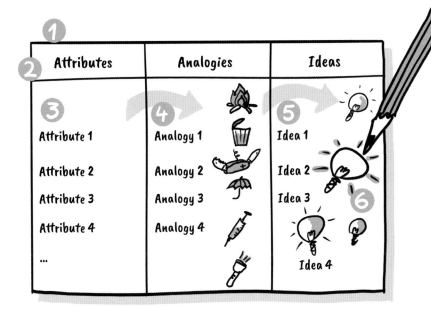

How the tool is applied...

To increase the creative output, we can use a combination of design by means of analogy technique and by sketches. In the work with analogies explained above, we also use sketch notes.

Step 1: Divide a large sheet of paper into three columns.

Step 2: Label the columns with attributes, analogies, and ideas.

Step 3: List the attributes about the problem or problem statement (see page 49).

Step 4: Ask the design team to find analogies for the respective attributes.

Step 5: Solve the problem in the group from the point of view of the analogy in the form of sketch notes. How to draw sketch notes is shown on page 174.

Step 6: Develop original and viable ideas for the problem statement or parts of it.

The creation of sketch notes is not just fun, it also allows the design thinking team to find great analogies.

Visual basic building blocks: By skillfully combining the individual building blocks, content can be visually displayed; it's a bit like combining letters into words and finally into stories.

Forms:

Nearly everything can be represented with dots, lines, and geometrical forms

Symbols:

Font:
1/5
3/5
1/5

Today we practice

Write letters rather close to one another

Gray Highlights:

Gray outside = 2-D, i.e. flat

Gray inside = 3-D, i.e. volume

Container:

Thoughts Speak Factual statement Emotional things Info

Figures:

The simplest form for a person...and a group

From a star...to a figure

Diversity and professions

Faces:

Emotions through the form of the eyes and mouth   Line of vision indicated in the position of the eyes

Structure:

If you say: "I can't draw!", then this is the right thing for you

Sketch note training

Position:
Senior Manager
Communications at B. Braun Melsungen AG

"Design thinking has revolutionized the way we create solutions for (future) clients and keeps evolving through everyday practice."

Why is it her favorite tool?

For me, working with analogies is the perfect complement to traditional brainstorming approaches. The tool helps with ideation and fits the design thinking mindset perfectly. Combining analogies with sketch notes is particularly enjoyable during the creation as well as for the viewer. They boost our creative effectiveness and our self-confidence. The combination of both techniques combines the best of both worlds.

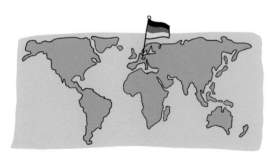

Country:
Germany

Affiliation:
B. Braun
Melsungen

Checked by: **Thomas Schocher**

Company/Position: CSS Versicherung, specialist for transformation

Expert tips:

Concentrate on the critical experiences and pains
When searching for analogies, we should concentrate on critical experiences, thus identifying new and intriguing aspects that we can apply to our problem.

Also look at absurd industries and concepts
Analogies and benchmarks that are far away from our industry or the problem at hand have often proven quite helpful; it means that at first glance there were few common aspects; nonetheless they helped in solving the problem.

If nothing comes up, just Google
Another way to discover analogies and be inspired is a Google image search. Enter "fast" and "comfortable," for instance, and you get thousands of objects with these characteristics.

Practice daily to train the mind
Daily practice improves the power of association. Hence it is useful to train the mind in finding similarities on a daily basis, for example, when watching TV or on the way to work.

Copying from others is allowed
Basically, every time a problem arises, we should ponder how other people solved it.

Use it spontaneously and often
Apply the association technique spontaneously, for example, during a brainstorming session. Ask participants, for example: How is the customer service solved in a 5-star hotel?

Description of the use case

- To increase creativity, Lilly's team wants to work with analogies and benchmarks.
- After an intense brainstorming session about analogies, thoughts come up about zoos, aliens, strange planets, off-road expeditions through Africa, and much more.
- Finally, decisive stimuli arise from the analogies regarding the topics of culture, the natural environment, and comprehension of new circumstances.

Key learnings

- Inspiration with analogies and benchmarks can add a lot to any ideation.
- Frequently, completely new approaches to a solution are found this way that we, as experts in our domain or industry, had ignored before.
- The combination of analogy and sketches heightens the creativity of design thinking teams.

Tool for download

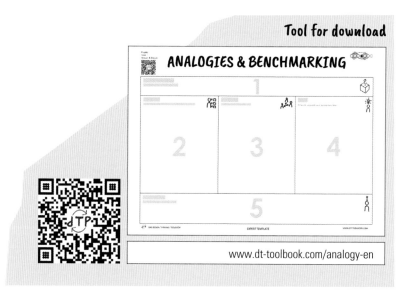

www.dt-toolbook.com/analogy-en

NABC
need, approach, benefit, competition

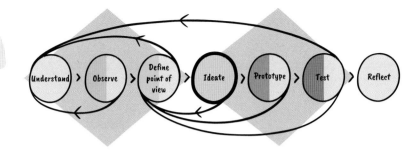
I would like...

to capture the core of an idea within a very short time and share it with others in a targeted way.

NEED   APPROACH

BENEFIT   COMPETITION

What you can do with the tool:

- Capture the core of an idea, a concept, or prototype quickly.
- Ensure that the focus is on the user/customer by starting with the question about the customer problem, followed by an intensive examination of the customer need.
- Look at an idea under four different aspects: need (problem), approach (solution, performance promise), benefit, and competition (alternatives on the market).
- Present an idea in an early phase and obtain important feedback.
- Compare different ideas/concepts.

Some information on the tool:

- The NABC is the minimal version of a business idea structuring method. It comprises the first four basic questions (need, approach, benefit, and competition) around the context of the idea.
- NABC can be applied in many phases, for example, in the "ideation" phase; it's also useful in the validation of prototypes or for a better understanding of the users.
- Often, NABC is used in documentation or after the ideation and in the presentation of business ideas and innovation projects with respect to feedback providers.
- In addition, NABC can be used in combination with an elevator pitch (see variation on page 179).

What tool can be used instead?

- To begin with, a simple idea communication sheet with title, description, and sketch can be used (see *The Design Thinking Playbook*, page 105).
- In principle, NABC can be inferred from any other business idea/business model structuring method or be further developed and deepened (e.g. business model canvas and lean canvas) (see page 251)
- Storytelling (see page 129)

Which other tools support working with this tool?

- Watering hole method with green and red feedback
  - Green feedback: What are the strengths of the idea? What should be retained?
  - Red feedback: What are the weaknesses of the idea? What should be improved?

Group size

1–6

- Usually, it is enough for one person to create the first draft of the formulation.
- More people review content and comprehensibility.

Typical duration

20–40 min.

- The typical duration depends strongly on the phase and on how much information already exists.
- In principle, you can describe an NABC in sufficient detail and in an understandable manner in 20 to 40 minutes.

Materials needed

- NABC cross, printed on A4/A3 paper format or in electronic form directly on the computer.
- Post-its, pens, markers

Template and procedure: NABC

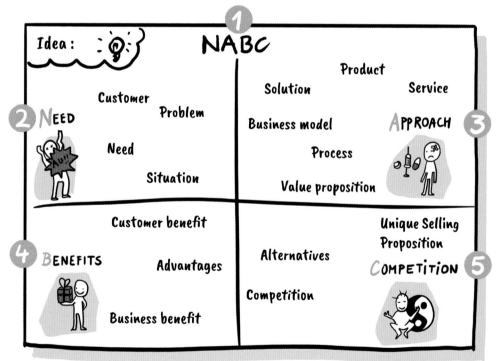

How the tool is applied...

- **Step 1:** Draw an NABC cross or use the template.
- **Step 2:** Begin with N as in need (problem) and describe
  - the problem that the customer has;
  - the typical customer who has this problem;
  - the typical everyday situation in which the problem crops up;
  - the need that results from it.
- **Step 3:** Go to A as in approach (to a solution) and explain
  - how to solve the problem, that is, what the approach to a solution/the performance promise looks like;
  - the product, service, or process;
  - how the business model looks or how it earns money.
- **Step 4:** Continue with B as in benefit and formulate in terms of both quality and quantity:
  - the benefit for the customer;
  - the benefits for you/your company.
- **Step 5:** Add C as in competition, that is, the alternatives and competitors existing today and in the future. In addition, list the unique selling points of the solution.

This is the favorite tool of Mathias Strazza

Position:
Head Future Banking, responsible for the PFLab (innovation lab) of PostFinance Ltd.; Lecturer for Innovation and Innovation Management

"The customer, his behavior, his problem, and thus his need constitute the focus. Today, customer experiences are even consciously designed. The term 'design thinking' groups together the process, the methods, and the mindset. Even non-professionals can bring it about that something new and customer-oriented quickly comes into being by dealing with the topic."

Why is it his favorite tool?

The NABC begins with the customer and his problem – and not with the solution. It is my favorite tool because the NABC succeeds in conveying the core of an idea in all its essential aspects and making it comprehensible to somebody even in a short presentation (pitch) of 5 minutes. In an early phase, initial important questions are raised; later, the method helps in reducing the wealth of information again.

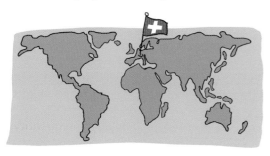

Country:
Switzerland

Affiliation:
PFLab
(PostFinance)

Checked by: Christine Kohlert

Company/Position: Professor at the Media Design University of Design and Computer Science

Expert tips:

Use the content of NABC according to your needs
- In support of the descriptions in NABC, always also use visualizations, sketches, and drawings.
- For us, storytelling often came in handy for conveying contents from the NABC.
- It is not imperative to stick to the NABC cross in a presentation. If PowerPoint is used, for instance, the sections can be shown one after another (one per slide).
- Not only ideas but also prototypes can be presented quickly this way.
- Once the problem has been described and a solution is known, we intentionally look for different, new solutions, in particular, when we are on the lookout for more radical changes.

Variation: NABC and the elevator pitch

- The elevator pitch is the shortest form of presentation and is used to convince somebody in the shortest possible time. Dividing the pitch into three parts has proven useful: The entry point (hook), the middle part (core), and the conclusion (close). The NABC is deployed in the middle part.
- The NABC pitch at a glance:

Entry point (hook):
- Attract attention with a statement, a keyword, a headline, a question. Provoke!
- Whet the appetite, kindle interest.
- Be different, unique, surprising.

Middle part (core): NABC

Conclusion (close):
- What comes next? What is to be achieved?
- Invitation and next steps.

Description of the use case

- On the basis of a known customer problem, various ideas are created. The ideas are then documented and visualized in an NABC.
- At a later point, the design thinking team presents the idea within the context of an NABC pitch and obtains feedback on it.
- Lilly's team uses the NABC often for a variety of applications. They deploy it, for instance, to define a focus or to present the prototype.
- Lilly frequently reminds the team to go beyond looking at obvious competitors when considering alternatives.

Key learnings

- The NABC normally fits on one page.
- Describe the needs, the approach, benefit, and the competition in terms of a potential solution.
- Use NABC also for the preparation of an elevator pitch or as an aid for the definition of a value proposition in the business model canvas.

Tool for download

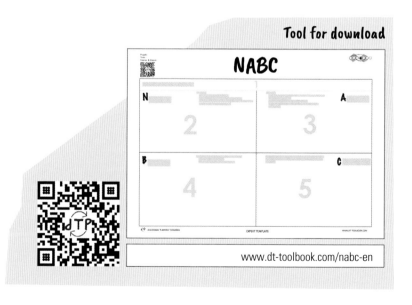

www.dt-toolbook.com/nabc-en

Blue ocean tool & buyer utility map

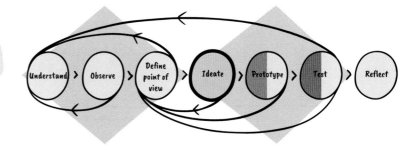

I would like...

to differentiate a product or service from the competition and open up new market opportunities.

Red ocean   Blue ocean

What you can do with the tool:

- Explore untapped market opportunities.
- Provide differentiated and new offers based on the user needs.
- Adapt a strategy to new market needs by understanding the competitive edge.
- Establish the right vision for the design challenge or a road map for step-by-step implementation and control mechanisms.

Some general information on the tool:

- Blue ocean and blue ocean shift, invented by W. Chan Kim and Renée Mauborgne, help in the definition of a unique value proposition.
- With a buyer utility map, the focus is put on the user/customer. His experience with services and products usually can be seen as a cycle that is broken down into six phases (purchase, delivery, use, accessories, maintenance, and disposal).
- Findings from the application of the tool also help to define a point of view or generate initial ideas after the competition and the needs of the users have been observed and analyzed.
- In the buyer utility map, we work with various levers that either reduce, eliminate, raise, or create factors of a proposition. The aim is to distinguish oneself from the competition and to craft innovative propositions.

What tool might be used instead?

- Lean canvas (see page 251)
- Value proposition canvas

Which tools support working with this tool?

- Persona/user profile (see page 97)
- NABC (see page 177)
- 2x2 matrix (see page 155)
- Competition analysis, including SWOT analysis
- Benchmark analysis of competitors

How much time and what materials do we need?

Group size

4–6

- It is easier to develop suggestions for the buyer utility map on smaller design teams than on large teams.
- Split large teams into several smaller groups, if needed.

Typical duration

30–120 min.

- Completing the buyer utility map usually takes 30 minutes.
- The complete implementation, including a comprehensive competitor analysis, takes several days.

Materials needed

- Some sheets of paper
- Pens, Post-its, markers
- Print templates in A0

Template and procedure: Blue ocean

New value curves with the four actions framework  ①

Raise ↗ ②
What factors might be raised far above the previous industry standard?

Reduce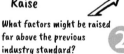
What factors might be reduced far below the previous industry standard?

Eliminate
What factors are defined in the industry and might be eliminated?

Create ⭐
What factors that the industry has not offered so far might be created?

Six phases of the buyer experience

	Purchasing	Delivery	Use	Extension	Maintenance	Disposal
Productivity			●			
Simplicity			●			
Convenience				●		
Risk						
Fun & image	●					
Sustainability						

● Current industry focus

● Blue ocean offer

③ ④ 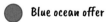  ⑤

New blue ocean value proposition

How the tool is applied...

- **Step 1:** Begin with the "four actions framework" (raise, reduce, eliminate, and create). The focus is on the definition of strategic factors, which direct or alternative competitors – or the industry as a whole – concentrate on with respect to a product or service (e.g. productivity, price, guarantee, etc.).
- **Step 2:** Determine which of these factors can be raised, reduced, eliminated, or which ones can be newly created. Choose the most critical factors.
- **Step 3:** Arrange these critical factors in the buyer utility matrix. First define the decision factors critical to the user/customer with respect to the offer known today.
- **Step 4:** Think about which factors can be reduced or eliminated. Now comes the creative part. Conduct a brainstorming session with the team to get to the unused factors. To do so, additional value ranges should be identified that a service or product may be able to cover.
- **Step 5:** Define the new "blue ocean" value proposition from the result.

This is the favorite tool of Alice Froissac

Position:
Co-founder & design thinking expert at Openers – ME310 Alumni d.school Paris

"Design Thinking allows you both to understand your users who are all unique and to work with people with other backgrounds than yours. By combining all those characteristics and differences, you can do amazing discoveries and be really creative and innovative. It is a great opportunity to make things happen."

Why is it her favorite tool?

Blue ocean as a tool that makes it possible to develop a differentiation strategy pragmatically. For me, this approach is an excellent combination of empathy with the customer and a competition/benchmark analysis. With a change in perspective, the offer of the competitor is neither scary nor do we have to copy it. It serves as an inspiration for our work of defining unique products and services. The buyer utility map helps with questioning the status quo and defining the value proposition when launching a new offer.

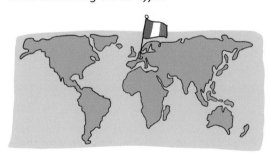

Country:
France

Affiliation:
Openers

Checked by: Sebastian Fixson

Company/Position: Babson College, Researcher | Teacher | Advisor on Innovation and Design

Expert tips:

Expand the buyer utility map and non-customers map individually
The activities of a customer can be expanded as required. For example: How did the user become aware of the product? Did he compare products prior to the purchase? What type of delivery does he prefer? Does information on the handling of returns have an impact? Were ongoing expenses an issue? Do the comments in social media influence the purchasing process? In terms of use of the product, attributes such as simplicity, convenience, and risk minimization can be crucial.

Red ocean	Blue ocean	Black ocean
Existing markets Strong competition	Non-competitive markets Few competitors	Ecosystem-driven markets Without competition

Variation: Black ocean/minimal viable ecosystem

- In addition to the shift from a red ocean strategy to a blue ocean strategy, we recommend also taking a black ocean strategy into consideration, as explained in *The Design Thinking Playbook* by Lewrick et al. (2018, p. 240 et seqq.) for the design of business ecosystems.
- The black ocean strategy aims at forming a system of actors in which the other competitors have no chance of competing in the long term.
- The procedure is based on an iterative process in which a minimum viable ecosystem (MVE) evolves across four design loops.
- The MVE serves as a basis for the optimization of the value streams and offers of each individual actor in such a way that competitors could not survive.
- In the definition of the offer, initially such offers are selected that have the greatest market penetration, fewest functionalities, and the greatest customer benefit.

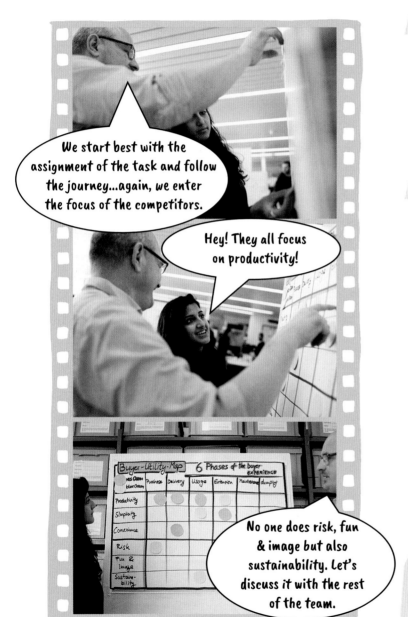

Description of the use case

- After Lilly's team has analyzed the competitors and observed the users, the time has come to analyze the findings about the focus of the market and the competitors.
- Lilly is in a mature market. The teams have found that most competitors focus on boosting productivity through digital transformation.
- This gives Lilly's team the opportunity to address other levers for increasing the benefit for the customer.

Key learnings

- Don't hesitate to interview users/customers regularly during the definition of a blue ocean strategy.
- Get experts from your own or other industries involved in order to identify the facts better and define new factors.
- It's best to fill out the buyer utility map on the team.
- Explore opportunities to be part of a black ocean strategy.

Tool for download

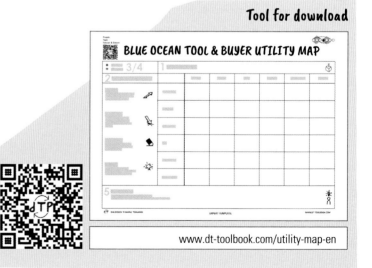

www.dt-toolbook.com/utility-map-en

Phase: Prototype

Building prototypes makes the selected ideas tangible and perceptible. Prototypes range from a simple critical function prototype to the final prototype. To build a prototype, we use simple materials that are good enough to test a function or an experience. The "prototype" phase is closely connected to the following "test" phase. The feedback from the tests is used to learn more about the user and to improve or discard the current prototype. This procedure is reflected in the design thinking motto: Love it! Change it! Or leave it! Early failure gives us the opportunity of learning and building a better prototype in the next iteration.

Frequently used kinds of prototypes

On the following pages, we briefly present the most popular variations of a prototype. For the prototypes, we use the terminology introduced in *The Design Thinking Playbook*, being fully aware that there are different terms for the variants. It depends on the context of the problem statement which prototype is used, how many prototypes are built, or how often a micro-cycle is run through until we have designed a final prototype.

For better illustration of the individual prototypes, we defined a simple design challenge as our example. It provides quick information on the focus of the respective prototype and how it changes across the design thinking cycle. As a rule, prototypes get a higher resolution and become more specific over time; initial ideas are usually still just simple sketches.

Design challenge:
HOW MUCH WATER TO CARRY?

THIRST!

What is the optimum solution for hikers who depend on fluids during a mountain hike and want to transport the daily requirement of water easily and safely?

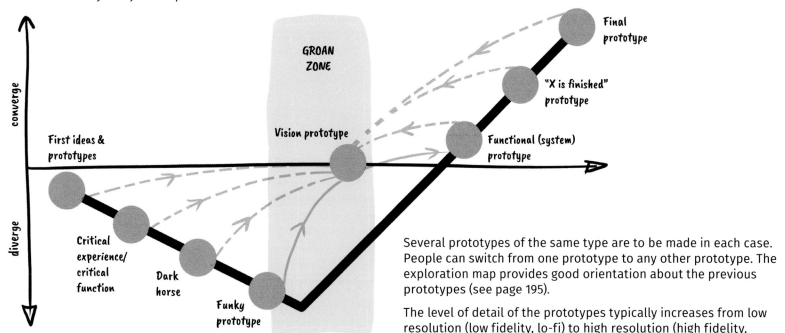

Several prototypes of the same type are to be made in each case. People can switch from one prototype to any other prototype. The exploration map provides good orientation about the previous prototypes (see page 195).

The level of detail of the prototypes typically increases from low resolution (low fidelity, lo-fi) to high resolution (high fidelity, hi-fi).

Focused experiments – Critical Experience Prototype (CEP) & Critical Function Prototype (CFP)

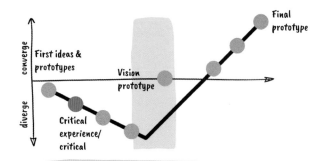

I would like...

to learn more about the user and his problem through experiments.

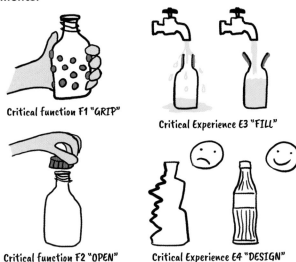

Critical function F1 "GRIP"

Critical Experience E3 "FILL"

Critical function F2 "OPEN"

Critical Experience E4 "DESIGN"

What you can do with the tool:

- Investigate and clarify elements that are critical to the project with users in little experiments.
- Create an experience that is critical for the overall design to learn more about the users.
- Simulate a function that is critical for the overall design.
- Arrive at a more profound understanding of the users' needs.
- Gain understanding of all aspects of a problem to the greatest possible extent.
- Provoke emotions in the user that are not accessible with a simple questionnaire.

Some information about this type of prototype:

- These critical experience prototypes (CEP)/critical function prototypes (CFP) are carried out at an early stage in a project, when the first steps of the "understand" and "observe" phases have been completed, or when initial contacts have been made in the form of interviews and the design team wants to learn even more about the user.
- The CEP/CFP can be performed several times over the design cycle, especially if the whole problem is not yet understood.
- CEPs/CFPs make sense when critical elements for experience or function are still unclear or need to be questioned.
- CEPs/CFPs are little prototypes that allow us to deal with the user on a more in-depth level.
- The direct exchange with the user about individual decisive elements reveals deeper needs and helps, among other things, to prevent misinterpretations of interviews.

Expert tips:

- It's not about solving the problem completely. Instead, the aim is to question elements of a possible solution. The experiments (or prototypes) should be created in a very short period of time.
- The critical items diagram tool (see page 145) can be used as a basis.
- Begin by building a prototype together with the team and integrating new ideas that emerge during realization. Building can also be understood as "thinking with one's hands."
- Many little experiments often yield more findings than one big experiment.

Crazy experiments – Dark horse prototype

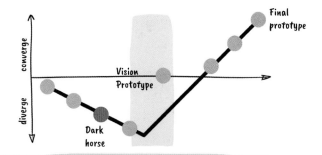

to learn even more about the user and his problem through peculiar experiments.

Water pill

Water infusion

"Rasta water"

What you can do with the tool:

- Clarify unusual or future questions and test them in the form of an experiment.
- Try out unorthodox ways.
- Consciously get off the well-beaten path.
- Cast light into the most distant dark corners of the problem space.
- Provoke strong emotions and reactions on the part of the user in extreme experiments.
- Dare to move out of your comfort zone as far as possible.

Some information about this type of prototype:

- "Dark horse" is a term used in athletic competitions or in politics. It describes the unexpected winner, who was not given a chance to win at the beginning, or the participant who is completely unknown.
- These experiments are carried out in the early phases of a project. With a dark horse prototype, you can test the reaction of the user to unusual approaches to a solution.
- For ideation, for instance, you might want to take a peek into the future: "What will the solution look like in 30 years?" Or turn previous assumptions around. The central questions often start with "What if...?"
- With the "dark horse" prototype, ideas can be tested that entail a high risk and have not been in use for the proposed application or have not (yet) been technically feasible until now.

Expert tips:

- It is usually impossible in this phase to create a functioning prototype. This is why a Wizard of Oz experiment or a video of it is a good form of implementation. In a Wizard of Oz experiment (also referred to as mechanical Turk), the test person pretends to be communicating with a technical system. In reality, of course, another person is hidden and creates the responses from the system. For example: A person keeps refilling the water for the water infusion.
- This risky experiment should be carried out in the early phases since then the failure of an experiment is allowed, if not encouraged.
- If there's a risk that the design team gets stuck mentally, the building of a dark horse prototype also helps to generate radical ideas.

Combined experiments - Funky prototype

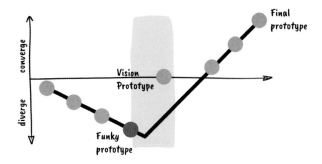

I would like...

to combine the findings of initial experiments in order to complete the exploration of the problem space.

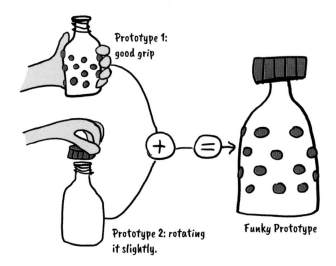

Prototype 1: good grip

Prototype 2: rotating it slightly.

Funky Prototype

What you can do with the tool:

- Begin with combining initial findings.
- Clarify remaining questions about the needs of the user.
- Test first overall functionalities and come to an initial vision of the final objective.
- Build and perform experiments that focus on the benefit.
- Gain certainty about the critical elements of the solution.

Some information about this type of prototype:

- For the funky prototype, the findings and ideas from various previous brainstorming sessions and prototypes (e.g. CEP, CFP, or dark horse) are merged.
- These more detailed experiments are intended to remove any remaining uncertainties about the elements that are critical for the solution. The main objective is still the collection of findings in the problem space. Finding a solution to the problem is still of secondary importance.
- First final functionalities of a possible solution are to be implemented in the most simple way. These experiments or first prototypes are made from simple materials or are based on existing prototypes or existing solutions.

Expert tips:

- The experiments (or prototypes) should be created in a short period of time; they continue to be simple prototypes.
- Using a morphological box, an overview of the results of all experiments and the findings from the "understand" and "observe" phases can be created. This allows for better combinations to be found faster.
- Together with the critical elements of the critical items diagram, it can be checked whether there are still open questions concerning the critical elements, which are to be answered with this step.

Imagining the future – Vision prototype

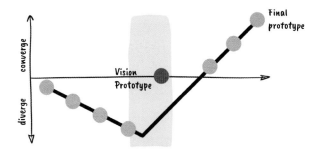

I would like...

to create a vision of the later solution based on all previous findings and test it.

Vision:
"Water, my constant companion: lightweight, always available, cool"

What you can do with the tool:

- Develop a first vision on how the problem is solved.
- Create a vision of what is to be marketed in the future.
- Make sure that the vision solves the identified needs and problems of the user.
- Design the transition from problem exploration to problem solution.

Some information about this type of prototype:

- The vision prototype is the first concept that attempts to solve all identified needs and problems of the user. The sketched vision usually has a rather distant time horizon that can be reached through a series of solutions in the form of products and/or services.
- This concept must also be tested and verified with the users. In this step, it is quite common that new insights about the user and his or her behavior emerge.
- The vision prototype is designed to help the team overcome the "groan zone" – the transition of the divergent phase of problem exploration to the convergent phase of problem solution.

Expert tips:

- A vision statement should describe in a single sentence the status aimed for. If this statement gets the attention and kindles the interest of the user, the path taken is promising.
- For the vision prototype, it is critical to find out the needs that are to be satisfied with a product, the target group, and the benefit that is provided.
- Extreme/lead users (see page 79) are excellent references when testing a vision prototype.
- A vision prototype has likewise a very low resolution. It can show the eventual solution scenario in a sketch or in a video.
- Again, it is worthwhile here to do several iterations to refine the vision of the future.

Prototype with a first function – functional (system) prototype

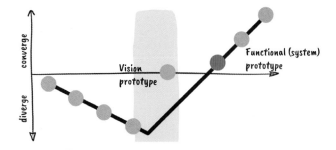

I would like...

to develop a first working prototype.

Vision:
"Water, my constant companion:
lightweight, always available, cool"

The prototype for the functions
"always with me" and "lightweight."

What you can do with the tool:

- Implement first steps of the described vision.
- Breathe some life into the later solution.
- Find out how a main function can be technically implemented and which solution variants there are.
- Get a step closer to the minimum viable product (MVP, see page 207) or even reach it.

Some information about this type of prototype:

- With the functional (system) prototype, one part of the previously emerged vision is implemented. The focus is on the part of the vision that can be achieved early on and easily. With a system of multiple functionalities to be implemented, it is common first to realize the main function of the later product.
- In the case of solutions with reduced functionalities, a minimum viable product (MVP) can already be achieved at this point.
- The main purpose of the functional prototype is making the main function of the later product tangible and perceptible. This main function should be implemented technically with simple means. The main function should be checked for its technical feasibility.

Expert tips:

- The basic functionality to be implemented should be kept as simple as possible and be reduced to its very core. Other functionalities will be automatically added later.
- After the phase of problem exploration with low-resolution prototypes and very fast iterations, the step toward technical implementation is often a barrier, since failure is likely. This is why this step needs some courage.
- A failure in this step should be understood as a learning success, true to the adage: "There is no failure, there's only learning."

Solutions in detail - "X is finished"

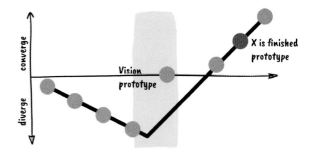

I would like...

to implement the important elements of the desired solution and go into details.

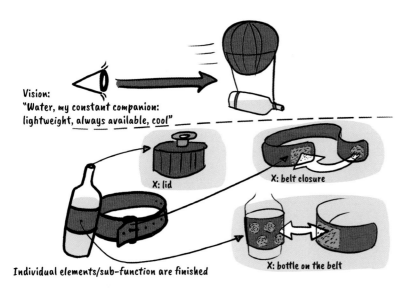

Vision:
"Water, my constant companion: lightweight, always available, cool"

X: lid

X: belt closure

X: bottle on the belt

Individual elements/sub-function are finished

What you can do with the tool:

- Gain certainty about important sub-functionalities.
- Describe the elements that are essential for the overall function of the solution in as much detail as possible.
- Take a big step toward the implementation of a solution.
- Obtain a good starting position for calculating the costs of the next steps, including implementation.

Some information about this type of prototype:

- "X is finished" is the phase in which the elements or sub-functions required for the overall functionality are implemented and realized. The goal is to have a functional overall system on hand after the conclusion of the phase whose main functions have been specified to the greatest possible degree.
- While both the vision prototype and the functional (system) prototype focus on the solution of the overall problem, more emphasis is put on the detailed solution for the most important elements in the "X is finished" phase.
- Especially for systems with multiple sub-functions, this phase is a crucial step toward a final prototype.

Expert tips:

- In this step, the focus is on the essential sub-functions (of a system).
- The knowledge gained in this step will help in the assessment of the later implementation.
- The technical requirements and possible development costs are estimated for the first time within this phase.
- In this step, it may be helpful to integrate third-party know-how of partners or potential suppliers.
- The sub-functions must be checked and tested for their user suitability as well. The "X is finished" solution usually also requires several iterations until the sub-system works really well.

(Hopefully) at the finish — Final prototype

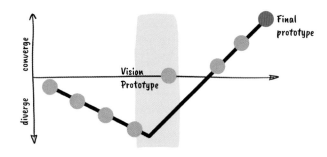

I would like...

to come to an end and put the finishing touches on the solution.

What you can do with the tool:

- Exit the prototype phase and thus the early innovation phase.
- Avoid overfulfillment of needs.
- Reduce all required elements to what is essential.
- Find intelligent combinations of sub-functions.
- Create an elegant ultimate solution for the needs and problems.
- Make the first marketable step toward the implementation of the vision.
- Try to convince the decision-makers of your final prototype, because this is the only way they can actually understand what the solution will look like and which needs are met with it.

Some information about this type of prototype:

- The final prototype concludes the phase of problem solving. When looking so closely at individual elements, you easily lose sight of the big picture. When the individual sub-functions are developed, there is a risk that they will diverge, become too large, and that the elegance and simplicity of the overall solution will be lost.
- Another thing to be done in this step is to check whether the proposed solution still matches the needs originally determined and the problem of the target group.
- At the latest in this step, the minimum viable product (see page 207) should be achieved. Depending on the complexity of the overall solution, this goal is reached earlier on or only with the final prototype.
- The final prototype shows the "problem/solution fit."

Expert tips:

- The reduction to the essence and the smart combination of individual elements and functionalities ensures elegance.
- It has stood the test of time to take another look at the defined elements, for example, CFP/CEP (see page 188), and to examine whether the desired ultimate solution matches them and which parts might be dispensed with.
- Make sure that only those functionalities that are really necessary are implemented and no overloaded solutions emerge.

Exploration map

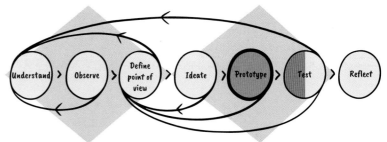

I would like...

to know what experiments I have done so far and how I can classify them.

What you can do with the tool:

- Make visible the types of experiments that were carried out and the prototypes that were realized.
- Get a quick overview of the experiments or prototypes that can still be performed.
- Record the delta between the expected and actual outcome of an experiment.
- Obtain a shared understanding of the experiments carried out so far.

Some information on the tool:

- The exploration map helps to keep track of all the experiments and prototypes already carried out.
- It normally has an experience and a function axis. The two axes symbolize known or existing as well as new or unexpected behaviors and functions.
- In addition, the feedback of the users/customers with respect to the experiments can be entered on the exploration map. This way, it can be determined whether the expected user behavior conforms to real-life experience.
- The exploration map shows – at the end of the entire design cycle – the path the team took to reach the ultimate solution.

What tool can be used instead?

- The experiments and their results can be documented in a more conventional way without the use of an exploration map.
- In this case, it won't become clear, however, whether really risky or unusual experiments were carried out, how creative the teams were, and how far they dared to go in the exploration of the problem space and in finding the solution.

Which tools support working with this tool?

- Feedback capture grid (see page 217)
- Solution interview (see page 225)
- I like, I wish, I wonder (see page 239)
- Testing sheet (see page 213)

How much time and what materials do we need?

Group size

- Design thinking core team.
- Ideal are groups of 4-6 people.

4–6

Typical duration

- The duration depends on the number of prototypes to be entered on the map and the intensity of the resultant discussion on the team.

10–45 min.

Materials needed

- A large sheet of paper
- Post-its, pens, markers
- A lot of creativity and fun to realize something tangible

Template: Exploration map

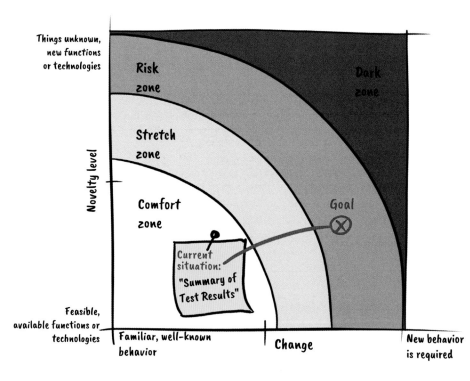

How the tool is applied...

The exploration map gives the team an overview of the experiments carried out and shows the areas in which experiments can still be made. It provides information on the expectations regarding an experiment and its effect on the target group.

- **Step 1:** Enter the experiments already carried out. They might have to be repositioned. Each experiment is recorded on the exploration map – it is best to do so with a name and an image (e.g. of the prototype and the testing).
- **Step 2:** Discuss the positioning of the experiment on the team. Have we really left our comfort zone? Based on the previous exploration and the previous experiments, the goal for a new experiment, for example, can be defined.
- **Step 3:** After the prototype has been built and the expectation regarding the result has been formulated, they are also entered on the exploration map and positioned accordingly.
- **Step 4:** After the tests, the reaction of the users and the findings of the tests can also be captured. The critical discussion of the feedback may change the position of the experiment on the exploration map.

The exploration map stimulates the discussion among team members, provides the basis for planning new experiments, and helps with the reflection after tests.

196

This is the favorite tool of Larry Leifer

Position:
- Professor of Mechanical Engineering at Stanford University
- Founding Director, HPI & Stanford Center for Design Research
- ME310 "Project-based Engineering Design, Innovation, and Development"

"Keep up the design thinking mindset and start hunting for the next big opportunity."

Why is it his favorite tool?

The exploration map helps the teams, because it is often difficult for teams to check whether they have really explored all aspects of the problem space with their experiments and prototypes.
I like this tool because the map shows in a simple way whether the problem has really been examined on a broad basis and what was learned from the individual steps.

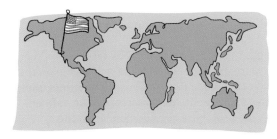

Country:
USA

Affiliation:
Stanford University

Checked by: Shwet Sharvary

Company/Position: Everything by Design, Innovation Catalyst | Insights Manager | Design Strategist

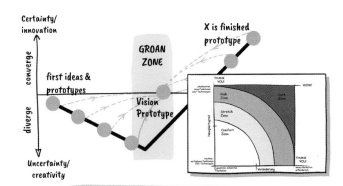

Expert tips:

At the beginning of the journey, the destination is not known
- We make sure that this activity is carried out with the entire core team and that a common understanding of the course of the experiments emerges.
- The exploration map should be supplemented after each experimenting phase. Groups from the core team working in tandem can acquire information from it on the results of other teams.
- When repositioning an experiment, the original expectation is also recorded. The difference stands for the misinterpretation of the needs. The following applies: The greater the difference, the greater the gain in knowledge.
- It might be helpful to keep two parallel exploration maps. The expectations with respect to the results of the experiments are marked on one of the maps; the reactions from the tests on the other. Otherwise, you quickly lose track if the number of experiments is large.

Pictures and visualizations say more than a thousand words
- We put the exploration maps in a place (e.g. as a huge poster), where they can be seen by all team members.
- The overview shows, throughout the design cycle, possible gaps in the exploration of the problem space.
- The exploration map is not a precise measuring device. It provides rough orientation. The time for the positioning of the individual experiments should therefore be kept very short.
- Pictures say more than a thousand words. It is advisable to use visualizations or photos of the realized prototypes to position them on the map.

Description of the use case

- With the initial iterations, Lilly's team had the goal of getting a real in-depth understanding of the problem and the customers. As a result, the team has acquired a very good sense for and understanding of the situation.
- Now they want to pull the user out of the comfort zone in the tests and try out more radical approaches.
- With a dark horse prototype, they plan to sound out the limits of what's feasible and dare to enter the "dark zone" of the exploration map.

Key learnings

- The exploration map helps to keep track of our experiments and see the point we have reached on our journey of exploration toward the next market opportunity.
- The map visualizes the intention of our experiments and shows how the results change over time.

Tool for download

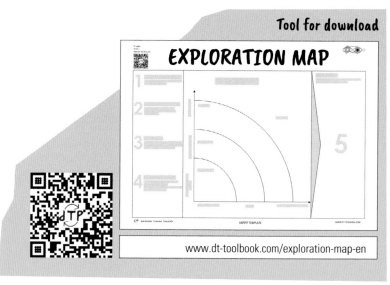

www.dt-toolbook.com/exploration-map-en

Prototype to test

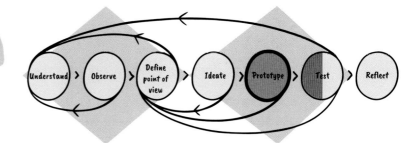

I would like...

to assess whether the needs of the user were met with the implemented ideas.

What you can do with the tool:

- Let the user experience the idea and observe how he/she interacts with the prototype.
- Deepen the understanding of the potential user.
- Validate needs and review assumptions.
- Acquire feedback on various dimensions of desirability, feasibility, and practicability.

Some information on the tool:

- With its focus on direct user interaction and feedback, the prototype to be tested is a fundamental concept of design thinking. After the "ideation" phase, the ideas are translated into prototypes and tested with real users.
- The point is to configure an experiment for the user in order to learn more about a feature or experience.
- There are many different kinds of prototypes (see pages 187-194). Choose the kind that best matches the phase in the macro-cycle, the idea, and the hypotheses to be reviewed.
- The potential user should interact with the prototype and experience it. This way, basic functional requirements for the solution can be identified.
- The feedback collected during the test is extremely valuable and constitutes the basis for further decisions, for example, the determination of the most promising ideas or of the functions that must be reworked.

What tool can be used instead?

- Interviews or online surveys can be an alternative for certain kinds of prototypes. But be careful: These methods do not guarantee the same findings since direct user interaction is lacking.

Which other tools support working with this tool?

- Empathy map (see page 93)
- Feedback capture grid (see page 217)
- I like, I wish, I wonder (see page 239)
- Solution interview (see page 225)

Group size

1—many

- A prototype can be created by one person or by a larger team.
- Experts and additional team members help to check that everything has been taken into account.

Typical duration

30 min.– many days

- The duration can vary depending on the degree of resolution.
- Low-resolution prototypes can be built within 30 minutes. A final prototype may require days or even weeks.

Materials needed

- Design thinking material
- Paper, Post-its, pens
- Whatever material it takes to create the prototype

Template and procedure: Prototype to test

Prototype to test – preparation

① Why?
What assumptions do we want to verify?

_____
_____
_____

② How might we make it tangible and perceptible for the user?

_____

③ What should we do? Outline possible variants

④ Choose the best idea and outline the experiment

How the tool is applied...

- **Step 1:** Before prototyping, we should ask ourselves what kinds of insights we want to gain and why we want to make an experiment. Therefore it is necessary to formulate assumptions to be tested and how the experiment is to be carried out.
- **Step 2:** Think about how interacting with the prototype will become an exciting experience for the user (test person) and how the test will result in new insights.
- **Step 3:** Determine the level of resolution and what exactly is to be done. Define different prototypes to be built. Often it makes sense to think in alternatives and then opt for one.
- **Step 4:** Choose a variant and outline the experiment, if necessary. Low-resolution prototypes focus on the insights with respect to needs, practicality, and functionality and are mostly used in the divergent phase. High-resolution prototypes concentrate on feasibility and profitability.

There are many different kinds of prototypes. Depending on the materials and the context of the idea, mock-ups, storyboards, scenography, or Wizard of Oz prototypes can be used. A list of prototypes with corresponding resolutions can be found in _The Design Thinking Playbook_ on pages 111–112.

This is the favorite tool of Patrick Deininger

Position:
Senior Consultant at delta Karlsruhe GmbH | Student Consultancy, Karlsruhe Institute of Technology (KIT)

"Design thinking helps to change one's mindset completely, broaden one's horizon, and challenge assumptions to come up with unconventional and disruptive ideas."

Why is it his favorite tool?

The prototype to be tested is indispensable for gaining deep insights into the users. I like to communicate with other people and greatly enjoy showing a prototype we created to users and watching their interaction. It is difficult to convey our crazy ideas (see, for example, dark horse prototype) to users. Prototyping helps us to visualize futuristic and disruptive ideas in such a way that the user comprehends the basic idea behind them. In this way, we can test a need in an environment that is difficult to capture otherwise. Of course, building prototypes is lots of fun.

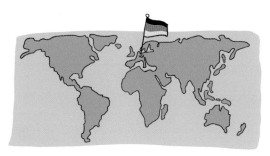

Country:
Germany

Affiliation:
Karlsruhe Institute of Technology (KIT)

Checked by: Justus Schrage

Company/Position: Karlsruhe Institute of Technology (KIT)

Prototype to test

FEEDBACK

Expert tips:

Difference between lo-fi and hi-fi prototypes
- The higher the resolution of a prototype, the less feedback we receive regarding desirability and functionality. The lower the resolution, the more honest the answer. So build prototypes from simple materials.
- Unfortunately, we all tend to fall in love with a prototype we created. When that happens, we will hold on to an idea, even though there might be better ones. This is why we keep searching, even if we already received perfect feedback. We dig deeper and find out whether the feedback was really honest.
- We never invest too much time in prototyping since that automatically increases the resolution or overloads the prototype with functions.
- We try to implement no more than one or two functions in each low-resolution prototype.
- The right time to test a low-resolution prototype is when we are still a little embarrassed to show this particular prototype.

Get inspired by other mock-ups, prototypes, and design teams
- There are many materials we can use. The best inspiration we receive is from other prototypes.
- Although we should not explain a prototype, it is often necessary to convey the context to the users. This is why it is useful to relate briefly what we intend to do with our design challenge.
- In order to ensure that we still pursue the "show, don't tell" approach, it is a good practice to separate the context explanation from the test itself in terms of time.

Description of the use case

- First, Lilly makes sure that her team first tests the right assumptions; next, she wants them to learn as much as possible as quickly as possible and would rather do several iterations, if needed.
- She motivates the team to think in variants instead of building away like mad and to think critically about the prototype only after the testing. Thinking in variants helped her to simplify many prototypes and test iterations, thus speeding up the project.

Key learnings

- Show, don't tell!
- Never fall in love with a prototype!
- Try to build prototypes with the lowest possible resolution. Test, even though you are embarrassed to show the prototype! If you aren't ashamed of your prototype, you have invested too much time in it.
- It's better to make many experiments with low-resolution prototypes than to test an ultimate solution that nobody needs or wants.

Tool for download

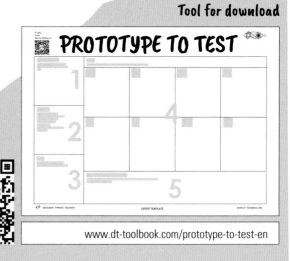

www.dt-toolbook.com/prototype-to-test-en

Service blueprint

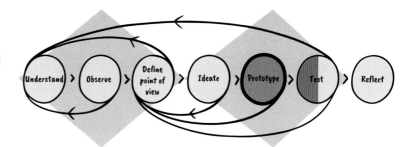

Understand > Observe > Define point of view > Ideate > Prototype > Test > Reflect

I would like...

to acquire a common understanding of the interaction and the processes that have an impact on customer satisfaction, target achievement, and efficiency.

What you can do with the tool:

- Expand the customer journey map by integrating supporting technologies, data, and customer interactions for each phase of the "journey."
- Tackle key issues in the development of new products or services, for example, whether a service covers all customer needs or whether all pains have been eliminated.
- Carry out a visualization of interactions with a customer at different levels (e.g. front stage, back stage, supporting processes).
- Define key performance indicators (KPIs) in terms of quality and time of the interactions.

Some information on the tool:

- The service blueprint is a comprehensive tool that helps to define or improve the interaction with a customer and the interfaces at a company for a product or service.
- With the advanced visualization of a customer journey map, it is possible to activate and motivate the entire organization because the service blueprint also takes into account back-office processes and supporting processes, as well as new regulations and technologies.
- A service blueprint can take into consideration various IT architectures, data layers, digital customer channels, and digital actions, which result in tailor-made interactions with the customer on the basis of artificial intelligence (e.g. chat bots).
- The tool offers easy handling, the integration of customer information, as well as the detection of different processes and the possibility of presenting them simultaneously.

What tool can be used instead?
- Customer journey (see page 103)
- Solution interview (see page 225)

Which tools support working with this tool?
- Customer journey (see page 103)
- Empathy map (see page 93)
- Persona/user profile (see page 97)

How much time and what materials do we need?

Group size

3–6

- The right group size is between 3-6 people.
- In the best case, take the relevant experts and process owners on board.

Typical duration

120–240 min.

- As a workshop format, the creation of a service blueprint takes about 4 hours.
- Beforehand, it must be determined which specific service creation process is to be optimized or designed and where the process limits are.

Materials needed

- Large wall or whiteboard
- Paper, pens
- Post-its

Template: Service blueprint

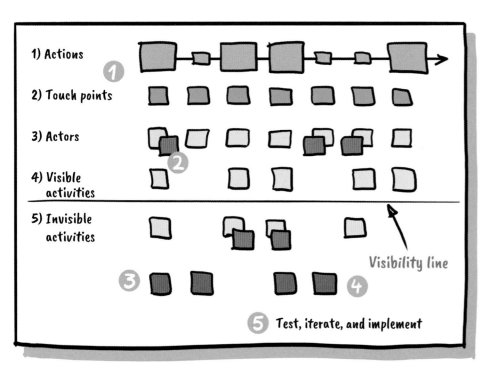

1) Actions
2) Touch points
3) Actors
4) Visible activities
5) Invisible activities

Visibility line

Test, iterate, and implement

How the tool is applied...

The service blueprint is a chronological representation of processes in which the respective effects are worked out with the customer. The discussions during the creation also help greatly to enhance the team's understanding of the context.

- **Step 1:** Look for a large wall and stick a long sheet of paper on it. Draw the lines (e.g. visibility line) and begin to fill in the steps and processes with Post-its. Start with the large blocks (actions and touch points).
- **Step 2:** Include the actual state of existing services. Create a rough process model for the design of new processes. Problems and errors are identified with color dots or Post-its.
- **Step 3:** Search for solutions together with the team in order to eliminate sources of error, streamline processes, and actively shape customer experiences. Use videos, images, sketches, and Post-its.
- **Step 4:** Distribute the open items to group work/ working in private. By working in tandem with the time boxing method, results are achieved faster.
- **Step 5:** Integrate the partial results of the groups on the service blueprint. Once the new service blueprint has been sufficiently refined, the individual elements as well as the end-to-end perspective can be tested, improved, and finally implemented.

This is the favorite tool of Beat Knüsel

Position:
CEO Trihow AG

"Design thinking can crack the three biggest problems in organizations: silo mentality, hierarchical hurdles, and lack of customer orientation."

Why is it his favorite tool?

A service blueprint overcomes departmental boundaries and focuses on customer benefits. It helps in realizing a corporate culture that is in line with transparency and active participation at all levels. This in turn creates a shared common understanding and a form of organization based on joint functioning. In digital transformation, well-defined blueprint processes help with simplification and automation, thus contributing to increased efficiency.

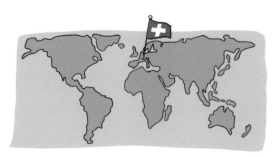

Country:
Switzerland

Affiliation:
Trihow

Checked by: Roman Schoeneboom

Company/Position: Credit Suisse, UX Design Systems Lead (VP)

Expert tips:

Extensibility and haptics
- Every service blueprint can be extended according to your own criteria and wishes. It can be completed with corresponding attributes, for example, KPIs regarding time, quality, and finance. We often found it useful to document different points of view with photos and videos since it helps to imagine the relevant situation.
- A service can be made tangible and perceptible as "theater" ("service staging") to test a service blueprint prototype. Putting yourself in the shoes of customers and suppliers is made easier, and situations can be tried out in a playful way.

Trigger questions
- Typical actions are, for example, attracting attention, informing, deciding, buying, planning, installing, using, maintaining, and disposing.
- Questions can be used to illuminate individual actions:
  - How do we imagine an ideal process? What are the process steps and interfaces that can be omitted?
  - Where can tasks be simplified or processed in tandem?
  - How and where can the customer's perception be improved?

Stumbling blocks
- Service blueprints need space. It is best to reserve a room for several days and leave the information there.
- Delineate the goal clearly at the beginning of the workshop. Otherwise, there's a risk of getting lost in the processes. Therefore, begin with the big picture.

Description of the use case

- Lilly's team has analyzed the customer journey in detail and visualized it on a large wall. The team has a clear understanding of the main phases and the associated actions and touch points.
- Together, they discuss the emotions and, above all, the pains along the journey. They ensure that all actors are mentioned and compare them to the stakeholder map.
- In the next step, the team completes the blueprint of the service. All visible and invisible activities are defined.

Key learnings

- By identifying, eliminating, or improving pain points, the first prototype of a blueprint emerges.
- A blueprint can help uncover silos or lack of transparency and integrate new technologies.
- A blueprint is a highly complex thing. It makes sense to divide the overall system into sub-systems and optimize the latter.

Tool for download

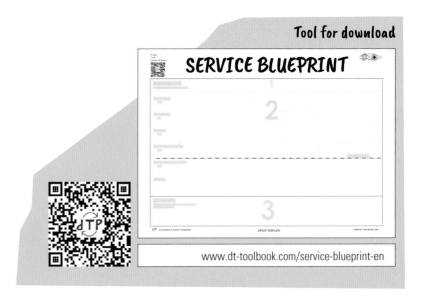

www.dt-toolbook.com/service-blueprint-en

206

MVP = Minimum viable product

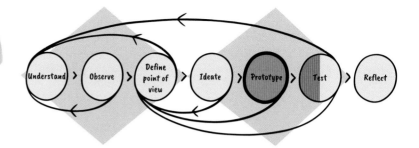

I would like...

to translate user needs into a simple, functional product and test whether the offer will be successful on the market.

This is an **MVP**:
You develop and test iteratively.

This is **not** an **MVP**:
Finished products or individual parts are not MVPs.

What you can do with the tool:

- Find out at an early stage whether the basic need is satisfied and the product attracts interest on the market.
- Find out through iterative testing whether the user need is met with a minimally functional product and how the product should be enhanced.
- Find out through user feedback how much demand there is for the product before developing further details and features.
- Minimize the risk of investing in a solution for which there is little demand on the market, thus saving time, money, and energy.

Some information on the tool:

- A minimum viable product (MVP) is a tool for the development of a product, service, or business model.
- The aim is to find out as quickly as possible (and with little effort) in an iterative process whether the solution satisfies the user needs in any meaningful way.
- This iterative process is characterized by a permanent alternation between the holistic solution of the problem (functional prototype) and the solution of individual details (X is finished; see pages 192-193).
- Typically, MVPs are prototypes of an already higher resolution and constitute the basis for launching a product or service on the market on a step-by-step basis.
- The results of the tests provide the foundation for the decision as to whether the MVP will be implemented, adapted, or eliminated.

What tool can be used instead?

- Functional prototype (see page 192)
- "X is finished" prototype (see page 193)

Which other tools support working with this tool?

- Ideation with a wide range of tools, for example, brainstorming
- Persona/user profile (see page 97)
- Feedback capture grid (see page 217)
- Exploration map (see page 195)
- Solution interviews (see page 225)
- Structured usability test (see page 229)

How much time and what materials do we need?

Group size

1–8

- Ideally, 2-4.
- Not only the team size counts but the skills of the individual employees do as well.
- Usually interdisciplinary teams.

Typical duration

Days – months

- Depending upon the product or service being developed, the time required for the development of an MVP varies.

Materials needed

- Depending on the MVP, different materials are required

Template and procedure: MVP

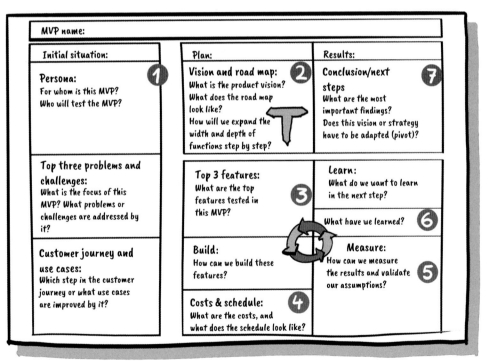

How the tool is applied...

- **Step 1:** Always focus on one MVP (not on several simultaneously) and describe the initial situation. Included in this are the persona, the top three problems and challenges, the customer journey, and relevant use cases.
- **Step 2:** Ensure that the design team is very clear about the product vision and the functional scope. Prioritize and focus on the core functionality when developing the MVP. Expand the functional width and depth step by step (T-shaped MVP).
- **Step 3:** Define the top three features to be tested in the next iterations of the MVP.
- **Step 4:** Plan the building of the MVP. Here you should keep an eye on the costs and the schedule. If the plan optimizes learning, define the measurement criteria and then realize the MVP.
- **Step 5:** Test the MVP on potential users/customers in a real context and collect as much feedback as necessary. The results should be measurable.
- **Step 6:** Summarize the learnings together and improve the MVP step by step. If the MVP flops, don't be disappointed. We can learn something from every iteration.
- **Step 7:** Summarize the overarching findings from the iterations. Must this vision or strategy be adapted?

This is the favorite tool of Esther Moosauer

Position:
Consultant in Technology Advisory at EY – Ernst & Young AG in Zurich

"I like most the FAIL FAST, FAIL EARLY, FAIL CHEAP mindset since this attitude fosters pragmatism and keeps perfectionism in check. Thanks to MVP tests, business model and investment decisions can be made very fast and with the focus on the user."

Why is it her favorite tool?

The MVP forces me to make quick decisions and focus on the essence of the idea. In my opinion, the "fail fast, fail early and often, fail cheap" mindset is a very efficient approach to the development of an idea into a product. In addition, the MVP makes it possible to find out whether we "are doing the right thing before we do it right." You get fast feedback from the market/user as to whether or not the product is valid and in demand. Moreover, users (especially early adopters) are often more satisfied with a product or service when they have the option of giving feedback and contributing to the continuous further development of the product or service.

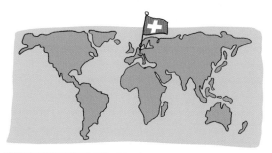

Country:
Switzerland

Affiliation:
Ernst & Young

Checked by: **Hannes Felber**

Company/Position: Invacare Europe, Innovation/Business Design Coach

Expert tips:

- For the building of an MVP, the 80/20 rule is a good yardstick: 80% of the proposition can already be presented to the user with 20% of the development effort.
- The solution of the problem should go hand in hand with low cost and little time expenditure.
- First, a good solution should be found for standard cases before turning to complex individual cases. The core of the solution idea is what counts.
- Make little preliminary tests! Show the proposition to colleagues who do not know it yet. If everybody comes up with the same questions, the value proposition is not yet as clear as it should be.
- T-shaped teams tend to develop a T-shaped MVP.

Minimum viable ⇨ earliest testable / usable / lovable / sellable

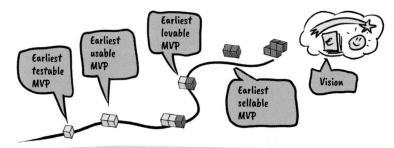

Variation: Minimum viable ecosystem (MVE)

- Digital products and solutions require an appropriate business model and a business ecosystem to create as much value as possible.
- The minimum viable ecosystem (MVE) (Lewrick et al. 2018) uses the MVP mindset to design a business ecosystem in the form of an MVE that ensures clearly defined goals and the efficient cooperation among the actors in the system.
- This procedure is used in the context of business models with new technologies such as DLT (distributed ledger technologies). A multitude of actors create a value proposition together, for example, as a data community or cooperative.

Description of the use case

- In countless iterations, Lilly's team has defined the customer needs and created many low-resolution prototypes. They have reached the problem/solution fit, so now they are going to expand the functionality step by step and test it.
- In the first step, the team has defined the scope of the MVP. The offer is reduced to a variant that is complete (viable) from the customer's point of view but absolutely minimal (minimum). They want to test the critical function of the voice guidance. Prior to building the MVP, they conduct one last interview so as to make sure that they are on the right track with the implementation of this solution.

Key learnings

- Use the MVP template and test one MVP after another.
- Always request feedback from the user/customer.
- The following applies to MVPs as well: Iterate, iterate, iterate!
- Fail fast, fail early, fail cheap!
- T-shaped teams are usually better with building MVPs.

Tool for download

MVP – MINIMUM VIABLE PRODUCT

www.dt-toolbook.com/mvp-en

210

Phase: Test

The test of the respective prototype takes place in the interaction with a potential user. This means we not only receive feedback on the prototype but also refine our view of the problem and the user. In addition, we are reconnected to the "understand" and "observe" phases, which in turn can yield a new point of view. This micro-cycle is repeated as often as desired and characterizes the iterative procedure in design thinking. Tools such as the feedback capture grid and feedback techniques such as "I like, I wish, I wonder" support the testing. In addition, there are different test procedures. Which of them is the most helpful depends on the kind of prototype. Of course, the presented tools for testing overlap in terms of their purpose (testing); nonetheless, each testing approach and each procedure deliver valuable information that helps us to improve the prototype in question.

Testing sheet

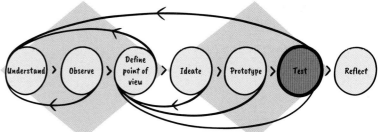

I would like...

to prepare the test sequence and document the test results.

What you can do with the tool:

- Plan a test systematically and define the roles.
- Document the test and the results so it's easy to use them for the next activities.
- Consider in advance which are the test criteria and in which cases the hypotheses are considered verified in order to validate the needs and to check assumptions.
- Develop empathy for the user.

Some information on the tool:

- Among other things, the point of testing is to learn as much as possible about the user and his/her needs by having the user interact with the prototype.
- It is worth planning the test situation and considering what the test sequence is, who has what role, and which key questions should be asked.
- With the testing sheet, we have a tool at hand that allows us to learn a lot in a short period of time and check whether our assumptions and hypotheses are correct.
- A test run is usually performed by two or three people. Not all team members have to be included. Much more important is the documentation of the tests (e.g. with photos and quotes or short videos) that allow us to share the findings with the team.
- It is crucial to observe the user keenly during the test and ask for his/her feedback.

What tool can be used instead?

- Structured usability test (see page 229)
- Solution interview (see page 225)

Which other tools support working with this tool?

- Powerful questions in experience testing (see page 221)
- Empathy map (see page 93)
- Feedback capture grid (see page 217)

How much time and what materials do we need?

Group size

2–3

- One person makes notes and documents the findings; the other performs the test. Optionally, one more person can observe.

Typical duration

10–30 min./test

- For low-resolution prototypes, 10-30 minutes per test are sufficient.
- The higher the degree of detail, the longer the tests take.
- With high-resolution prototypes, tests can stretch over a few weeks.

Materials needed

- Notepad and pen
- Camera (for photos and videos)
- Prototype (which is to be tested)
- Some prototyping material
- Template for test documentation

Template: Testing sheet

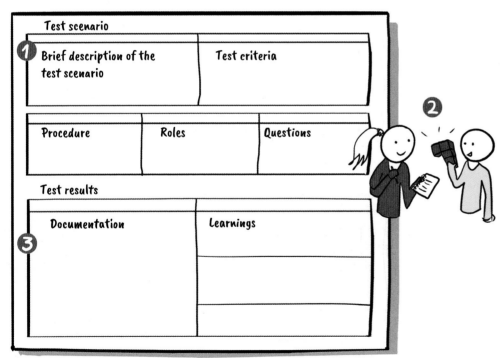

How the tool is applied...

The prototype has already been built. Now the test scenario must be planned.

- **Step 1:** Test planning:
  - Think about where the test should take place. It is best to carry out the test in the context of the problem on site on the user's premises.
  - Define the test criteria prior to the test. What are the criteria for a thesis to be considered as verified?
  - Plan the sequence, assignment of roles, and the key questions of the test.
  - Define who will ask the questions, who makes notes and documents the test, and who observes.
- **Step 2:** Test procedure:
  - Run the test and observe the user keenly during the test. Ask for feedback. It is very valuable and constitutes the basis for further decisions on the development of the prototype.
  - Write down the most important quotes.
- **Step 3:** Test documentation:
  - Document the test with photos or, better yet, short videos of the most important statements.
  - Summarize the main findings and learnings.

Position:
Lecturer in Industrial Design, Lucerne University of Applied Sciences and Arts; Program Director CAS Design Thinking Co-founder of Entux GmbH

"The 'bias toward actions' mindset is not only a recommendation but a must. If you don't experience design thinking yourself, you won't be able to estimate its benefits. Not infrequently, I have had the pleasure of getting positive feedback even from the most stoic of skeptics after they've taken part in one of my workshops."

Why is it her favorite tool?

Design and experimentation have always been an integral part of my work. I firmly believe in pursuing a minimalist approach in the early phases to review the ideas and problem solutions. The test must be carefully planned and designed in order to make optimum use of time and resources.

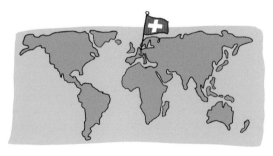

Country:
Switzerland

Affiliation:
Lucerne University of Applied Sciences and Arts

Checked by: **Brittany Arthur**

Company/Position: designthinkingjapan.com | Design Thinking and Innovation Consulting

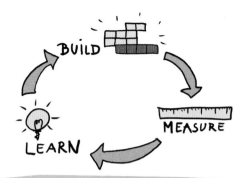

Expert tips:

Testing gives us important insights for the next steps
- The testing sheet can be used as a basis for any types of tests (e.g. usability tests, experience tests, solution interviews).
- Allowing enough time for testing is the most important aspect of planning.
- During preparation, it is vital to think up questions that are relevant to attaining our test objective. "Powerful questions in experience testing," for instance, can be helpful here (see page 221).
- In the case of digital prototypes, there are two ways to carry out the testing. For one, it can be done online. The test can be integrated directly on the website, and we can ask the user specific questions. The traditional way is to stay close to the user and observe precisely what he is doing.

Bring prototyping material to the test
- Take along some prototyping material to the test. With adhesive tape, Post-its, and other things, the test person or the team can adapt the prototype immediately.

Document the tests and share the results with the team
- If the users don't think the solution is any good, we recommend listening even more closely and finding out why. Then we are often able to explore exactly the piece of the puzzle that had been missing or that will make all the difference. Ask "Why?" several times.
- We use the testing sheet template for the documentation of all tests. If you want to make videos and photos, always ask permission first. If there's a need for further use, have a data use agreement signed.

Description of the use case

- Lilly's team tests simultaneously the customer needs and the existing interest as well as the functionality with various prototypes and, later, MVPs.
- The team knows that the tests are extremely important. The better the tests are planned and carried out, the better the findings. They always do the testing in the context and at the users' premises, if possible.
- The test criteria, sequence, and the roles in the test have been defined. The team works well together, so roles can be swapped sometimes. If, for example, the person who has been assigned to observe and take notes has a better rapport with the test person, the observer and the tester can swap roles.

Key learnings

- Through the tests, we get feedback on the prototype and on the user as well.
- Plan the test situation, think about what the test sequence will be like and which team member will play which role.
- The documentation of the tests is important so the results can later be shared with the team. The test sheet template can help in this regard.

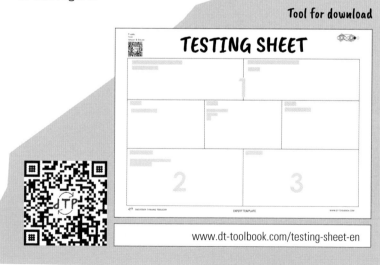

Tool for download

TESTING SHEET

www.dt-toolbook.com/testing-sheet-en

Feedback capture grid

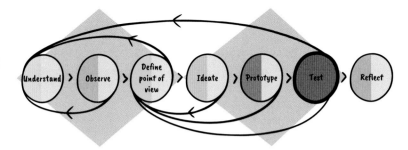

I would like...

to test my prototyped ideas quickly and simply and write down the results for further development.

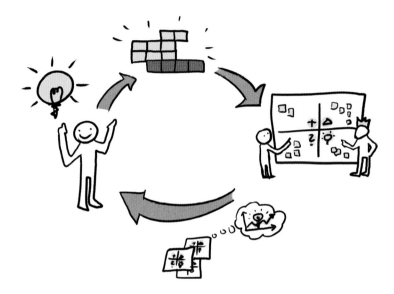

What you can do with the tool:

- Test the first prototypes quickly and easily using four defined questions.
- Write down, collect, and cluster the test results.
- Narrow down theses on problems as well as solutions, personas, and ideas and further develop prototypes on the basis of the findings.
- In general, make quick and simple structured notes of the feedback on ideas, presentations, and so on.

Some information on the tool:

- The feedback capture grid supports the testing of ideas using prototypes because it allows us to document test results in a very simple form.
- It is primarily used when it comes to finding out how well an idea solves a previously identified user problem.
- The feedback capture grid aims at acquiring profound understanding as to whether the problem can be solved and how it can be solved and whether the idea actually is the right approach to a solution.
- It can be used in general for obtaining feedback on the process, a workshop, or other things.

What tool can be used instead?

- Testing sheet (see page 213)
- Empathy map (see page 93)

Which other tools support working with this tool?

- All kinds of prototypes (see page 187–194)
- Ask 5x why (see page 67)
- Lean canvas as an information base for testing or to summarize the results after the test (see page 251)
- 5W+H questions (see page 71)

How much time and what materials do we need?

Group size

At least 2

- Tester 1: interviews, observes, and demonstrates the prototype.
- Tester 2: documents the results and asks further questions, if needed.

Typical duration

30–60 min.

- A test takes approx. 10-15 minutes. As a rule, we need several tests to be able to make accurate statements.
- If possible, always perform 2-3 tests

Materials needed

- Visualization of the idea as a prototype, MVP, digital prototype
- One printed or drawn feedback capture grid per tester and interview; the optimal size for the printout is A3

Template: Feedback capture grid

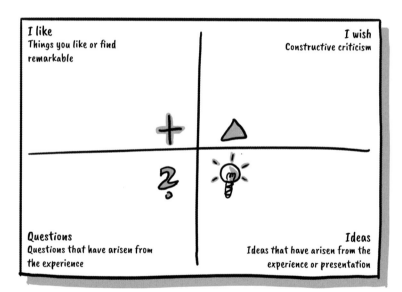

How the tool is applied...

A rudimentary prototype (e.g. a low-fidelity prototype), has already been created. We have developed information about the persona, need, and problem hypothesis over the last design thinking phases.

- **Step 1:** Draw the feedback capture grid on a sheet of paper or print out the template.
- **Step 2:** Always begin a test with the tester seeing and experiencing the prototype.
- **Step 3:** Ask the tester (user/customer) to think aloud.
- **Step 4:** Fill in the fields of the grid with these thoughts. They can be written in directly or using Post-its. In the upper left field note what the user liked, on the right what he might not like so much; in the lower left field note the questions that were asked as well as new ideas that the user or we ourselves had while observing.
- **Step 5:** Ask "Why?" questions (see Ask 5x why, page 67) to understand the answers of the tester even better. Pay attention to emotions, conflicting body language, and initial reactions.
- **Step 6:** Collect the feedback capture grids from the various interviews and work out similarities or major differences together with the design thinking team; they can be used for the further development of ideas and prototypes.

Position:
Innovation Consultant

"For me, design thinking as a method supports the implementation of the agile mind set: Cross-functional teams that understand the problems of users as well as the rapid testing of the solution ideas on the market result in real growth potential."

Why is it her favorite tool?

In innovation projects, I frequently stumbled over the fact that, starting with an idea, an (expensive) development project was launched and the testing was only done at the end. The solution was often developed out of sync with market requirements, and valuable resources were wasted. For me, design thinking – starting with a problem and quick, simple testing – is the procedure I had searched for so long. The feedback capture grid is a tool for the simple structuring of test results, and then the work can be continued with it. It also supports the communication of test results within the company.

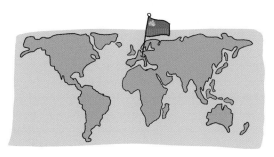

Country:
Liechtenstein

Affiliation:
Independent
Consultant

Checked by: **Roberto Gago**

Company/Position: Generali | Customer & Distribution
                       Experience Manager

Expert tips:

Get into the shoes of your customers
- The best way is to choose different places and user groups for testing.
- People who are not yet customers are particularly valuable suppliers of ideas in this phase.
- Again, we should not under any circumstances attempt to "sell" our idea to the user; instead, we must learn from the feedback we receive.
- The rule when testing is: Listen, watch, and try not to ask questions at first or explain the prototype.
- We also write down direct quotes and immediate reactions from the user.
- Testing is need finding. The same rules apply as with the interview.

Take a step back and reflect on the collected results
- We always should reflect on the test results together with the design thinking team. A new point of view can be formulated this way that helps us with the further development of our idea or prototype.
- Grouping the completed feedback capture grids according to answers and personas has often proven helpful.
- As always: Iterate, iterate, iterate!! – until our potential users are happy.

Description of the use case

- Lilly's team uses the feedback capture grid in almost all phases of the design thinking cycle. They use it mainly for the documentation and summary of the tests with the users.
- Lilly and the design thinking team also like to use it for reviewing an iteration as part of the retrospective.
- Lilly highly values the direct, open feedback and constructive criticism. It enables her to learn quickly and improve the project both in terms of content and of process.

Key learnings

- Always conduct interviews with two people.
- Don't sell the idea but listen with curiosity, observe, and learn.
- Discuss the findings with the team and formulate a new shared point of view from them.

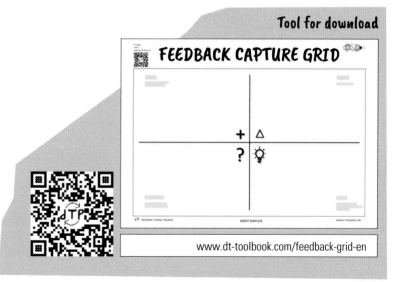

Tool for download

FEEDBACK CAPTURE GRID

www.dt-toolbook.com/feedback-grid-en

Powerful questions in experience testing

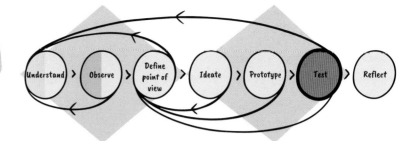

I would like...

to evaluate ideas, prototypes, services, or a product by testing them with real customers or users.

What you can do with the tool:

- Leave the world of imagination and conquer the real world by exploring the prototype with real customers.
- Find out whether it actually works for the users/customers like it was intended.
- Find out whether the idea will lead to success or not.
- Obtain feedback: "love it," "change it," or "leave it."
- Gather qualitative and quantitative data by asking the right questions in order to discern whether problems occur with the experience or with the use.

Some information on the tool:

- "Powerful questions" is a great tool for gathering more findings in a test.
- As early as with low-resolution prototypes, we should pose the right questions and develop them for high-resolution prototypes.
- The testing should always be done based on a specific prototype, however (first ideas, lo-fi to hi-fi prototypes, see page 187).
- During the test experience, the test person should interact as much as possible with the prototype. The observers watch and listen attentively and write down the results.
- A simple test plan with goals, test environment, process, moderation, and test participants is created.
- More exact methods are used in later development, for example, unit test, integration test, functional test, system test, stress test, performance test, usability test, acceptance test, regression test, beta test.
- The heuristic evaluation can be used as an informal appraisal to evaluate or check a product based on a number of agreed-upon best practices, standards, or guidelines.

What tool can be used instead?

- A/B testing to collect data (see page 233)
- "I like, I wish, I wonder" (see page 239)
- Feedback capture grid (see page 217)

Which tools support working with this tool?

- Brainstorming: why, how, and what should be tested by a highly heterogeneous team (see page 151)
- Personas/user profiles (see page 97)
- Empathy map (see page 93)
- Different kinds of prototypes (see page 187–194)

How much time and what materials do we need?

Group size

3–6

- A moderator and several observers, for example, members of the design team.
- Depending on the setting, not too many observers, though, since it might intimidate the users.

Typical duration

60–90 min.

- Depending on the complexity, 60-90 minutes for planning: Why, how, and what is to be tested.
- For example: at least 5 users participate in each test lasting 15 minutes.

Materials needed

- Observation rooms with recording software
- Guerrilla testing: Camera (sound & image), Post-its, flip chart, or whiteboard
- The more natural the environment, the more truthful the results

Ask the right questions when testing

❶ Test lo-fi prototypes

At this stage, we might have no more than a rough idea or the proverbial sketch on the napkin. For the validation of those ideas, the following questions have proven useful:

- What is the problem your idea solves?
- How do users solve this problem today?
- Can the user think of another product with similar characteristics?
- What made other solutions fail?
- Do the users understand the benefits of the product or service?
- How does the user rate the product or service?
- Can the user think of competing products?
- What has the app/website/function, etc., been designed for?
- Does the potential user actually have a need for this product?
- What other objects or interactions does the user himself imagine?
- What use scenarios can he/she imagine?

❷ Test med-fi prototypes

Based on the feedback, we designed initial wireframes for our rough concept. They are neither interactive nor functional but they illustrate what should be used and how it should be used. Good questions help steer the project in the right direction and address the sequence and simple elements in the respective experience.

- Does the prototype do what is expected of it?
- What is the users' reaction to the product design?
- As soon as we show the prototype, does the user understand what it does?
- How does the prototype meet the expectations of the user?
- What features are missing?
- What is in the wrong place or unnecessary?
- How does it feel to the user when he uses the prototype?
- If the user had a magic wand, what would he change on the product?
- How high is the probability that the potential user will use the finished product in the future?

❸ Test hi-fi prototypes

Through further iterations, the resolution of the prototype has improved. It is usually a simple copy of the ultimate solution, that is, a semi-functional prototype. The prototype should be interactive and be able to carry out the functions we have planned. What is missing is the glamour and beauty of a final product. Questions:

- Does the prototype do what it is meant to do?
- Does the design of the product match its purpose?
- What would the user like to do first with the product? Does this possibility exist?
- Is the user confused when using the product?
- Is the user distracted by something when using the product?
- Are there any functions that are completely ignored by the user?
- Is the navigation sensible and intuitive?
- Do the users feel that the product was developed for them?
- What would prompt the user to use this product more often?
- How likely is it that the user recommends the finished product to a friend?
- How would the user describe the product in his own words?

This is the favorite tool of Natalie Breitschmid

Position:
Chief Experience Enthusiast at SINODUS AG, lecturer at Lucerne University of Applied Sciences and Arts

"Testing is doing. Doing is like wanting, just more blatant. To become successful, choose the earliest day possible to prove whether your idea works or not."

Why is it her favorite tool?

We all have great ideas. However, frequently customers do not use what we have come up with, or else our idea was simply bad and nobody will ever use this solution. Powerful questions in experience testing is my favorite tool because with it we can challenge whether we are investing our energy in something the world really needs. We should also not forget that no proposition has any intrinsic value: The only person assigning value to a product or a service is the customer.

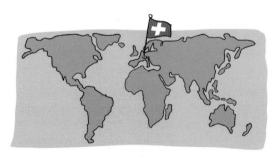

Country:
Switzerland

Affiliation:
Sinodus and Lucerne University of Applied Sciences and Arts

Checked by: Gaurav Bhargva

Company/Position: Iress, user experience expert, design thinker

Expert tips:

Test, test, and test again
- Test and test, again and again: Don't skip the testing due to time pressure or for other reasons. Testing is too important.
- Allow for enough time for testing. It is the most important phase. Here is where you learn.
- Don't tell or show the test participants how it works; it would automatically influence the way they see the prototype. So let them do it and watch them closely. Ask them why and how they think about it.
- Hand the prototype over to the users to take it with them for 1 day or even a week, so they use it as often as possible and we get the most accurate feedback. You can also ask the users to be filmed or live record themselves while using the prototype.

Use online testing tools or digital methods where appropriate
- If the prototype is a service (app or website), user validation can be done much quicker. Online surveys are an option here. The survey on the service can be integrated into the app or website in order to get even more feedback.
- Of all start-ups, 90% fail (Patel, 2015). Over 40% fail because there is no market demand for their product (Griffith, 2014). This is why it is so important to observe the customer/user exactly and carry out interactions. Improve the prototypes, from the initial concept to lo-fi to hi-fi prototypes: The more we focus on the essence of a real customer problem and real customer need, the more successful we will be.

Description of the use case

- After various low-resolution prototypes, Lilly's team has programmed a small robot to test the human-robot interaction.
- Before the tests, the design thinking team went through a lot of brainstorming regarding the test requirements, so that later the results of the experience testing actually correspond to the desired experience.
- The valuable test findings are immediately integrated by the team into the next prototype, and that is done until customers love the prototype.

Key learnings

- The only person assigning value to a product or a service is the user/customer.
- Ask the user in a targeted manner and give him the feeling that his answers are valuable.
- Have the user/customer think aloud during the test.

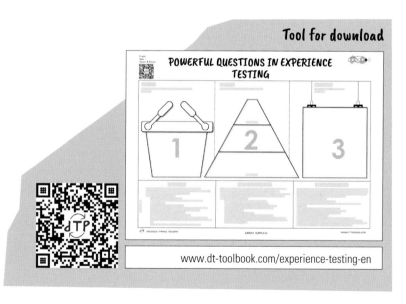

www.dt-toolbook.com/experience-testing-en

Solution interview

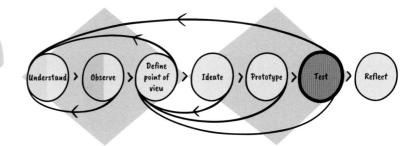

I would like...

to find out whether a solution is accepted by the user.

> It feels good. In this size, I would spend 100 dollars on it.

What you can do with the tool:

- Understand whether an intended solution is valued by users, that is, whether it is convincing in terms of functionality, user-friendliness, and user experience.
- Question the underlying task of the project, that is, examine whether you are focusing on the crucial issues in the project.
- Understand the needs, behaviors, and motivations of users/customers more deeply.
- Measure the value of the solution for the user.

Some information on the tool:

- As the name suggests, solution interviews are a tool used in the test phase with advanced (high-resolution) prototypes.
- The goal is to test solutions that were developed in the project and see whether they are accepted by the users addressed.
- In order to make a clear distinction from the testing tools already presented, the solution interview is mainly used in the solution space.
- This is why we focus on the "acceptance" of a final prototype or MVP.
- In this late phase, solution interviews supply insights on the acceptance of a solution by the user, right up to the pricing.

What tool can be used instead?

- Feedback capture grid (see page 217)
- Testing sheet (see page 213)
- A/B testing (see page 233)

Which other tools support working with this tool?

- "How might we..." question (see page 125)
- Persona/user profile (see page 97)
- Various kinds of prototypes (see page 187 and what follows)

How much time and what materials do we need?

Group size

2–3

- Teams of 2 are ideal.
- One person is the interviewer; the second person makes notes, observes, and follows up on questions.
- If appropriate, a third person takes photos or films.

Typical duration

20–30 min.

- 30 minutes is a good orientation for a solution interview.
- The perceived gain in knowledge is the qualitative criterion for the duration of the interview.

Materials needed

- Interview guide
- Prototype of the solution
- Paper, pencils; if needed, some prototyping material
- Recording device, video camera, or mobile phone

Template and procedure: Solution interview

Solution: Solution to be tested

Context

Task
- Design challenge of the project
- "How might we..." question

Goal
- Interview goal
- Key question that should have been answered after the interview

Persona
- Personas and their needs (focus of the solution)
- Point of view statement

Interview planning

Interview candidates
- Identify interview candidates that are similar to personas
- Determine the number of interviews required

Interview team
- Size of the interview team
- Role assignment

Material
- Core equipment
- Reference to the last interview
- Supplementing materials

Interview guide

Agenda
1. Warm-up (time span:)
2. Introduction to the context (time span:)
3. Experience the solution (time span:)
4. Summary (time span:)

Content
- Discussion points
- Specific questions
- Form of presentation of the solution

How the tool is applied...

Solution interviews are used to gain knowledge through feedback from the user/customer on an almost finished solution.

- **Step 1:** First define the interview goal. Reflect on the task and the persona that the solution should address.
- Depending on the current phase in the macro-cycle, the goal is to check the impact of the solution or measure the value of the solution.
- **Step 2:** Determine the interview team, including role assignment.
- When selecting the interview candidates, make sure they resemble the persona for which the solution is intended.
- Think about what you should take along with you to the interview (e.g. reference points from previous discussions).
- **Step 3:** Plan the interview guide in four phases: warm-up, introduction to the context, experience the solution, summary.
- **Warm-up:** Create an atmosphere that allows for uninhibited statements. Check the similarity between interviewee and persona.
- **Introduction to the context:** Define what context information about the usage scenario should be given to the interviewees.
- **Experience the solution:** Let the interviewee work out the solution by himself; ask him to "think aloud."
- **Summary:** Summarize the statements of the conversation partners in your own words. Watch the reaction.

226

This is the favorite tool of Niels Feldmann

Position:
Lecturer for Service Design Thinking at Karlsruhe Institute of Technology (KIT)

"At Ideo, they say design thinking is 'enlightened trial and error.' Enlightenment through trial and error? Or trial and error controlled by enlightenment? I like the quote because it highlights the iterative character of design thinking in a few words while simultaneously emphasizing the importance of thinking, the aspect of deep insight."

Why is it his favorite tool?

Solution interviews are a moment of truth. We have already tested several prototypes in the previous steps. We have interpreted the data situation, developed solutions for our interpretation, and created prototypes for our solutions. In the solution interview, we now compare our interpretation of reality with reality itself – a moment of truth. After the solution interviews, we have a changed initial situation for the next iteration in our project.

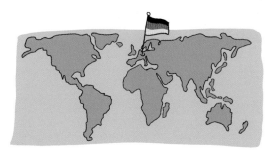

Country:
Germany

Affiliation:
Karlsruhe Institute of Technology (KIT)

Checked by: **Roger Stämpfli**

Company/Position: Aroma AG, Creative Director

Expert tips:

Attention
One of the greatest challenges is to avoid misleading statements of the interviewees on account of politeness.

Select interview candidates
Mix people who are known from the problem interviews with unbiased people who now test the solution.

Define an interview team
Use third parties as interviewers if the (technical) language is not known. Specialist staff, children, and minorities give different answers to their peers than to nonspecialist colleagues, adults, or members of the majorities.

Choose the material carefully
The prototype should be suitable for achieving the interview goal. Unlike the tests in earlier phases, where paper mock-ups are used deliberately, a high-resolution prototype is needed (e.g. to test the monetary value of a solution).

Get a feel for the other person
Check that the interviewees are similar to your persona. Also consider personality traits: Innovators give different answers than the early majority, for instance.

Interview – experience solution: "Study and don't sell!"
Let the people who are interviewed explore the solution themselves. Demonstrations put interviewees too easily on preconceived paths. To have few discussion points is helpful in the early phases; specific questions are helpful in later phases. Let the interviewee tell you how he would use the solution.

Record keeping
Film the interview if possible. Behavior reveals much truth beyond the spoken words.

Description of the use case

- The solution interview helps the team to validate the solution idea. Lilly uses it to challenge the ideas of the team.
- The team frequently has a hard time letting go of their own ideas. She likes saying, "Love is for people, not for prototypes," but that is of little use here.
- It is far more helpful when the customer says it. At times, Lilly and her team have used the solution interview in earlier project phases to question the solution or throw it overboard. But mainly they use solution interviews in later phases for a thorough test of the solution.

Key learnings

- Solution interviews are used to gain knowledge – not to sell something.
- Well-thought-out solution interviews lead to meaningful and compelling answers.
- Statements not only deliver insights but also observations.
- The result is the interpretation of the data, not the data itself.

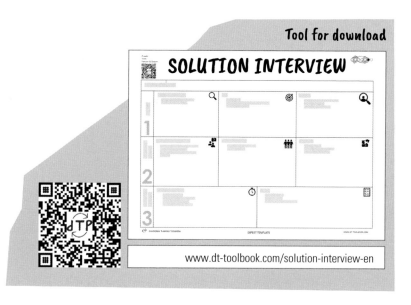

Tool for download

SOLUTION INTERVIEW

www.dt-toolbook.com/solution-interview-en

Structured usability testing

Understand > Observe > Define point of view > Ideate > Prototype > Test > Reflect

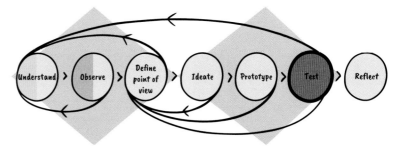

I would like...

to test my prototypes with potential users at defined and uniform conditions.

Video

User who uses the product

Observerr

Product to be tested

"THINK ALOUD"

Facilitator

What you can do with the tool:

- Observe the interaction between user and system (prototype) in defined test scenarios (tasks).
- Check and compare the correctness of the assumptions, solutions, and concepts made with the user.
- Get new inputs for improvement or completely new ideas.
- Gain deeper insights into the problem by testing existing products.
- Improve the suitability for use iteratively through testing and subsequent optimizing.

Some information on the tool:

- Anything that is "operable" can be tested; this applies to both physical and digital products.
- With usability testing, it can be checked whether something works effectively, efficiently, and satisfactorily for the user.
- The testing should be as specific, frequent, and as early as possible.
- This requires real users who perform given specific tasks with the prototype at defined and uniform conditions. Observe everything and document it with video or tracking software, whenever possible.
- The uniform structure allows for testing and comparing several ideas or variants on the basis of the same criteria.
- Before testing is started, it is important to be aware of what is to be tested and how it is to be measured.
- There are many different variants and versions of the usability testing tool: hallway, guerrilla, laboratory test, field test, and so on.

What tool can be used instead?

- Solution interview (see page 225)
- A/B testing (see page 233)
- Consumer clinics
- Focus group

Which other tools support working with this tool?

- Various kinds of prototypes (see page 187 and what follows)
- Persona/user profile (see page 97)
- 5W+H questions (see page 71)

How much time and what materials do we need?

Group size

>2

- At least 2 people.
- One person guides and supports the user; another or several other persons observe and document the test.

Typical duration

40–90 min.

- Varies depending on the complexity of the prototype and the task to be performed.
- The tasks and the sequence must be defined beforehand.

Materials needed

- Prototype (hardware or software)
- Camera for video and sound recordings
- Script (guide) with defined test scenarios (tasks), material to take notes, and evaluation grid

Template: Structured usability testing

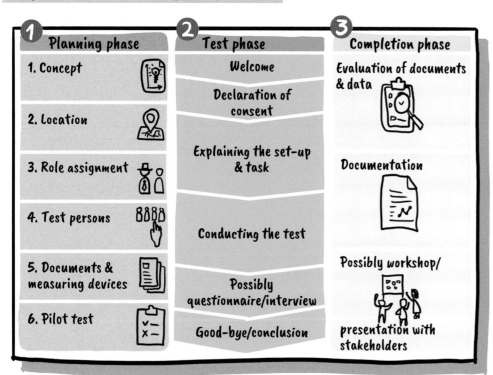

How the tool is applied...

The implementation of a structured usability testing has three phases:

- **Step 1: Planning phase:** Prepare the testing. First draw up a concept that roughly describes what it is all about; what the test object is; what exactly is to be found out; which assumptions and hypotheses already exist; and what the chronological sequence should be. Then choose the location, define the roles (moderator, observers, etc.) and test persons; define the exact test scenarios (tasks). Prepare the documents and finally conduct a "dry run" to verify that everything works as it should.
- **Step 2: Test phase:** Conduct the actual test with users/subjects. Try to stick to the sequence and test scenarios as closely as possible and always provide all test persons with the same information.
- **Step 3: Final phase:** Evaluate the collected findings, document them and, if desired, present the results to the relevant stakeholders. Use the results to continue improving usability.

Position:
Project Manager in the innovation management team at Helbling Technik AG

"The direction in which the development of a product is meant to go is frequently influenced by internal factors. But since it is not the management that buys the products but the customers, making their needs the entry point is crucial. This is exactly where the strengths of design thinking lie in the early phase of product development."

Why is it his favorite tool?

The structured usability testing is my favorite tool because it helps to move away from discussions about assumptions. Thanks to the structured approach, it gives the project team an empirical basis on which the product or the idea can be improved. It forces the design team to implement the ideas as quickly as possible. In addition, the direct contact with the customer/user is inspiring and motivating. "Remember that your system will be tested for usability – even if you don't do so yourself." – Jakob Nielsen

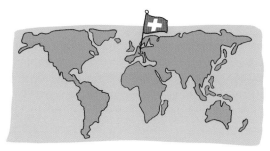

Country:
Switzerland

Affiliation:
Helbling

Checked by: **Mladen Djakovic**

Company/Position: Q Point, user experience designer

Expert tips:

Right test scenarios and prototypes
- Test scenarios (tasks) must be clearly defined. They help to determine which aspects of the prototype should be tested.
- Success factors per task can be rated as "success," "struggle," or "fail" to make subsequent evaluation easier.
- The level of detail of the prototype must be matched to the test scenarios. Particularly in the case of fundamental questions (e.g. about the operation sequence), unnecessary details should be omitted.

Never fall in love with your prototypes
- Don't waste too much time on details. Otherwise, you'll have a hard time saying good-bye to your idea later.
- Even an existing product or competitive product can be tested in a very early phase of a project.

Right test users and moderation
- The selection of the test users is of great importance. They must match the selected personas to the greatest possible degree.
- The moderation is best done by an independent person who is not involved (objectivity).
- A positive and grateful attitude with regard to the test person is vital because the system is tested, not the person.
- The test persons should think aloud, that is, relate everything they think.
- No leading questions! (For example: "Can you click it anywhere else?" already tells the user that he can click it somewhere else.)
- If a user gets stuck, don't help but ask what should happen next.

Meaningful test documentation
- A digital screen capturing or video is helpful in the case of physical products for communicating the results.

> Is the test structure right this way? So we can really test the usability? What do you think?

> Stop, guys! Come now! We discussed long enough. Let's test it with real users.

> Cool. Can it also operate a vacuum cleaner?

Description of the use case

- Lilly's individual teams want to bring more structure to the testing of their prototypes.
- The team begins with drawing up specific tasks (test scenarios) for each prototype. Simultaneously, the team has already begun to look for test persons who match the target customer (persona).
- The team's plan is to have the test persons conduct all tests in interaction with the prototype during one whole day.

Key learnings

- Set clear-cut goals for the usability test.
- Select test persons from the target group and urge them to "think aloud." The test persons should relate everything they think.
- Avoid asking any leading questions. It's better to run first tests early on with only a few subjects/users than later with many.

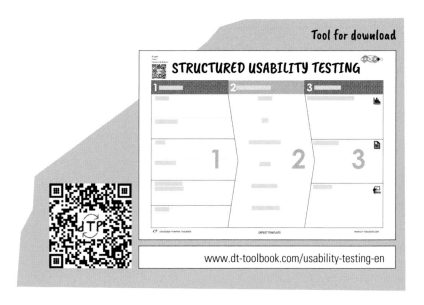

Tool for download

STRUCTURED USABILITY TESTING

www.dt-toolbook.com/usability-testing-en

A/B Testing

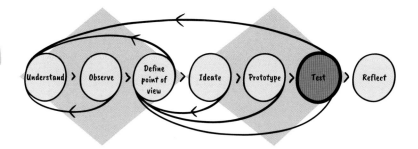

I would like...

to review an assumption or compare two variants (in terms of quantity or quality) to find out what the preferences of the users/customers are.

What you can do with the tool:

- Perform a true A/B test or several variants of a prototype in the form of a multi-variants test or as split testing.
- Do a quantitative evaluation.
- Carry out a qualitative survey and evaluate the number and content of feedbacks.
- Compare individual variants of a function or a prototype (e.g. buttons, visuals, arrangement).

Some information on the tool:

- The A/B test can be used as a stand-alone test or as an expansion of a prototype test.
- The A/B test is a simple tool for testing two variants of a prototype simultaneously. The test of the prototype usually answers a question with different characteristics.
- This test is quite well suited to advance an existing prototype/MVP or to test a new variant in comparison with a basic prototype. It is important to make it very clear before the test what is to be tested and compared (e.g. by means of key figures).
- Most users find it easier to give feedback when comparing two prototypes than when they are asked to comment on one prototype.

What tool can be used instead?

- Structured usability test (see page 229)
- Solution interview (see page 225)

Which tools support working with this tool?

- Powerful questions in experience testing (see page 221)
- Online tools support the entire process of an A/B or multi-variant test, including the evaluation.

233

How much time and what materials do we need?

Group size

1–2

- Depending on the procedure and tool support, at least 1-2 people per test.
- With tools, 1 person suffices; without, at least 2 people.
- Test group(s) (different sizes).

Typical duration

5–15 min.

- Depending on the number of users and the use of a tool or the manual evaluation.
- Make time for preparation and follow-up

Materials needed

- Depending on the prototype, different materials
- Pen and paper to capture the feedback
- Online prototype via software and voting tool

Procedure: A/B Testing

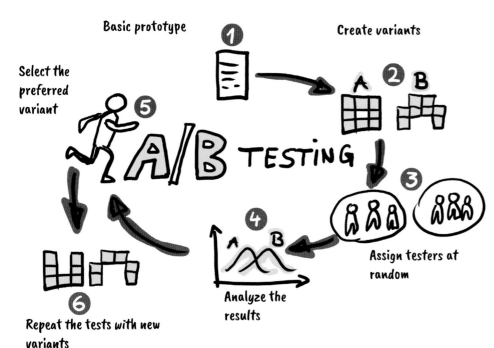

Basic prototype ① Create variants

Select the preferred variant ⑤

A ② B

③ Assign testers at random

④ Analyze the results

⑥ Repeat the tests with new variants

How the tool is applied...

A/B testing is quick and easy. It must be decided at the beginning what is to be tested and how it is to be done:

- **Step 1:** Define the basic prototype and decide who is to be the test group (selection of the target group).
- **Step 2:** Consider variants of the prototype and make a decision for two of them to be compared with each other. Define key figures for what kind of testing is to be done (whether quantitative or qualitative test).
- **Step 3:** For quantitative tests, assign the users at random and conduct the test.
- **Step 4:** Evaluate the results.
- **Step 5:** Use the preferred variant for improving the prototype.
- **Step 6:** Repeat the tests with new variants or perform another test for validation.

Note: Differentiation of the test procedure: Quantitative A/B test: The user group is divided (x% variant A, y% variant B). Qualitative A/B test: The variants are tested against one another (all users see variants A and B).

This is the favorite tool of Christian Langrock

Position:
Innovation Manager of Hamburger Hochbahn AG

"Agility and design thinking are based on a similar mindset that helps us focus on the customer again and develop the right products and services for and with the customer in the VUCA world."*

*VUCA is an abbreviation for volatility, uncertainty, complexity, and ambiguity.

Why is it his favorite tool?

In IT, A/B testing has been a vital tool for many years. It allows us to obtain key figure-based customer feedback (quantitative testing) quickly. In design thinking, it is not yet so common to test prototypes against each other. Usually, one prototype that is favored by the team is tested. With an A/B test, two variants that were developed by the team can be compared by the user (quality testing). It helps with giving feedback, because the users can compare two variants. A/B testing can provide important information for the next prototype.

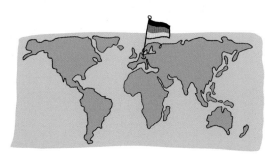

Country:
Germany

Affiliation:
Hochbahn

Checked by: Regina Vogel

Company/Position: Disruptive design thinker, leadership coach

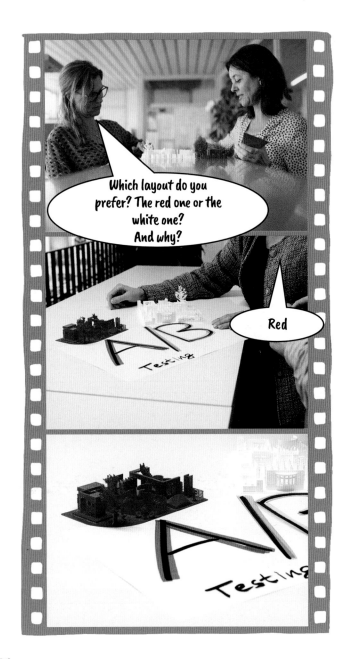

Description of the use case

- Lilly uses A/B testing only for quantitative online tests, for example, when she wants to investigate which landing page brings a higher conversion.
- Lilly's teams, however, also use the tool for the test of physical prototypes, for example, to find out which property is important for the customer and is more appreciated by the target group. For this purpose they create two variants that differ only in one property.
- After the actual test, the team learns many intriguing aspects of the users' needs, especially during personal conversations.

Key learnings

- A/B testing does not mean testing two different ideas but two variants of a prototype.
- The test target groups should match the target persona.
- Make a decision on the setup prior to the test, that is, whether qualitative or quantitative feedback is needed.

Tool for download

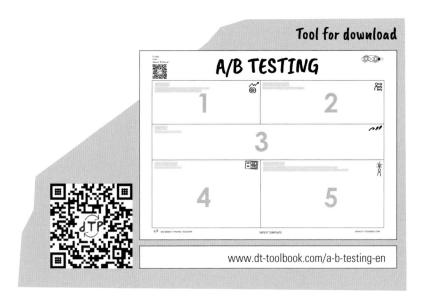

www.dt-toolbook.com/a-b-testing-en

Phase: Reflect

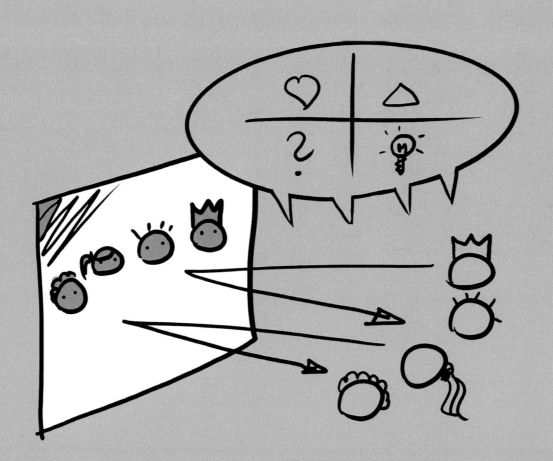

The last phase — "reflecting" — helps on several levels. We can reflect on our procedure; the work on the team; the involvement of the relevant stakeholders; or whether the mindset is lived. For us, the steps of reflection and learning are of vital importance; this is why they have become an integral part of our work as designers. Various techniques such as "I like, I wish, I wonder" and the retrospective sailboat help with the reflection on the procedure. Tools such as the lean canvas or "create a pitch for presentation" help with the reflection on and documentation of project content and its continuous further development.

I like, I wish, I wonder

[IL, IW, IW]

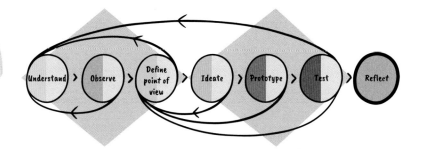

I would like...

to provide constructive feedback and keep a positive mood.

> I liked the numerous visualizations in the Toolbox and in the Playbook.

> I wish for a second Design Thinking Toolbox with more tools.

> I wonder about the fact that design thinking is not used more often to shape the way we live our lives.

What you can do with the tool:

- A feedback ritual is established by the team in which only "I like, I wish," supplemented with "I wonder" (in short: IL/IW/IW), is permitted as feedback.
- Celebrate small successes achieved with this method in an iteration, with a prototype or in a test.
- Make it a part of reflection and ideation; it can be expanded by "What if..." and a parking lot for ideas.
- Give and receive written and spoken feedback.

Some information on the tool:

- We need feedback throughout the entire design thinking process for the improvement of prototypes, stories, and business models.
- "I like, I wish" is particularly suitable for sensitive projects. By maintaining a positive mood, a relationship that is based on partnership evolves between the feedback provider and the feedback recipient.
- It can be used in the context of reflecting on the collaboration as well as for a specific result. For example: "I like how you motivated us to conduct another customer survey"; or "I wish that the prototype were tested in other cultures as well."

What tool can be used instead?

- Red and green feedback (use adhesive dots. red = attention; green = all ok)
- Lessons learned (see page 255)
- Feedback capture grid (see page 217)
- Retrospective sailboat (see page 243)

Which tools support working with this tool?

- Design thinking mindset (see page 6)
- Brainstorming (see page 151)

How much time and what materials do we need?

Group size

3–5

- Ideally, feedback is given by several people.
- It can also be used with 2 people (feedback provider and feedback receiver).

Typical duration

15–90 min.

- "I like / I wish" can be deployed after small iterations and in large feedback sessions with multiple participants.

Materials needed

- Post-its and pens
- Large sheet of paper

Template: I like, I wish, I wonder

TEAM/ PROTOTYPE	I LIKE…	I WISH…	I WONDER…	WHAT IF…?
Team X Prototype 1				
Team Y Prototype 2				
Team Z Prototype 3				

How the tool is applied…

- Take a large sheet of paper and draw a table with 5 columns. The column headings are: Team/prototype, I like …, I wish …, I wonder …, and What if …? Enter the names of the teams and their prototypes in the rows.
- To obtain feedback on a prototype that was presented, each participant is given at least three Post-its. Each participant is encouraged to complete the sentence on the X-axis ("I like," "I wish," "I wonder").
- For an interaction to emerge, each participant should read aloud what's written on the Post-its before sticking them on the grid. Then everybody places his or her Post-its containing the feedback on the grid.
- Once all the Post-its are sticking to the sheet of paper, the time has come to reflect on the findings and ask whether there are any insights that are important for the next iteration.
- Starting a discussion as the recipient of the feedback should be avoided. It would change the mood, and the positive attitude is lost. The application of this tool aims at avoiding ad hominem criticism and maintaining a positive mood.
- The feedback should be seen as a gift by the feedback recipient.

This is the favorite tool of Lena Papasz

Position:
Self-employed design thinking coach and marketing consultant

"Albert Einstein has aptly put it: 'Problems can never be solved with the same way of thinking that created them.' Design thinking opens up new horizons and helps to view things from different angles."

Why is it her favorite tool?

"I like, I wish, I wonder" offers a wide range of applications in both professional and private environments. It is my favorite tool because it can be learned quickly and is reliable and absolutely effective. Its child's play to implement it in your daily life.

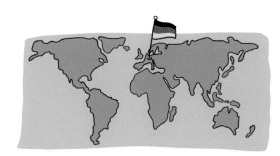

Country:
Germany

Affiliation:
Design Thinking Freelancer

Checked by: Helmut Ness

Company/Position: Co-founder of Fuenfwerken Design AG

Expert tips:

Give feedback on a regular basis
- Replace "I wish, I wonder" with "How to…" in order to generate not only ideas but also initial solution proposals.
- Integrate the tool in feedback interviews (1:1).
- Conduct weekly team meetings with IL/IW/IW (I like, I wish, I wonder) so as to involve all team members, ensure that tasks are taken seriously, and recognize concerns early on.

Feedback is a gift
- As a feedback provider, we must always show respect and consider: How would we feel about this feedback? When giving personal feedback, look the other person in the eye.

- If we receive feedback, we should show respect and listen carefully. Hearing other people out and, if necessary, asking again will distinguish you as a good listener and show that you are really interested. We should always say thank you for feedback.

Positive attitude
- Lessons learned – IL/IW/IW can not only be used during the project phase but also toward the end. By adding "I learned," personal key learnings can be recorded and used for upcoming projects (see page 255).
- Moreover, we can start our day with "I like, I wish, I wonder" and "What if…," thus setting ourselves daily goals. In this way, we can use the questions for ourselves and integrate them in shaping our own life (also see "Design thinking life," page 289).

Description of the use case

- Lilly and her teams have practiced a positive feedback culture right from the onset. In every interaction, feedback in the form of "I like, I wish" is provided. In the beginning the team often fell back into old patterns, but in the meantime everyone has internalized the principle.
- Their template also has columns for "I wonder" and "What if…" that are used as the situation requires it. Especially when documenting the feedback, this can still yield significant stimuli.

Key learnings

- Practice a positive feedback culture. The use of "I like, I wish, I wonder" helps in maintaining a positive mood.
- It is important to write down the feedback and reflect on it later with the design thinking team.
- Feedback is a gift – always say thank you.

Tool for download

www.dt-toolbook.com/i-like-feedback-en

Retrospective "sailboat"

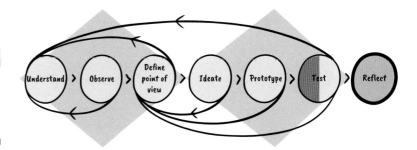

I would like...

to reflect on the procedure and learn something new to improve myself (or the procedure) for the next iteration, at the end of each iteration, and at the end of the project.

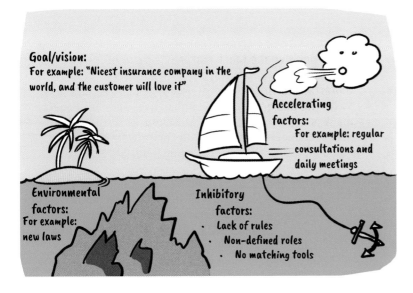

Goal/vision:
For example: "Nicest insurance company in the world, and the customer will love it"

Accelerating factors:
For example: regular consultations and daily meetings

Environmental factors:
For example: new laws

Inhibitory factors:
- Lack of rules
- Non-defined roles
- No matching tools

What you can do with the tool:

- Improve interaction on the team and collaboration – in a fast, targeted, appreciative, and structured way.
- Take a retrospective look back to check what went well and what could be improved.
- Reflect upon the question of which factors can be changed and which factors must be accepted.
- Foster a positive mood, since all team members are listened to and can make a contribution; this, in turn, nurtures the mindset of self-organized teams.

Some information on the tool:

- The "sailboat" retrospective is frequently used with the SCRUM method in the context of the reflection on a sprint. It can also be drawn as a retrospective board with four quadrants (see page 245).
- It is also very suitable after any design thinking phase or after a project has been completed.
- It can also be used for 2 persons only, for example, as a "post-mortem" after the joint moderation of a workshop.
- The tool responds to accelerating, inhibitory, and environmental factors.
- It also promotes the "failure mindset" in which mistakes are not seen as failures but as an opportunity to change and learn.

What tool can be used instead?

- Feedback capture grid (see page 217)
- "I like, I wish, I wonder" (see page 239)
- "Water cooler chats" with colleagues

Which other tools support working with this tool?

- Ask 5x why (see page 67)
- Feedback capture grid (see page 217)
- Lessons learned (see page 255)
- Sketch notes (see page 173)

How much time and what materials do we need?

Group size

- Ideal with teams of 4-6.
- Large teams can be divided into sub-groups.

4–6

Typical duration

- Depending on the objectives and the need for discussion, the retrospective can be kept shorter.

60–120 min.

Materials needed
- Flip chart or whiteboard
- Post-its
- Pens, markers

Procedure: Retrospective "sailboat"

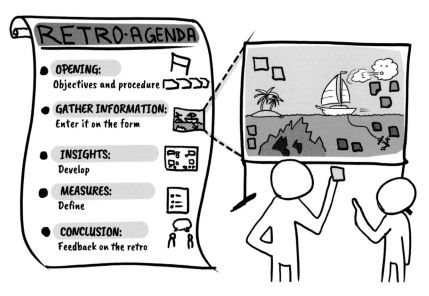

How the tool is applied...

Typical sequence of a retrospective session:

- **Step 1: Opening:** Introduce the objectives and the sequence of the retrospective session.
- **Step 2: Collect information:** Collect information on Post-its that are stuck to the corresponding fields of the sailboat template. Typical questions:
  - What happened recently? What was good? What gave us some wind at our backs (WIND)? What didn't work so well on the team and slowed us down (ANCHOR)? What are the hazards and risks against which the team has no power (CLIFFS) (e.g. market, new technologies, competitors)? What shared common vision and motivation does the team have (ISLAND)? Everybody reads his or her Post-its aloud.
- **Step 3: Cluster and prioritize findings:** Select and deepen the most important topics. Get to the bottom of things, that is, identify causes, so that more than just the symptoms are tackled. The aim is also to address unpleasant issues and create the basis for improvements.
- **Step 4: Define measures:** In the last step, the measures are formulated. This means that we document precisely anything to be changed or tried out in a following iteration.
- **Step 5: Conclude the retro:** Everybody gives a brief feedback on the retro, for example, with a feedback capture grid (see page 217). Ultimately, the group should part with good feelings.

This is the favorite tool of Achim Schmidt

Position:
Design thinking coach & sketch note trainer

"We do design thinking every Tuesday from 2:00-4:00 p.m.! – I have actually heard somebody say that in a company. To me, design thinking is a mindset that views things holistically and is related to many areas and life as such! My motto: Always use common sense!"

Why is it his favorite tool?

The success of most projects depends on motivation, fun, the mood, group dynamics, and communication within the team. The sailboat retrospective makes a huge contribution to making things work between team members – in an appreciative and well-structured way. I like it because it is quite effective and requires little time for preparation and implementation. The template is also convenient for documentation.

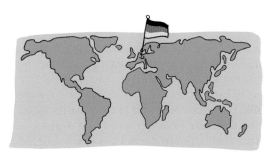

Country:
Germany

Affiliation:
business-playground

Checked by: Elena Bonanomi

Company/Position: Die Mobiliar | Innovation Manager

Alternative: Retrospective board with four quadrants

Things we continue to do in the same way	Things we will do differently next time
Things we want to try out	Things that are not relevant

Expert tips:

Create a positive mood!
- Pay heed to a positive mood and constructive criticism.
- Always start with positive feedback and insights.
- No blame game!
- Everybody must be heard out. Everybody should be able to make a contribution.
- A major retro session (e.g. at key milestones or in difficult situations) should be conducted by an external moderator or an employee who is not on the team.
- The choice of a different location can affect the retrospective: Get out of the everyday working environment and meet at a coffee place or in a public park.

Build trust
- Build trust. Especially with sensitive issues or when hierarchical differences exist. Anonymity can help.
- Explain that we apply the "Las Vegas principle": "What happens in this room stays between us for now!"
- Are there any "unspeakable" things or taboos that hold back the team?

Don't skip it
- If the team members know one another well, the retrospective is often omitted. That's a pity. It's worthwhile conducting one anyway because it helps in fostering a good mood.
- Implement small changes and measures; they frequently trigger big things.
- You can start the retrospective with the question: "Why do we conduct a retrospective?" Write down all the answers and make the findings visible to all. This retro already offers a huge potential for change!

Description of the use case

- After each iteration, Lilly's teams sit down for a moment and look back on what went well and what wasn't so great.
- It's important to Lilly that the chemistry on the team is right and that new things are tested again and again.
- In every iteration, she tries out new techniques and methods, accepting the possibility that not all of them work as desired. If something doesn't work out, the team has learned to laugh about themselves.

Key learnings

- Conduct a short retrospective in each iteration as well.
- Everyone writes down something; at a minimum, something he or she wants to try out.
- Make sure that the mood is positive and that there is trust. Remember, it's about continuous improvement.

Tool for download

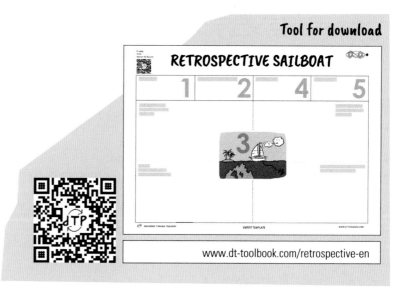

www.dt-toolbook.com/retrospective-en

Create a pitch

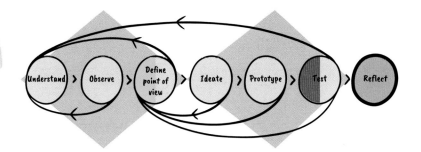

I would like...

to share the results and insights with the team at the end of an iteration, and also at regular intervals with the stakeholders.

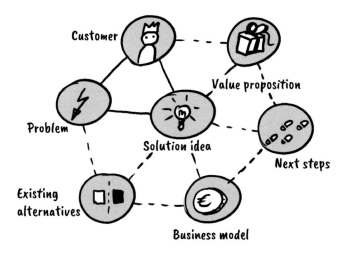

Customer
Value proposition
Problem
Solution idea
Next steps
Existing alternatives
Business model

What you can do with the tool:

- Show the team and stakeholders the current status of a prototype, a project, or the ultimate solution.
- Structure ideas and highlight core information.
- Obtain feedback on the solution and important functions, the customer needs, or the value proposition.
- Convince the audience or decision-makers of the project to get approval and resources for further steps or the implementation.

Some information on the tool:

- The term "pitch" actually comes from the advertising industry and refers to a presentation in front of a potential customer. Agencies often compete in persuading the client and thus getting the contract. The term "pitch" also became established in the start-up scene. Here a pitch describes the presentation of one's own business idea in a short time in front of investors or a panel of judges.
- In design thinking, we use "pitch" for the brief presentation of the results before the teams or the stakeholders.
- There are different types of pitches. They differ in terms of length, for instance. The elevator pitch is the shortest type of presentation. The point is to convey a summarizing and informative outline of the idea within a very short period of time (often no more than approx. 30 seconds or 1 minute).
- Usually, only a few PowerPoint slides are used, or none at all. In many pitch presentations, real prototypes are shown, making the presentation more vivid.
- Depending on the project phase, the focus is on different questions.

What tool can be used instead?

- NABC (see page 177)

Which tools support working with this tool?

- Lean canvas (see page 251)
- Stakeholder map (see page 83)
- Road map for implementation (see page 259)
- Storytelling (see page 129)

How much time and what materials do we need?

Group size

4–6

- The entire team.
- Or one person does the main presentation, and the others support him or her and add details.

Typical duration

60–120 min.

- The more impressive and short the pitch, the longer the preparation time.
- A short preparation time of about 1 hour suffices for an intermediate presentation. For the final presentations or an investor pitch, considerably more time is needed.

Materials needed

- Post-its and pens
- Prototypes
- Videos and photos of tests, customer feedback, and testimonials

Template and procedure: Create a pitch

Elements	Possible key questions of a pitch
Entry point (story)	• Attracts attention with a story
Problem	• What is the greatest problem? • Why is it a problem?
Customers	• Who is affected by the problem? • For whom is it a problem? (your persona) • What is the extent of the problem? (How great is the potential for a solution of the problem?) • Who are the early adopters? With whom can we do co-creation?
Solution/idea	• What is our solution? (prototype, demo, including test feedback) • What is the value proposition? What makes us unique? • Why are we better than the existing alternatives? • Why can only we implement the solution?
Business model	• How can we make money? • What are the challenges and risks?
Next steps	• What are we going to do next? • What do we need for the next steps?
Summary	• Why is it worthwhile to solve the problem? Why now? • Possibly introduce team at external pitches

How the tool is applied...

Step 1: Rough planning

Answer the following questions for the rough planning:
- Who are the listeners? What do they know already? Where can I meet them? What do they want to know?
- What's the framework? How much time do we have? What are the options for the presentation?
- What is my goal? What is my message?
- Then plan the rough sequence (e.g. with Post-its). Define the content, form, and who does or says what.

Step 2: Break down into details

Break down the pitch into details in several iterations:
- Use stories and arouse emotions.
- Follow KISS (keep it short and simple) with a maximum of 10 slides.
- Use key figures. Figures say more than words!
- Pictures say more than words, and videos more than pictures.
- Standard is boring! Don't use PowerPoint, if possible.
- Show the prototype in the pitch, give a demonstration, show how it works.
- Repeat the key messages at the end of the pitch.

Usually, a listener cannot remember more than 2 or 3 facts.

Step 3: Test, practice, and improve

- Test the pitch, practice the sequence, and improve it iteratively.
- After the pitch, the team should be prepared for all sorts of questions.

This is the favorite tool of Patrick Link

Position:
– Professor of Product Innovation, Lucerne University of Applied Sciences and Arts
– Design thinking and lean innovation coach – Co-founder of Trihow AG

"Design thinking complements our analytical culture as well as our problem-solving and decision-making processes. Especially in combination with other approaches such as systems thinking, data analytics, lean start-up, design thinking can be effective and help implement new, radical ideas."

Why is it his favorite tool?

It is incredibly difficult to present a radically new business idea in 1 minute and instill enthusiasm for the idea in the audience. It's all the more wonderful when we succeed and take positive feedback or useful information with us on our journey. Pitching must be practiced. Use every opportunity to practice – be it after work with friends in a bar or at events. A good pitch deck is much more than just colorful PowerPoint slides.

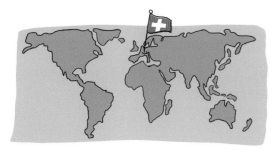

Country:
Switzerland

Affiliation:
Lucerne University of Applied Sciences and Arts, Co-Founder Trihow AG

Checked by: **Maria Tarcsay**
Company/Position: KoinaSoft GmbH, innovation accelerator

Expert tips:

Be prepared
- The shorter the pitch, the more difficult it is to prepare, because in this case we have no chance to catch up or add something later.
- Each presentation should be oriented toward the listeners. What do they already know? What do we need for the next steps?

Avoid PowerPoint
- Avoid PowerPoint slides with text. If you want to show slides nonetheless, observe Guy Kawasaki's rule for good pitches: "10, 20, 30," that is, 10 slides, 20 minute presentations, and font size 30.
- The audience can listen or read but not both at the same time. Don't use animations that distract the audience.
- Role-playing, in which the prototype or the persona takes center stage, has proven valuable here.
- Short videos or customer statements can also be intriguing. Make sure that the sound and the video work! If possible, test everything and have backup scenarios up your sleeve (e.g. in the event the projector fails or there's no sound).

Be passionate
- Exhibit enthusiasm for your product, service, and the target market during the pitch. It is not only about the idea but about the team's ability to implement the solution as well.
- The lean canvas yields valuable clues for relevant content (see page 251).
- Have answers to all relevant questions and prepare additional information as a backup.

Description of the use case

- To Lilly, presenting the idea well has top priority. She knows that the listeners do not want any endless PowerPoint presentations.
- Her team normally begins with a little role-playing game that makes the problem clear and tangible to the listeners. The team plans the presentation story, moving from the rough outline to the details. Whenever possible, Lilly wants to integrate into the pitch the prototype and the feedback from the users.
- The conclusion is as important as the entry point. The team plans the entry point and conclusion very carefully.

Key learnings

- Test the pitch deck and get feedback.
- Standard is boring! Don't use PowerPoint, if possible.
- Tell a story based on a persona or show a prototype.
- Show the enthusiasm of the customers/users in the interaction with the solution.
- The team is crucial here. Enthusiasm and commitment are always a winner.
- Repeat the important key messages at the end of the pitch.

Tool for download

www.dt-toolbook.com/pitch-en

250

Lean canvas

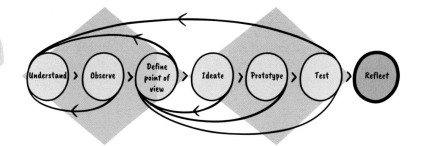

I would like...

to translate a problem into a solution that takes into consideration both the customer needs and my own business context.

What you can do with the tool:

- Summarize the results of the design thinking iterations so everybody gets a clear picture of the innovation project.
- Visualize and structure the hypotheses to review them afterward and capture the findings in an overview.
- Think and make observations about the implementation or the business model to identify risks entailed in the implementation.
- Compare different variants and business models.

Some information on the tool:

- The canvas supports us with structuring and visualizing our innovation project. The completed lean canvas documents the ultimate "problem/solution fit."
- The blocks of the lean canvas lead through a logical sequence, from customer problems to unfair advantages.
- The canvas is better suited for designing the solution than for exploring a problem.
- We use the lean canvas primarily to review the "problem/ solution fit" and adjust it if necessary. This means that the collected data is compared to the best solution that fits the behavior and challenges of the customers.

What tool can be used instead?

- Business model canvas
  We advise working with the lean canvas first since it takes greater account of the validation of the solution as a minimum viable product (see page 207) and is comparably less inside-out oriented than the business model canvas.

  Once the lean canvas is valid and optimization of the cost structure becomes more important, we switch to the business model canvas.

Which tools support working with this tool?

- NABC (see page 177)
- Problem to growth & scale innovation funnel (see page 263)
- MVP (see page 207)
- Persona/user profile (see page 97)

How much time and what materials do we need?

Group size

1–4

- Ideally, no more than 3-4 people work on a canvas.
- With larger groups, people should be assigned to several canvasses; later, the results are consolidated.

Typical duration

60–120 min.

- The initial creation of the lean canvas takes approx. 60 minutes. In most cases, the focus will then be on steps 1 through 5.
- In iterations, the lean canvas is supplemented and advanced step by step with the new findings.
- An update takes 10-15 minutes.

Materials needed

- Lean canvas can be printed on A0
- Pens and markers
- Post-its in various colors and sizes (e.g. different colors per customer segment/stakeholder)

Template and procedure: Lean canvas

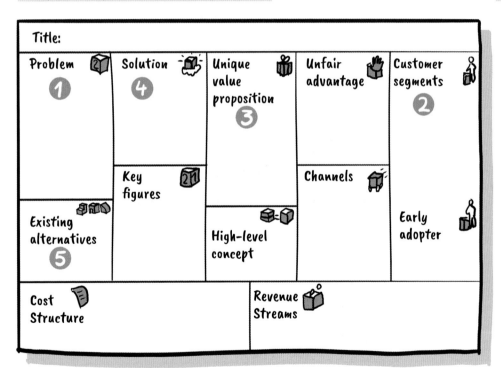

Note: Adapted from A. Maurya, *Running Lean* (2013)

How the tool is applied...

Print the lean canvas on A0 paper and provide Post-its of various sizes.

- **Step 1:**
  Fill in the lean canvas step by step and supplement it with new findings. In the early phases, the focus is on steps 1 through 5 to review the "problem/solution fit" (problem, customer segments, value proposition, solution, and existing alternatives). Tip: First, iterate these five steps until a stable image has emerged.
- **Step 2:**
  Complete the other steps in any order.
  Tip: Depending on preferences, use Post-its of different colors for different customer segments or according to risks (e.g. pink = high risk, must be tested quickly; yellow = medium risk; green = already tested or low risk).
- **Step 3:**
  Identify the most risky assumptions and test them in experiments.

Position:
Innovation Coach at creaffective and guest lecturer at various universities

"Many good ideas do not fail because we cannot implement them. They fail because we invest a lot of time, money, and effort to develop good solutions for the wrong questions. Design thinking ensures that we build products that really address the needs of customers and users. Lean canvas as a tool can effectively support us in this approach."

Why is it his favorite tool?

The lean canvas allows us to summarize all results. It contains all important factors to provide a simple and easy-to-comprehend description of the innovation project. It helps the team identify gaps and the next steps which should be tested next by experiments. It focuses on the solution. Moreover, it gives us a rough outlook of a possible implementation or business model.

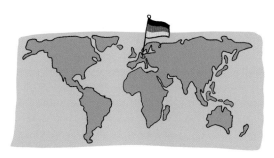

Country:
Germany

Affiliation:
Creaffective
GmbH

Checked by: Patrick Link

Company/Position: Lucerne University of Applied Sciences and Arts & co-founder of Trihow AG

TOO THIN   **TOO FAT**   **LEAN START-UP**

Expert tips:

Don't lose track of what's what
- What has worked well for us before is to have 3 to 4 Post-its per field with one statement each.
- Too many Post-its on a field indicates a lack of focus.
- If the field is empty or almost empty, it should be worked on further.
- We usually use Post-its because they can be changed and moved easily.

Record the content after each iteration
- We recommend that you document progress and record changes on a regular basis (e.g. with photos).
- At a later point, when fewer major changes (pivots) are made, an electronic version can be used.

Use the KPIs common in the relevant industry
- Every company, regardless of industry and size, has some key figures that can be used for the performance review. In order to make it easier for the team, we recommend using Dave McClure's AARRR (pirate metrics).

Get feedback from outside
- Naturally, external inputs and opinions of third parties are quite valuable.
- Once the lean canvas is valid and there is no need to change it anymore, the outcome can be easily transferred and expanded into the business model canvas (if necessary or desired).

Customize the lean canvas
- Add the customer profiles and experiment reports to the lean canvas (see www.leancanvas.ch).

Description of the use case

- Lilly's team uses the lean canvas to document the problem/solution fit and prepare the pitch.
- The lean canvas shows contradictions and open items very well. After Lilly's team has completed the lean canvas, they think about where the greatest uncertainties and risks lie. Once identified, the team tests them first because they want to make effective and efficient use of their time.
- Lilly's team still sees the greatest uncertainty in the value proposition and would like to test it again next.

Key learnings

- It is vital to solve a problem that is relevant to the customer with the product idea.
- To find the right solution for the right problem and for the right customer is a challenge. We will hardly discover it the first time around. Therefore: iterate – iterate – iterate!
- As soon as the first lean canvas is done, the assumptions can be tested. Begin with the riskiest one.

Tool for download

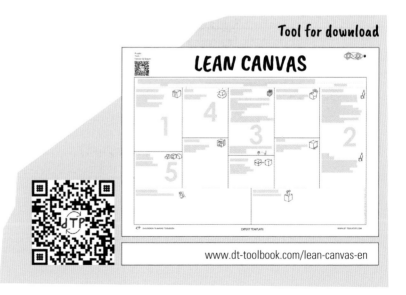

www.dt-toolbook.com/lean-canvas-en

Lessons learned

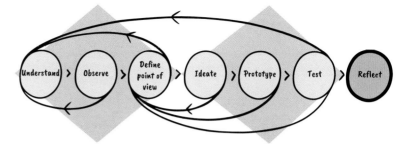

I would like...

to reflect on and record the insights gained during and at the end of a design thinking project.

Learn and develop

Repeat your successes

Mistakes can be something positive but try to avoid making the same mistake twice.

Don't reinvent the wheel, perfect it

What you can do with the tool:

- Collect and appraise experiences made in the project in a structured manner.
- Learn from experience and make use of it in the next project.
- Facilitate a positive attitude toward mistakes and appreciate progress.
- Identify and document the findings; make them applicable and usable.

Some information on the tool:

- The term "lessons learned" originates from project management.
- Lessons learned means the written recording and systematic collection and appraisal of positive and negative experiences, developments, findings, mistakes, and risks during a project.
- Different levels are considered, for example, technical, content, emotional, social, and process-related.
- The goal is to learn from the actions and decisions in order to design future projects better.
- Thus lessons learned map the experience, knowledge, insights, and the understanding the participants developed in the context of project implementation.
- Design thinking projects usually produce a wide range of insights since the methods are always applied in the context of the problem statement, so each design challenge takes a different course.
- The tool helps to reflect on one's own actions and learning. For more extensive projects, its use is also recommended during the project, not only at the end.

What tool can be used instead?

- Feedback capture grid (see page 217)
- Retrospective sailboat (see page 243)

Which tools support working with this tool?

- Lean canvas (see page 251)
- Create a pitch (see page 247)
- "I like, I wish, I wonder" (see page 239)

How much time and what materials do we need?

Group size

design team

- Core team and, if necessary, other stakeholders for reflection at project level.
- Reflection at the meta level; participants working individually.

Typical duration

40–60 min.

- The exercise for the group typically lasts 40-60 minutes (depending on the project length).
- The longer the project, the more time should be planned for reflection.
- The more time is scheduled for group work, the easier the individual work.

Materials needed

- Log book (kept by each participant during the project in preparation for the workshop)
- Template or flip chart
- Post-its and pens

Template and procedure: Lessons learned

① Project level

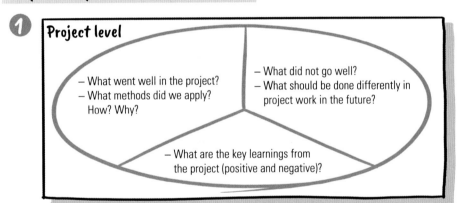

- What went well in the project?
- What methods did we apply? How? Why?

- What did not go well?
- What should be done differently in project work in the future?

- What are the key learnings from the project (positive and negative)?

② Meta level

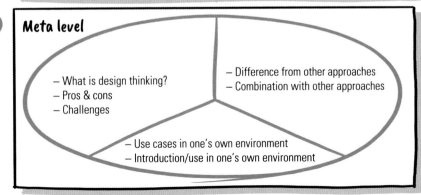

- What is design thinking?
- Pros & cons
- Challenges

- Difference from other approaches
- Combination with other approaches

- Use cases in one's own environment
- Introduction/use in one's own environment

How the tool is applied...

- The most common method is that all relevant project stakeholders jointly review the project in the form of a workshop exercise.
- Reflection should take place at two levels: the project level and the meta level.
- **Step 1:** At the project level, the focus is on answering the following questions:
  - What went well in the project and what did not
  - What methods did we apply? How? Why?
  - What should be done differently in future project work? What should or must change?
  - What are the key learnings from the project (positive and negative)?
- **Step 2:** At the meta level, the following questions take center stage:
  - What does design thinking mean to me? What are the pros and cons? Challenges?
  - How is design thinking different from other approaches?
  - How can design thinking be combined with other approaches?
  - How could design thinking be applied in my environment/my company? Which use cases might be of interest?

This is the favorite tool of Stefanie Gerken

Position:
Design thinking program lead, workshop specialist & coach, HPI School of Design Thinking

"For me, design thinking is a holistic approach, a matter of attitude, of how to deal with your environment and not just a methodology used for single projects."

Why is it her favorite tool?

To me, lessons learned or other reflection methods are crucial for the success of a project. It is important for us to reflect regularly and infer from the results appropriate measures for action, so problems are identified early in the process and positive aspects can be intensified.

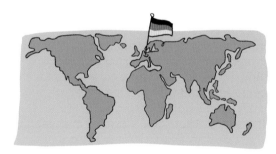

Country:
Germany

Affiliation:
HPI School of Design Thinking

Checked by: Marc Fetscherin

Company/Position: Rollins College | Professor of Marketing

The only mistake in life is the lesson not learned!

Albert

Expert tips:

Address key questions in a lessons learned session
- The following questions are useful in the preparation of the workshop:
  - What specifically do we want to look at, and when?
  - Where is the focus? What is the goal of the client? How will coordination with the client take place?
  - Who will moderate the workshop?
  - Which project participants should be invited?
- Wait with holding a lessons learned session if the mood after the project is rather bad. It has often worked for us to wait 6 weeks in such a case; seen from a greater distance, many issues can be looked at without stirring up too many emotions.

Lessons learned should be part of the project plan
- Typically, a lessons learned session is held after the completion of a project as part of the project completion documentation and should be an integral part of project planning.
- In addition, we should collect lessons learned during the project (e.g. halfway into the project or at crucial milestones), so they can be integrated into the next phases.

Less is more when it comes to defined actions
- Less is more: Emphasize the things that have proven successful and those that failed; define actions and measures based upon this.
  Important: Do not focus only on the negative aspects and don't get personal!
- Lessons learned is also a good foundation for the definition of the design principles (see page 53). or they can be used as part of "define success" (see page 137).

Description of the use case

- Lilly's teams reflect on their projects at regular intervals and at pivotal milestones.
- The lessons learned at the meta level are consolidated with the learning of the other teams, so that the design principles can be adjusted, for instance, or collaboration be improved.
- The questions on the technical level and in terms of content, at the emotional/social and process-related level, however, often vary greatly per team and project objective.

Key learnings

- Use lessons learned on multiple levels (the technical level and in terms of content, at the emotional/social and process-related level).
- Hold reflection sessions during the project with the help of a log book at project level. Include the meta level at the end of the project.
- Prepare some key questions for the reflection session with the team.

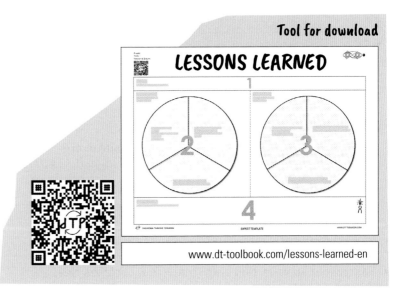

www.dt-toolbook.com/lessons-learned-en

258

Road map for implementation

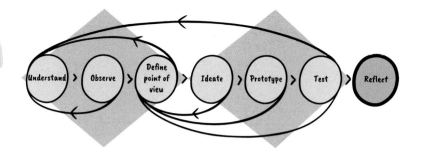

I would like...

to put the focus on the successful implementation of potential market opportunities right from the onset.

What we had planned...

Where we stand...

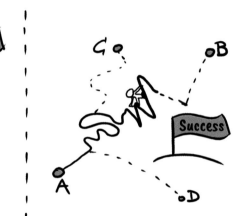

What you can do with the tool:

- Use the road map for implementation as a guide in order to define the current position (A) and the destination (B): "Where should the journey take us?"
- Don't lose track; determine whether the right target area and target group are being looked at during the journey.
- Share the road to the destination in common with others.
- Work out the basis for a checklist with the most important factors of success.
- Ensure that an uncertain path from A to B becomes clear over the course of the journey.

Some information on the tool:

- The "road map for implementation" is, as it were, the road to success. With the open approach of a complex problem statement, it is crucial to gain clarity about the context as quickly as possible.
- The tool helps determine the critical factors that are relevant to the planning of the implementation project.
- The aim is to get a holistic view of the subsequent implementation as early in the process as possible, to identify the critical path and possible risks in order to determine the necessary next steps.
- The road map is created as early as possible, reviewed after each step, and adjusted if necessary.
- It is our compass, so to speak, for realigning the project again and again to an initially vague and moving target.
- The execution of the implementation plan usually takes place later. Project management methods, as they are used within the organization, help here.

What tool can be used instead?

- Scenario techniques
- Game plan
- Reality check

Which tools support working with this tool?

- Define success (see page 137)
- Stakeholder map (see page 83)
- NABC (see page 177)

How much time and what materials do we need?

Group size

5–7

- Ideally, the project manager, a designer, business or product managers, representatives of the users or customers, investor or sponsor, developer and challenger, if appropriate.

Typical duration

60–120 min.

- The road map is created step by step; it can be done in portions over several days.
- Determine several meetings of 60 to 120 minutes for the iterative and incremental creation of the road map.

Materials needed

- Large sheet of paper or A0 template
- Pens, Post-its
- Camera to capture the road map

Template and procedure: Roadmap for implementation

① Define goals ② Stakeholder ③ Fields of action

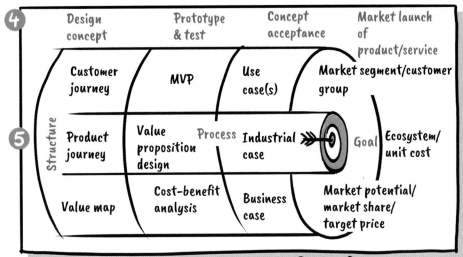

④ Design concept / Prototype & test / Concept acceptance / Market launch of product/service

Customer journey / MVP / Use case(s) / Market segment/customer group

⑤ Structure — Product journey / Value proposition design / Process / Industrial case / Goal / Ecosystem/ unit cost

Value map / Cost-benefit analysis / Business case / Market potential/ market share/ target price

⑥ Assignment of the persons implementing the solution

How the tool is applied...

- **Step 1:** First define goals and build a control system; if possible, quantify relevant decision-making criteria (KPIs); determine budget, schedule, milestones, etc.
- **Step 2:** Draw up an overview with all participants. For this purpose, tools such as the stakeholder map (see page 83) are useful for checking the goals for their suitability for implementation and, above all, for putting together the right team.
- **Step 3:** Define the structure, the main fields of design, and perspectives. The "standard perspectives" are desirability, feasibility, and viability (see page 20). Depending on the problem statement, they can be further specified, for example, by dimensions such as sustainability and environmental compatibility.
- **Step 4:** Describe the process steps or phases. Depending on the applied methodology, they may be concept design, prototyping, and testing (iteratively) as well as concept acceptance.
- **Step 5:** Fill in all fields with tasks, first in terms of quality; then enter the results of the individual tasks, for example, by means of a customer journey (see page 103) for concept design usefulness.
- **Step 6:** Here, it is important to position on the map all people implementing the solution or needed for the implementation, since it might be necessary to win them over later.

This is the favorite tool of Markus Durstewitz

Position:
Head of Method Development, Innovation and Design Thinking at Airbus Strategy - New Business Models and Services

"In the end, the only thing that counts is the result (deliver or die). Design thinking is not a workshop format but a holistic approach to problem solving. Design thinking helps to do the right thing, that is, recognize the expectations, desires, and needs of users and potential customers."

Why is it his favorite tool?

The road map for implementation sketches the path to successful innovation using the design principles. It is, as it were, the compass for my journey from the original business idea to a successful market launch. Tools such as the stakeholder map help us with the definition of the key persons to make the initiative a successful one.

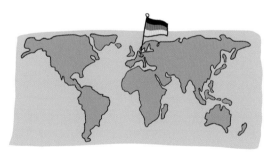

Country:
Germany

Affiliation:
Airbus

Checked by: Ute Bauckhorn

Company/Position: Schindler Aufzüge AG | Head of Safety & Health

"The road to success"

Who will use it?

Who pays for it?

Who will build it?

Expert tips:

Who will implement the solution is a critical question
- The implementation of new market opportunities is complex and has many pitfalls. In our experience, it helps to apply methods and tools in a targeted manner to complete the "journey" successfully.
- We have found it very helpful to start with the question "Who needs the solution? Who is the user/customer? Who will build it? Whom do we need for the implementation? Who pays? Who is funding the project? Who pays for the solution?"
- If we are not yet able to name all those involved, it usually indicates that our goal is not really clear yet.
- In addition, it is always important to choose the right method for every step. The tool must fit the context.

Know the sponsors, their needs, and adapt the pitch to them
- In the end, we want to achieve a positive decision in favor of implementation. The road map helps us to cover all areas, starting with the use case, to the industrial case, on up to the business case. They must be coordinated with one another.
- When we prepare a pitch (see page 247) for a decision board, it is vital to know the needs of the decision makers and what kinds of "stories" are "in" at the moment. The pitch should meet the needs of all participants in terms of content; it can comprise additional beneficial elements such as visualizations, posters, or videos. A structure according to NABC (see page 177) helps with the preparation.

Description of the use case

- The road map for implementation is created jointly by Lilly's core team. Since usually not all people involved are identified from the beginning, they can be brought in at a future time with later adjustments.
- In addition to the tasks, the people implementing the solution must be named. Once the road map is complete, it is a good indicator of the project's level of maturity.
- Lilly thinks about the implementation at an early stage. Only in this way is she able to involve the relevant stakeholders.

Key learnings

Step-by-step procedure to the road map for implementation:

- Define goals and criteria.
- Select tasks and methods.
- Assign people.
- Adjust road map after each step and each iteration if necessary.

Tool for download

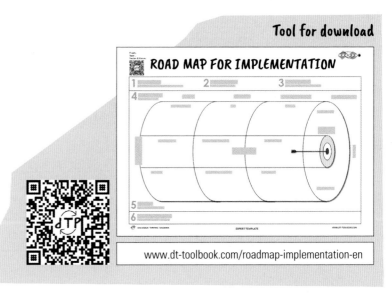

www.dt-toolbook.com/roadmap-implementation-en

Problem to growth & scale innovation funnel

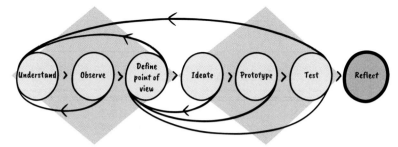

I would like...

to make the growth initiatives transparent in a "funnel."

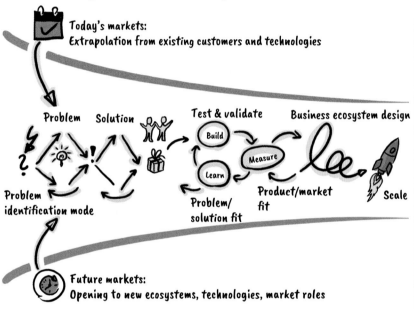

Today's markets:
Extrapolation from existing customers and technologies

Problem — **Solution**

Test & validate

Build

Measure

Learn

Business ecosystem design

Problem identification mode

Problem/ solution fit

Product/market fit

Scale

Future markets:
Opening to new ecosystems, technologies, market roles

What you can do with the tool:

- Document a portfolio of existing customer requirements (today's markets) and future customer requirements (future markets).
- Put the focus on the contribution margin and the revenue with regard to existing customers and technologies by extrapolation.
- Follow the opportunities in new ecosystems, technologies, and market roles by retropolation.
- Visualize the market validation of the prototypes, proof of concept, and finished solutions over time.
- Replace existing innovation funnels by contemporary terminologies and approaches.

Some information on the tool:

- The "problem to growth & scale framework" constitutes the basis of a modern, contemporary innovation funnel.
- It is not based on many different ideas that are filtered through gates (as with classical innovation approaches); instead, it starts with the "problem identification mode." The problem identification mode is controlled by two factors. First, by the exploration of existing customers and technologies, and second, by retropolation, a way of looking at future ecosystems, technologies, and market roles.
- The various initiatives for solving present and future problems are visualized over time and presented in a portfolio.
- Initiatives that are discontinued remain in the funnel. At regular intervals, the causes are examined in the context of a retrospective, for instance (see page 243) .

What tool can be used instead?
- Road map for implementation (see page 259)

Which tools support working with this tool?
- Trend analysis (see page 111)
- Lean canvas (see page 251)
- Vision cone (see page 141)
- Stakeholder map (see page 83)
- Retrospective sailboat (see page 243)
- Pictures of the future (by Siemens)
- Minimum viable ecosystem (see *The Design Thinking Playbook*, page 240 and what follows)

How much time and what materials do we need?

Group size

- The inputs for the topic and the current status come from the strategy, design, and implementation teams in an organization.

1–2

Typical duration

- Gathering the information initially requires some effort.
- The updates should be no longer than 30-60 minutes.

30–120 min.

Materials needed

- The funnel can be used as an A0 poster in a work room or kept electronically in a PowerPoint presentation
- Possibly state-of-the-art collaboration tools such as Trello, Teams, OneNote...

Template: Problem to growth & scale innovation funnel

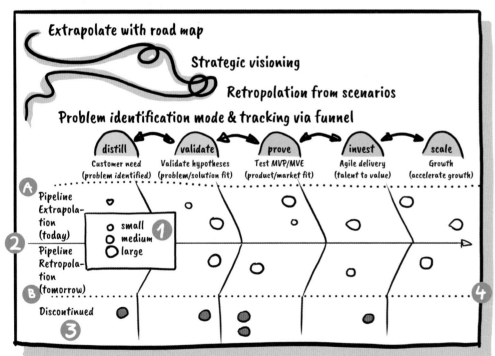

How the tool is applied...

- The funnel is a very good tool for documenting the individual activities and arranging them chronologically in terms of their maturity level.
- It gives us transparency on current prototypes, MVPs/MVEs, ultimate solutions, and discontinued activities.
- **Step 1:** Enter a name for all projects and establish a scale for the size or the contribution of the project to the success of the company (e.g. < 5 million, 5-50 million, > 50 million). The things being measured are adapted to the value system of the respective organization (e.g. top line vs. bottom line).
- **Step 2:** Place the current projects on the time axis and differentiate between existing business (A) and future topics (B). This differentiation shows us how much activity is invested in the development of the sustainable future of an enterprise.
- **Step 3:** Projects that were discontinued are also traced, so we are able to examine the reasons for it at regular intervals.
- **Step 4:** Update the funnel through regular control (e.g. on a monthly basis), and discuss on this basis resource allocation and sales and profit targets.

This is the favorite tool of Michael Lewrick

Position:
Best-selling author, speaker, innovation and digitization expert

"The mapping of initiatives, including the corresponding development levels, allows for a quick overview of the innovation and growth portfolio."

Why is it his favorite tool?

The "problem to growth & scale innovation funnel" picks up the basic idea of the lean canvas and tracks potential growth initiatives, from the identified customer needs up to scaling. It shows clearly the maturity level of a portfolio and which revenue and contribution margins the organization can expect.

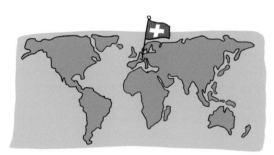

Country:
Switzerland

Affiliation:
Innovation and
Digitization Expert

Checked by: Markus Blatt

Company/Position: neueBeratung GmbH, Managing Director

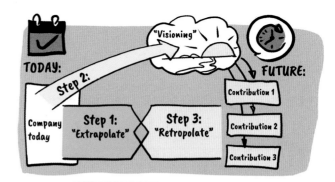

Expert tips:

For the extrapolation and especially the retropolation, tools like "pictures of the future" can be used.

How do we extrapolate?
- We extrapolate from the world of today; and our starting point is the daily business of our company. We look at the trends, from which we extrapolate how the near future of our company may look. This takes place by the analysis of data and information from different sources, for example, industry reports and interviews with experts.
- The fastest way for reaching our goal is to fall back upon the known trends in an industry, for example, using internal trend reports and market analyses, which are freely available on the Internet.

How does strategic visioning work?
- For this, we choose a positive, constructive, and profitable scenario and ask ourselves: "How might our company make a maximum contribution to this scenario? What would we have to do and offer?"
- We stay in the future in our thoughts and don't allow the processes and structures of our company today to influence us.

How does retropolation from tomorrow's world take place?
- With retropolation, we draw conclusions for the present from the "well-known" facts of the future scenario. We juxtapose the results from the two other activities, combine them, and infer from that what it means, in very specific terms, for the alignment and direction of our company today. In which directions should we innovate and do research? What skills need to be built?

Description of the use case

- Lilly wants to use a simple tool in order to depict the initiatives that were worked out over time in a funnel.
- The "problem to growth & scale innovation funnel" offers her the advantage that she can stay within the methodology of lean start-up and design thinking.
- In addition, she quickly realizes which initiatives were discontinued at what time and how many growth topics and their market potential are in development.

Key learnings

- Always think in problems and not in ideas when creating a funnel.
- Take both the problem/solution fit and the problem/market fit into account.
- Sub-divide the funnel into existing business fields and future fields of activity.
- For example, use "pictures of the future" to explore the topics of the future.

Tool for download

PROBLEM TO GROWTH & SCALE INNOVATION FUNNEL

www.de-toolbook.com/funnel-en

Applications

The application of the design thinking mindset is multi-faceted. Toward the end of our Design Thinking Toolbox, we would like to present selected applications that cover the entire breadth of design thinking. The initiatives range from programs at universities, such as the legendary ME310, to intrapreneurship programs that give employees the opportunity of realizing their own ideas. Moreover, design thinking can be used in the context of "design your future," that is, for the design of one's own life planning.

Universities

ME310 at Stanford University

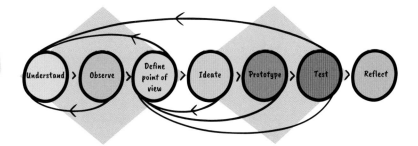

I would like...

to have a complex problem for my company solved by a group of international students.

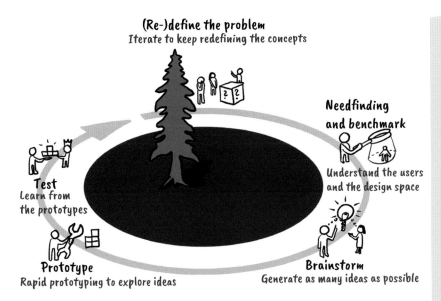

(Re-)define the problem
Iterate to keep redefining the concepts

Needfinding and benchmark
Understand the users and the design space

Test
Learn from the prototypes

Brainstorm
Generate as many ideas as possible

Prototype
Rapid prototyping to explore ideas

What can such a program achieve?

- International student teams find solutions for complex problems of companies
- Building and transferring design skills to the corporate partner
- Access to the international design thinking community
- Intercultural collaboration of student teams
- Application of the design thinking mindset in problem solving
- Conveying design methods and skills

Some information on ME310:

- An international team of students takes on a design challenge from a corporate partner over a period of 9 months.
- The students have been tasked with designing a complete system, taking into account desirability, feasibility, and viability.
- During the run time of the project, the students substantiate the problem statement, generate a broad variety of ideas, build and test prototypes, and present, at the end of the program, a final prototype that serves as the proof of concept for the idea.
- In each ME310 project, student teams from Stanford University collaborate with teams from foreign universities. The aim is the emergence of groundbreaking innovations through collaboration and diversity.
- In recent years, companies and institutions such as IBM, 3M, Siemens, Swisscom, BMW, VW, GM, Honda, Volvo, NASA, HP, Intel, Pfizer, Thales, Baxter, Bosch, SAP, Apple, and many others had student teams develop design challenges with great success.
- Partner universities include the University of St. Gallen, Aalto University, HPI Potsdam, KIT Karlsruhe, Kyoto Design Lab, NTNU, Porto Design Factory, TUM, University of Zurich, Linköping University, Trinity College, Dublin, University of Science and Technology of China, and many more.

How much time and what materials do we need?

Group size

- 2-3 teams, each made up of 4-6 students at various universities.

8–18

Typical duration

- The ME310 lasts 9 months. Often, the process begins some months in advance with the definition of the problem statement together with the corporate partner.

9 months

Materials needed

- Material for prototypes
- Pens, Post-its
- Infrastructure for teams
- Communication tools for the teams

Procedure and schedule

"Hunting"

A

B_f

"Transport"

B_0

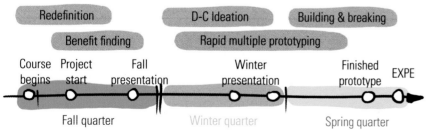

| Redefinition | D-C Ideation | Building & breaking |
| Benefit finding | Rapid multiple prototyping | |

Course begins · Project start · Fall presentation · Winter presentation · Finished prototype · EXPE

Fall quarter · Winter quarter · Spring quarter

What is the philosophy of ME310?

The learning concept of ME310 follows the design thinking process. The program distinguishes between two large areas: "hunting" and "transport," in which the student teams act. According to the design philosophy of ME310, it takes both behaviors for the discovery of innovative solutions.

The ME310 mindset includes:

- Hunting is not "wandering" (you must have a purpose).
- Never go hunting alone (multi-capability teams).
- Don't give up too early (patience in the event of failure).
- Don't confuse transport with hunting (announce and explain the behavior).
- Bring it home (deliver results).

Many of the tools and methods presented in *The Design Thinking Toolbox* are applied in ME310. The tools help the teams in the analysis of problems, the drafting of various options, and with the synthesis that helps to get to the bottom of problems and combine different ideas. Frequently, unique solutions evolve between the poles of different options.

The most important element in ME310 is the building of physical prototypes that help to achieve a real interaction with a potential user.

270

This is Larry Leifer's program

Position:
- Professor of Mechanical Engineering, Stanford University
- Founding Director, HPI & Stanford Center for Design Research
- ME310 "Project-based Engineering Design, Innovation, and Development"

"If you think of design thinking as an iceberg, then the tools and methods that are easy to learn form the peak. The design thinking process can also be learned and experienced. The most important thing, however, is the design thinking mindset, that is, to think and work like a designer."

The reasons why he swears by the ME310 concept

Me310 lives the design thinking mindset. Various tools help in finding and selecting ideas, and the design thinking process helps to see where the teams currently stand. But what's most important is that the hunt for the next market opportunity does not follow a clear-cut pattern. At the beginning of the journey, the solution is anything but clear. This means that we learn to handle uncertainty, put trust in the teams, so in the end we bring forth a "WOW!" moment.

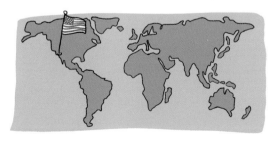

Country:
USA

Affiliation:
ME310 Stanford University

Checked by: **Sophie Bürgin**

Company/Position: INNOArchitects, User Researcher & User Insight Lead

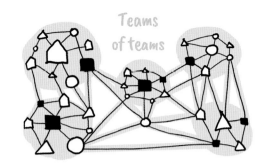

Teams of teams

Expert tips:

Cooperative adaptability is essential to high-performing teams
- Design thinking works best on a team. It is pivotal for ensuring that the teams are made up of people with different experience and backgrounds, so that there is a broad range of different perspectives on the problem and its solution.
- Teams of teams is another great approach. It is conveyed to the teams that each team is doing the right thing. In an international project like ME310, we consciously empower the individual teams to act and decide independently. If each team has the freedom to act without the consent of the other teams, the decisions are better balanced.

Powerful teams have the ability to think and act as a seamless unit
- In this approach, the teams have no direct control over other teams in the network; instead they collaborate with them.
- The idea of teams of teams is built upon network thinking, which makes it possible to disseminate information and results quickly. A traditional hierarchical structure does not allow for such quick responses, because information is consciously filtered.
- Collaboration should result at the end in a "Wow!" moment, not just: "Thank you very much. I received the information." A "Wow!" moment means that a team has met or exceeded expectations. When you understand how teams work together well, you'll achieve greater success in innovation.

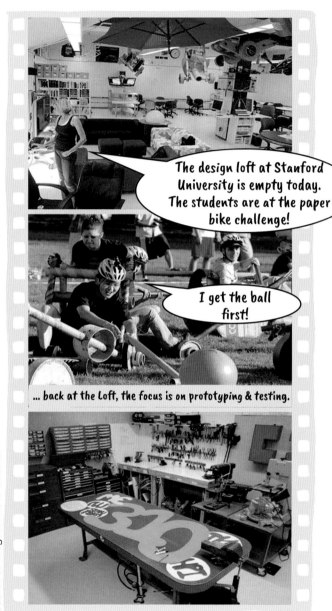

The design loft at Stanford University is empty today. The students are at the paper bike challenge!

I get the ball first!

... back at the Loft, the focus is on prototyping & testing.

Description of the use case

- For many students, the ME310 Design Loft at Stanford University is the place where, for a year, problem statements are understood and ideation and prototyping take place.
- The course has been in existence since 1967. Over the last few decades, many companies had teams of students work on their design challenges.
- One of the highlights of every program year is the "paper bike" challenge. This exercise boosts creativity and finding a solution with students. The basic idea is to build a vehicle with a limited range of materials that remains functional in changing game conditions.

Key learnings

- Use design thinking teams at universities and technical colleges for the solution of complex problem statements.
- What you get are simple, high-definition prototypes that help accelerate the product or service development cycle.
- The collaboration with students should also be considered a recruiting tool.

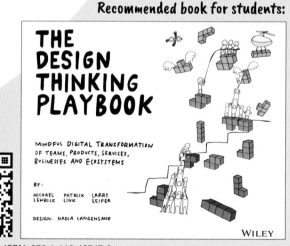

Recommended book for students:

THE DESIGN THINKING PLAYBOOK

MINDFUL DIGITAL TRANSFORMATION OF TEAMS, PRODUCTS, SERVICES, BUSINESSES AND ECOSYSTEMS

BY: MICHAEL LEWRICK PATRICK LINK LARRY LEIFER

DESIGN: NADIA LANGENSAND

WILEY

ISBN Print: ISBN: 978-1-119-46747-2 ,
available as paperback and e-book, in English and many other languages

Companies

"Co-creation toolbox" by Siemens

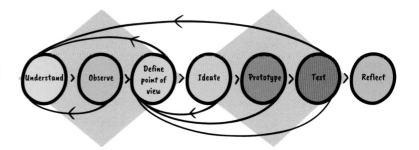

I would like...

to help our Siemens colleagues by imparting to them relevant design thinking methods and a user-centered way of thinking so they will be more successful in shaping the collaboration with customers and other stakeholders (e.g. suppliers, academic partners, and Siemens colleagues).

What you can do with this co-creation toolbox...

- Plan a project from the kick-off up to implementation, then go through it with the selected tools and templates.
- Gain an understanding about how to use the methods in a meaningful way and in which project phase.
- Select individual method cards and combine them according to the requirements of a project.

Some information on the tool:

- Co-creation is a wonderful approach for developing solutions together with stakeholders, simultaneously raising the level of innovation, accelerating the development process, and minimizing the risk.
- Design thinking is the methodical approach, both from a process point of view and in terms of the application of the individual tools.
- When implementing co-creation projects, people often don't know how to proceed in a structured manner and which methods should be deployed at what point.
- The User Experience Design Department at Siemens Corporate Technology has selected, described, and visualized 65 relevant methods for the implementation of co-creation projects.
- The individual methods were allocated either to the industrial design thinking process or the customer value co-creation process and color-coded accordingly.
- The cards are available in digital form and printed in a box or as a brochure.
- Matching templates were created for each method.

How much time and what materials do we need?

Group size

At least 5

- 4-16 people.
- Depending on the size of the group, 1-2 method coaches.
- 1-2 people from each important stakeholder group (customers, market, or technology experts).

Typical duration

3 days—
150 days

- Depending on the complexity and scope of the project.
- A short text is written on each card that explains the method, the purpose, the procedure, and gives an example.

Materials needed

- In addition to the method cards and printed templates, you need the typical design thinking materials (Post-its, timers, etc.). Another important aspect is an inspiring and collaborative work environment.

Procedure with the co-creation toolbox

Description and result of step

Design thinking process step with its own color

Overview of selected methods

Integration in co-creation project

Example

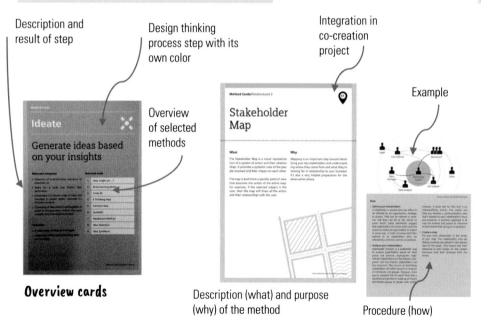

Overview cards

Description (what) and purpose (why) of the method

Procedure (how)

Method cards

How the tool is applied...

- Design thinking and co-creation experts are handed the entire set of tools (folder, box, templates) in printed and digital form. The experts decide on the material and the form in which it is relevant to the respective application context. They have the option of adapting the content to the respective project and the respective event.
- The toolbox can be made available digitally to a larger target group that is dealing with the topic for the first time. The toolbox helps to disseminate the knowledge that was collected by the experts across the entire organization as well as to motivate colleagues to try out some of the methods and manage co-creation projects themselves.
- The method cards are predominantly used in workshops and projects. Many colleagues, however, also use them to read about individual methods in peace and quiet as well as to collect additional information.
- The tool set provides support in all phases of the co-creation process: introduction to the topic of co-creation; definition of the framework conditions and resources; preparation of the co-creation activities (definition of the subject area, identification of suitable partners, collection of relevant information); implementation of the co-creation project; up to sustainable implementation.

This is the favorite tool of Bettina Maisch

Position:
- Senior Key Expert Consultant at Siemens Corporate Technology
- Lecturer at the University of St. Gallen

"Basically, design thinking is common sense. We cannot do business in a sustainable way if we don't produce something that gives the customer a compelling added value. By means of co-creation, we collaborate closely with the customer, articulate his needs, and generate sustainable added value through technology innovations."

Why does she swear by the "co-creation" concept?

Co-creation and design thinking overlap in many ways. In the co-creation process, design thinking helps from the very onset to understand the needs and limitations of the other party better and, from that point of departure, generate beneficial ideas and implement them iteratively. Our toolbox helps individual teams to use tried-and-tested design thinking methods for a successful project implementation. In addition, the tool makes you want to implement co-creation projects.

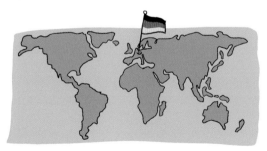

Country:
Germany

Affiliation:
Siemens

Checked by: Lucas Bock

Company/Position: Design Thinking Consultant at Siemens Corporate Technology.

Expert tips:

Co-creation is a team sport
- Involve all relevant internal stakeholders in the compilation of a co-creation toolbox and identify its structure and content together.
- Find your own visual language for your co-creation and design thinking activities.

Select the methods that are most relevant in the project context
- Conduct a little study on which tools were used most frequently and most successfully in co-creation projects at your company.
- Describe and visualize the methods in an attractive and comprehensible way. Test with colleagues whether they are able to make use of the description.
- Provide the methods both physically and digitally and distribute them to decision makers at your company.

Templates simplify and accelerate the application
- For the simplified and accelerated application of the methods and tools, templates should be provided.

Practice the methods in a safe environment with experienced coaches
- Offer simultaneous training sessions for the presentation and practice of the methods prior to the beginning of the project.

Description of the use case

- When preparing a project, the teams at Siemens use the toolbox to select the relevant methods for the project.
- The heading and color on the front of each method card help in integrating them in the design thinking process.
- A brief description explains the method (what) and what it is used for (why). At the back of the card, the approach is explained step by step, and an application example is given.

Key learnings

- Don't underestimate the visual design – it makes the methods attractive.
- Physical cards are still quite popular.
- Texts should be short, concise, and comprehensible to everybody.
- Application examples are extremely important.
- There are many inspirational examples of good method tool sets.

Intrapreneurship

"Kickbox" by Swisscom

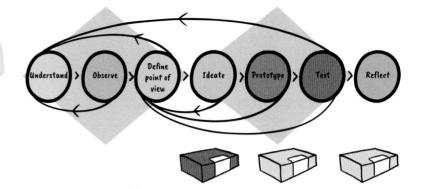

I would like...

to establish an intrapreneurial culture in the organization or company.

What you can do with the tool:

- Achieve a transformation in corporate culture and an innovation.
- Slim and customer-oriented validation and development of ideas.
- Enable all employees to develop ideas.
- Explore customer problems and open up new business opportunities.
- Build an alternative talent pool of employees who think as entrepreneurs.
- Make innovation tangible by means of a physical innovation box.
- Introduce a gamified approach that takes away the fear of innovation and failure.

Some information on the tool:

- The kickbox was originally developed by Adobe. Adobe used the approach to increase the speed of innovation for internal initiatives. By now, many companies have adapted the procedure.
- The idea behind "innovation in a box" is to give employees the chance to become self-efficient. Employees are given everything an innovator needs: funds, time, methods, and tools (like the ones presented here in the Toolbox), lots of coffee, other beverages, fruit, nuts, and sweets.
- The Swiss ICT company Swisscom makes three boxes available to its employees: red, blue, and gold. The boxes follow the design thinking process, from the "understand" phases up to the implementation of the final prototype.

What tools are part of a kickbox?

- Persona/user profile (see page 97)
- Problem statement (see page 49)
- Brainstorming (see page 151)
- Lean canvas (see page 251)
- Different kinds of prototypes (see page 187–194)
- Prototype to test (see page 199)
- Interview for empathy (see page 57)
- Solution interview (see page 225)
- Storytelling (see page 129)
- Create a pitch (see page 247)

How much time and what materials do we need?

Group size

1st Phase: usually 1 person.
2nd Phase: additional team members.
3rd Phase: permanent team. Idea owner remains during the whole process and acts as the "CEO."

1–n

Typical duration

1st Phase: 2 months
2nd Phase: 4–6 months
3rd Phase: 12–24 months

24 months

Materials needed

- Physical kickboxes with the necessary materials are provided to the teams by Swisscom
- Pens, Post-its and design thinking material

Procedure: Kickbox

Ideate it! → **Validate it!** → **Implement it!**

RedBox	BlueBox	GoldBox
20% of the time over 2 months	20% of the time over 4–6 months	100% full-time
CHF 1,000 project budget	CHF 10,000–30,000 project budget Innovation sprints & coaching	CHF 100,000–500,000 project budget
Innovation process & experts		Company founding & up-scale

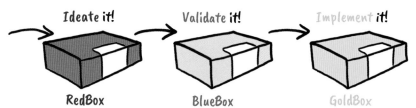

Scorecard	Customer value		Company Value					Company Fit				Risk 1 = high risk, 5 = low risk		
Concept	Convincing customers needs	Convincing solution	Competitive advantage	Addressable market size	Future market growth	Potential profit	"Wow!" value	"Go to market" fit	Technology fit	Brand fit	Implementation fit and process fit	Demand/sales	Technical feasibility	Can be tested incrementally

How the tool is applied...

RedBox: Validation of ideas with the RedBox (phases: understand, define point of view, and ideate)

Each employee in the company can get a RedBox. It also contains information on the time frame and a small budget for the exploration of a problem or an idea. The "kickboxer" is also allowed access to experts. At the end of the phase, the employee presents his or her idea in order to convince sponsors and thus reach the next level (BlueBox) of the kickbox process.

BlueBox: Experiments (phases: prototyping and testing)

The aim of this phase is the building of a prototype and the conducting of an experiment with real customers. The kickboxer is also given access to additional resources, coaching, support in the company, and with the analysis of the experiment; as well as access to a wide range of innovation services on a virtual market place.

GoldBox: Implementation and scaling

Employees have reached the GoldBox when their final prototype/MVP is a success and a decision is made to scale the project. The employee has created a new field of growth (internally or externally). The GoldBox phase includes support in the building of a company, a spin-off, or joint venture; or, if the project is close to the core business, the creation of an internal department.

Template: The individual prototypes and ideas are evaluated with a kickbox scoreboard. The logic follows the lean start-up methodology.

This is the favorite tool of David Hengartner

Position:
Innovation Lab Manager & Head of Intrapreneurship at Swisscom / Lecturer at ETH Zurich (Lean Startup Academy)

"Talk to real customers as early on and as often as possible to challenge their assumptions. Get out of the building!"

The reasons why he swears by the "kickbox" concept

I like that all employees have the opportunity of working on their business idea. This promotes their entrepreneurial way of thinking and opens up new perspectives. It also stimulates an overall culture of innovation and brings forth entrepreneurial executives who are not afraid of failure. The program is slim, data-driven, customer-oriented, and designed by entrepreneurs for entrepreneurs. After only 3 months, the open source community kickbox.org already has 1,200 signups of employees of global enterprises.

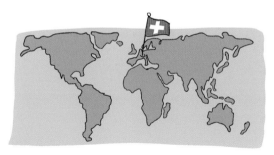

Country:
Switzerland

Affiliation:
Swisscom

Checked by: **Michael Lewrick**

Company/Position: Innovation and digitization expert

No Blah, Just Do!

Expert tips:

- **C-level support:** Top-down support, ideally from the CEO, is a crucial factor of success. Communicative measures and events together with top management are valuable activities.
- **No blah blah blah, just do:** In large companies, there is often a risk that things are endlessly mulled over and never started. Therefore the process must be in short steps, quickly and iteratively.
- **Guerrilla marketing:** Guerrilla marketing appeals to lateral thinkers. Launch impertinent advertising and break new ground. The rule is: the more unconventional the measure, the more attention it attracts!
- **Obtain working time:** Kickboxers drive their projects alongside their job. Intrapreneurs should negotiate their time budget with their supervisors themselves. It makes them all the more motivated.
- **Use internal experts:** Every enterprise has experts who can support intrapreneurs. It doesn't always have to be a costly external consultant; frequently, in-house skills are sufficient.
- **Kickbox community:** The intrapreneurs constitute a valuable community for exchange of information and ideas. Events help to keep the community alive and promote communication.

Supported by professional marketing, the kickbox has significance beyond the boundaries of the company.

Description of the use case

- Kickboxes of any size can be used in companies; and they work just as well at universities and for NGOs.
- The decentralized, bottom-up ideation with the RedBox, in which all employees of a company or an organization can participate, makes this program so powerful.
- It inspires the collective spirit of innovation in a company and transforms the corporate culture clear across departments and hierarchies.

Key learnings

- With the kickbox, a mixture of cultural transformation and business innovation can emerge.
- Each and every employee can start their own kickbox project.
- A lean start-up approach is followed systematically: begin small, test early, iterate fast!
- Many of the resources in the kickbox originate from *The Design Thinking Toolbox*.

Transformation

"Digital transformation road map"

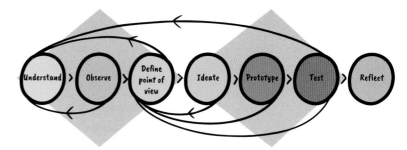

I would like...

to transform a business model and implement digital transformation professionally.

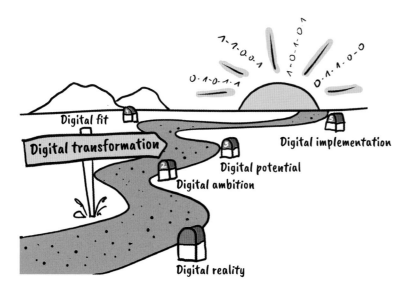

Digital fit

Digital transformation

Digital implementation

Digital potential

Digital ambition

Digital reality

What you can do with the tool:

- Transform a business model based on new technological requirements.
- Realize a competitive advantage.
- Meet customer needs, increase efficiency, and reduce costs.
- Redefine physical and digital channels and offer the customer a one-of-a-kind experience.
- Initialize the realignment of a company to remain viable in the future.

Some information on the tool:

- After initial product and service ideas are developed and tested in the form of prototypes, they can be integrated into the existing business model by means of the digital transformation road map in order to develop a future business model.
- The digital transformation refers to individual business model elements, the overall business model, the value chains, as well as the networking of different actors in a value creation network.
- Within the digital transformation, enablers (e.g. large amounts of data) are used to realize new applications and services such as on-demand forecasts.
- In addition, both from an economic and time-to-market point of view, the purchase of sub-services from partners (make or buy decisions) should be considered.

What tool can be used instead?

- Trail map (past)
- Storytelling (for the description of the future and the vision) (see page 129)
- Objectives and key results (OKR)

Which tools support working with this tool?

- Empathy map (see page 93)
- Customer journey (see page 103)
- Lean canvas (see page 251)
- Problem to growth & scale innovation funnel (see page 263)
- Road map for implementation (see page 259)

How much time and what materials do we need?

Group size

4–6

- A team consists of 4–6 people.
- Ideally, several teams participate at the same time, and a facilitator guides them through the process.

Typical duration

1- many weeks

- The duration depends on the complexity of the project, the team dynamics, and the desired level of detail of the solution.

Materials needed

- Design thinking material
- A lot of space
- Several work islands
- A0 poster templates for the individual phases and tasks

Procedure and template: Digital transformation roadmap

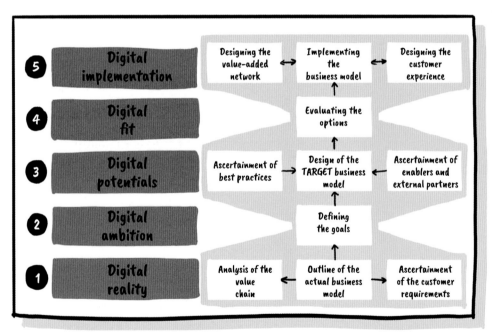

How the tool is applied...

The theory behind the road map is based on system thinking.

- **Step 1: Digital reality:** Outline the existing business model; analyze the value chains and associated actors as well as the customer requirements. The aim is to understand the reality in various dimensions.
- **Step 2: Digital ambition:** Define goals for the digital transformation in the dimensions of time, finance, space, and then prioritize them. The digital ambition shows the goals of the business model.
- **Step 3: Digital potentials:** Determine best practices and enablers for the transformation, and derive your own options from them.
- **Step 4: Digital fit:** Evaluate the options, for example, on the basis of the criteria "fit with business model" or "meeting customer requirements." Then the evaluated options or combinations are worked out in more detail. Criteria such as time, budget, feasibility, competitors, AI, corporate culture, and so on, are also considered.
- **Step 5: Digital implementation:** Find out for the implementation which actions regarding the design of digital customer interactions are necessary; which partners are to be integrated and how it's to be done; and the consequences the implementation has on processes, required resources, and the skills of employees, IT, contractual agreements, the integration in the group structure, and so on.

This is the favorite tool of Daniel Schallmo

Position:
Author, founder, and shareholder of the
Dr. Schallmo & Team GmbH and Professor at the
University of Applied Sciences of Neu-Ulm

"I love design thinking and the instruments and
procedures entailed in it. It makes it possible
to develop customer-oriented solutions in the
context of digital transformation."

Why is it his favorite tool?

*The road map for the digital transformation facilitates the
transformation of existing business models in a structured
way. One valuable aspect is that all participants can orientate
themselves to one procedure, which in turn makes for greater
transparency. Many methods and tools in this book support the
work of digital transformation.*

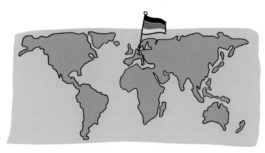

Country:
Germany

Affiliation:
University of Applied
Sciences of Neu-Ulm

Checked by: **Gina Heller-Herold**

Company/Position: beku-Consult, Senior Consultant and owner

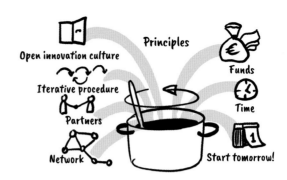

Expert tips:

Digital transformation has much to do with change. It begins in
the minds of the leadership team and with the understanding of
the project and its goals on the part of the employees.

An open innovation culture is central
We have had excellent experience with an open culture of
innovation. The following ten principles help in the design of the
digital transformation.

1. Give top priority to digitization, communicate directly, keep
   an eye on the corporate culture and your key performers.
2. Provide enough resources in terms of time, funds, space, and
   keep the employees free of too many other obligations.
3. Infer digital potential, initially on the basis of knowing the
   current business model. Don't hesitate to think far into the
   future to lay the right foundations in the corporate culture
   for things like AI and data analytics right now.
4. Don't lose track of the factors that push forward the
   digitization of a business model.
5. Keep track of the value chain of the relevant industry.
6. Learn from best practices in relevant as well as other
   industries.
7. Build necessary skills and practice the right mindset on the
   leadership team and with employees.
8. Cooperate with other actors in the business ecosystem and
   build an integrated value-added network.
9. Test ideas on a small scale (in the form of MVPs and MVEs) to
   reduce risks and enhance acceptance. Stay in direct contact
   with your customers and integrate customer feedbacks in
   the next test phases.
10. Start tomorrow at the latest!

Description of the use case

- The cornerstones of digital transformation are communicated.
- The evaluation of strategic options takes place in iterations with the building of MVPs and MVEs.
- In addition, a change takes place in the minds of management and employees. It is allowed to fail and act on the basis of self-efficacy. The rooms offer multiple ways for ad-hoc collaboration and starting experiments together.
- Lilly's team also helped in setting up a lab in which co-creation takes place and proofs of concept are implemented.

Key learnings

- Set clear goals to be attained with digital transformation.
- Allow enough time for the procurement of information and analysis.
- Be active, start and work iteratively.
- Use the tools from *The Design Thinking Toolbox*, for example, for the ascertainment of the customer requirements and needs.

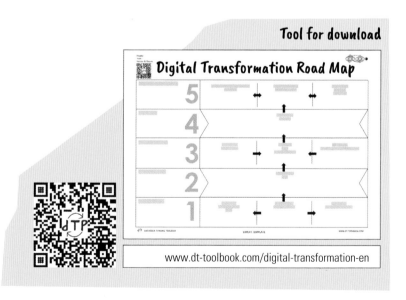

Tool for download

www.dt-toolbook.com/digital-transformation-en

Promotion of young talent

"Young innovators"

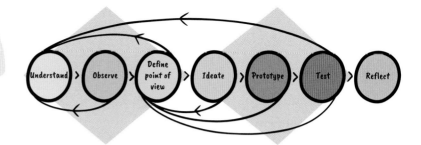

I would like...

to form a "community" for young people across the boundaries of organizations and companies and develop products or services for young customers, for example, or design the working environment of tomorrow.

What you can do with this program:

- Get to know, promote, and make use of the needs, ideas, and skills of the next generation.
- Deploy the "Young Innovators" as lateral thinkers and have them develop or test fresh ideas.
- Challenge the ideas of senior management or employees.
- Draw up the working environment of the future and promote young professionals.

Some information on the tool:

- "Young Innovators" stands for communities of young adults, from about 18 to 25 years of age, who have design thinking capabilities in addition to their heterogeneous skills and can be deployed for design challenges and innovation projects.
- As a rule, Young Innovators are cross-company communities. In large companies, it has proven worthwhile to build Young Innovators as an in-house community.
- The targeted use of "Young Innovators" in different design thinking phases has a number of advantages, especially if you want to achieve the following:
  1. Development of products and services for a young target group.
  2. The (re)design of products and services, for which fresh and innovative stimuli are purposefully searched and young lateral thinkers provide inspiration.
  3. The company wants to continue to be seen as an attractive employer in the future. Young Innovators help in the development of new working environments and provide stimuli for the transformation of the corporate culture.
- Working with "Young Innovators" can be helpful in any phase of the design thinking process, from the identification of problems up to the testing of prototypes. In addition, entire design challenges can be given to the community by several teams working on the same problem statement.

How much time and what materials do we need?

Group size

At least 5

- The larger the Young Innovators community, the better.
- Sub-teams can be formed, for example, to divide up the problem statements.

Typical duration

90–120 min.

- 1–2 hrs. for a minor design challenge.
- The duration varies depending on the scope of the design challenge.
- Complex problem statements lasting 1 week or longer.

Materials needed

- Post-its, paper, pens
- Design thinking material (e.g. for prototypes)
- Inspiring rooms

Procedure: "Young Innovators"

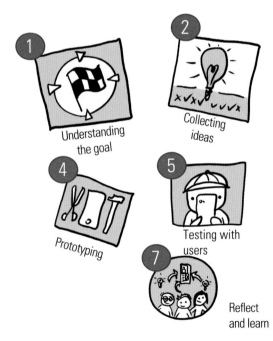

1. Understanding the goal
2. Collecting ideas
3. Deciding on the direction
4. Prototyping

5. Testing with users

6. Present solution
7. Reflect and learn

How the tool is applied...

Medium-term and long-term:
- Establishment and community building of the Young Innovators.
- The Young Innovators can even be involved in community building.
- Search for a sponsor in the company who has internalized the design thinking mindset and is aware of the added value of such a measure.

With each design sprint:
- **Step 1:** Formulate the design challenge as clearly as possible and point out its meaningfulness. Communicate the wishes and expectations of Young Innovators. Create the right mood for the Young Innovators with warm-ups.
- **Steps 2-5:** Work on the design challenge within the group; prompt participants to collect ideas and then test them with users/customers.
- **Step 6:** Pitch first prototypes and approaches to a solution before the client.
- **Step 7:** Give feedback on results and process. All this has a very important learning and motivational effect on the Young Innovators; enough time must be allowed.

Position:
Founder & CEO of Superloop Innovation, initiator of "Young Innovators"

"Design thinking has been a game changer for me. But the most important thing for me is that with design thinking we have a mindset and a method with which we can not only produce 1,000 new consumer goods but solve the great challenges of our time for a sustainable society and economy as well. For me, that is meaningful innovation."

The reasons why he swears by the "Young Innovators" concept

Fun and meaning, that's what it's all about for me! I enjoy working with these young lateral thinkers. Fresh ideas, an approach that is often quite unconventional, and the cool energy that inspires us all. So many surprising things crop up. With "Young Innovators," I also want to equip the young people with new ways of thinking. Along the design challenges, they can acquire crucial skills needed in the working environment of tomorrow. As a design thinker, everybody has the opportunity to develop meaningful and sustainable solutions.

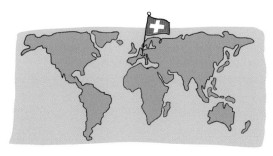

Country:
Switzerland

Affiliation:
Superloop
Innovation

Checked by: **Semir Jahic**

Company/Position: Salesforce

Expert tips:

Young Innovators community building:
- Build up a strong and heterogeneous Young Innovators community that uses the design thinking tools and methods in a targeted way.
- Ideally, this is done together with other companies. That brings diversity! A company's HR department and Talent Management should be involved here; that has proven to be quite valuable.
- The challenges should always be accompanied by experienced senior facilitators and mentors, though.
- It is important to demand the commitment of each individual "Young Innovator" and to make it clear that the group together has the responsibility for the challenge.

What makes the young generation tick is different from what made us tick:
- Meaning: Young people always want an answer to the "Why?" question. This is why it is important to formulate the intentions of the design challenge clearly and unambiguously.
- Freedom: Let the Young Innovators have enough freedom to do things "their way." But make sure that everybody understands the design principles (see page 53).
- Pitch: Let the Young Innovators pitch their results themselves.
- Collaboration: Make it a rule that outspoken ideas and opinions are welcome even when working with senior management.
- Feedback: Conclude every design challenge with a round of feedback (see page 239, for instance: "I like, I wish, I wonder"). This is an important element for the learning and motivation of Young Innovators.

Description of the use case

- When adults develop ideas and services for the young target group, they almost always get it wrong. A humanitarian organization asked the Superloop Young Innovators if they should use Snapchat. After all, it's the cool thing to do.
- The Young Innovators quickly learned the opinions and social media behavior of 500 young people, rejected the NGO's thesis, and provided them, in full self-organization, with completely different results than expected.
- Between us: No, Snapchat is not always cool.

Key learnings

- Use the Young Innovators network to harness the creativity of young people and integrate their skills across the entire design thinking cycle.
- Building your own Young Innovators community is time-consuming but it's worth the investment. New and fresh solutions emerge frequently!
- The community can also be used as a recruiting tool to identify innovative minds and to position yourself as an attractive employer.

Personal change

"Design thinking life"

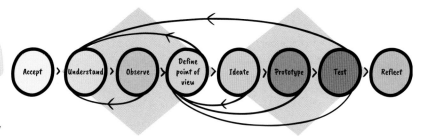

I would like...

to use the design thinking mindset to strengthen my self-efficacy and to redesign my life.

What you can do with the tool:

- Find a way to change, based on your own needs.
- Define different fields of action on which you want to actively work, such as relationship, leisure time, work, and health.
- Initiate change and strengthen your self-efficacy.
- Develop a better awareness of problems and issues that can be solved.
- Design and test different life plans.
- Achieve more well-being and satisfaction.

Some information on the tool:

- "Design thinking life" (DTL) runs through all phases of the design thinking process. Additional components consist of the phase of accepting facts and a comprehensive self-reflection, which is the basis of self-efficacy.
- "Design thinking life" is based on the principles of design thinking. It adapts this mindset, together with strategies from coaching and systemic psychotherapy, to the shaping of one's life.
- When you are able to recognize solvable problems and experiment with ideas, you will find out more quickly what makes you happy. It is often the small changes that help us to gain more vitality.
- In addition to personal use, the method is used as an accompanying measure to point out development perspectives in companies, universities, and coaching programs.

Which methods support working with this tool?

- AEIOU (see page 107)
- Brainstorming (see page 151)
- Special brainstorming (see page 167)
- Retrospective sailboat (see page 243)
- And many tools from the "understanding" and "observing" as well as "reflecting" phases.

How much time and what materials do we need?

Group size

1–5

- Larger groups have the advantage that the participants can support one another.
- Often, the life concepts are mutually inspiring.

Typical duration

3 days – 2 months

- The duration varies with the set-up of such programs. Usually 6–8 weeks are needed for a cycle.

Materials needed

- Post-its, pens, markers
- Large sheet of paper
- Inspiring rooms

Procedure: Design thinking life

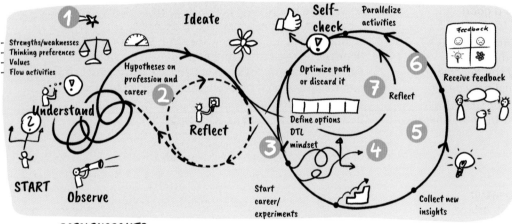

How the tool is applied...

The "design thinking life" process follows the design thinking process. However, it has been enriched with two crucial process steps: **acceptance** and **self-reflection**.

In the application of "design thinking life" in the context of career planning, we have had positive experience with the following steps:

- **Step 1:** Start by exploring personal values, thinking preferences, environmental factors, and identified flow activities.
- **Step 2:** Draw up hypotheses about a personal career plan.
- **Step 3:** Design different paths and possibilities.
- **Step 4:** Test and explore the possibilities.
- **Step 5:** Evaluate the options and reflect on whether they are consistent with your ideas and possible consequences.
- **Step 6:** Plan the implementation in small steps.
- **Step 7:** Reflect regularly on whether the current tasks still satisfy you; otherwise, you should optimize your life plan or define new options.

Position:
- Best-selling author, speaker, innovation and digitization expert

"Companies are surprised that the transformation into an agile enterprise does not happen with top-down-driven change management programs. Successful change, however, begins with how every single employee lives, thinks, and acts – a mindset that is based on the self-development of his or her skills and personality. 'Design thinking life' is a good start."

The reasons why he swears by the "design thinking life" concept

Company bosses frequently ask me what would be a good approach to the establishment of a new mindset. To that, I have two answers. First, exemplify it day after day, because only then is our desire for change authentic. Secondly, give the people in your organization enough freedom so that they can become self-effective and use their skills optimally. We must provide all employees with techniques and strategies in order to strengthen their self-efficacy. Only then will they support us with enthusiasm and energy in the transformation process.

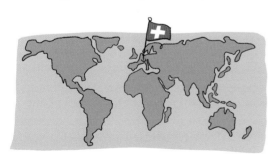

Country:
Switzerland

Checked by: Jean Paul Thommen

Company/Position: Independent Coach, Professor of Organizational Development and Business Administration

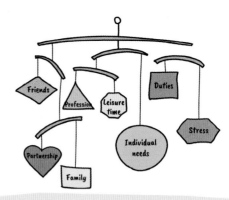

Expert tips:

Self-efficacy is the key strength of the future
- The "design thinking life" mindset is a targeted starting point to strengthen the capacity of employees to act.
- Using "design thinking life" for major transitions at companies has proven very valuable.
- It provides employees with easy access to the design thinking mindset, and they are motivated to practice this mindset on their team and in their projects.
- For HR managers, "design thinking life" is an ideal strategy and technique that aims at strengthening the skills and talents of employees instead of matching people with existing patterns and job descriptions.

Life is a constant process of change
- This means that "design thinking life" is a development tool, starting with pupils who must opt for a course of studies, to students who choose the next stage in their career during or right after their time at the university.
- In particularly difficult business or private situations of a participant, it is important that the moderator can deal well with emotional outbursts or is prepared for them.

Small changes can make a big difference
- That's why I give the tip: Everybody should initiate small changes on his/her own to achieve great things. It is important to always look to the future, in which everyone can write the script of life themselves through self-efficacy or adapt it to the new circumstances.

Description of the use case

- Use the "design thinking life" mindset to make your life the way you always wanted it to be.
- Get to the bottom of things through self-reflection.
- Learn to distinguish between solvable problems and facts.
- Try to initiate small changes to make a big difference.
- Look to the future by writing the script of life itself through self-efficacy or adapting it to the new circumstances.

Key learnings

- Design thinking aims to solve complex problems with creative ease – and where are there more complex questions than in our lives?
- However, "design thinking life" is not just about changing the individual – every stage and change has an impact on many people in our environment.
- As in design thinking, the path only becomes apparent when we begin to walk it.

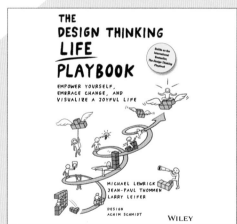

www.dt-playbook.com

ISBN Print: 978-1-1196-8224-0
ISBN E-Book: 978-1-1196-8225-7

Closing words

Closing words

Our final word is very brief:

> **Do it and don't just talk about it, because design thinking lives from the application!**

This book about Design Thinking methods and tools has satisfied the need of many users and students to understand the most popular design thinking tools in their full breadth and depth. Thanks to the expert tips in this Toolbox, a unique exchange of knowledge within the global design thinking community was realized. For us, it was important to describe the tools in a way that you can become effective, no matter whether you do it with a warm-up or a first observation of users.

Nevertheless, everyone has to find their own way as a design thinker on how to best use the tools depending on the problem, workshop dynamics, and knowledge of the participants. Each design thinking workshop will be different, and we will only be successful if we adapt to each new situation individually. The basis – our design thinking mindset, a positive feedback culture, regular reflection, and many other elements – are the foundation for all the tools we use in our daily work.

We would like to take this opportunity to thank the global design thinking community once again. First, for participating in our initial "International Survey on Design Thinking Methods and Tools" and then for the numerous expert tips that made it possible for us to realize such a Toolbox.

We look forward to receiving feedback on the tools, experiences with the design thinking mindset in your projects, and a lively exchange of information about the use of design thinking.

Michael, Patrick, & Larry

And remember....

Build on the ideas of the others

Establish a positive feedback culture and do not criticize ideas prematurely

Focus on the design challenge and the problem to solve

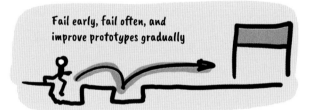

Fail early, fail often, and improve prototypes gradually

Visualize and build physical prototypes

Listen and hear others out

Place the user/customer at the center of considerations

Leave many ideas to the diverging phase

Build and test even wild ideas

... to get the most out of the Design Thinking Toolbox!

Authors & contributors

Michael Lewrick

Best-selling author, speaker, innovation and digitization expert

Patrick Link

Professor of Innovation, entrepreneur, and lean start-up expert, co-founder Trihow AG

RÉSUMÉS

Michael has had different tasks over the last few years. He was responsible for strategic growth, acted as Chief Innovation Officer, and laid the foundation for numerous growth initiatives in sectors that are in a transition. He teaches Design Thinking as a visiting professor at various universities. With his help, a number of international companies have developed and commercialized radical innovations. He postulated a new mindset of converging approaches of design thinking in digitization.

Patrick has been Professor of Product Innovation at the Institute for Innovation and Technology Management at Lucerne University of Applied Sciences and Arts – Technology & Architecture since 2009. He studied Mechanical Engineering at ETH Zurich, then worked as a Project Engineer before receiving his doctorate in the field of innovation management at ETH Zurich. After eight years at Siemens, he now teaches product management and deals intensively with the advancement of agile methods in product management, design thinking, and lean start-up. He is co-founder of Trihow AG.

WHY ARE YOU A DESIGN THINKING EXPERT?

I came into contact with design thinking for the first time in 2005. At the time, it was a question of supporting start-ups in the development and definition of new products. In recent years, I attended to various company projects, seeing them through at Stanford University. In the context of my various functions in different industries, I was able to initialize a multitude of co-creation workshops with major customers, start-ups, and other actors in the ecosystem and thus advance various methods and tools.

When I first became acquainted with design thinking, I quickly realized the potential of this approach for interdisciplinary collaboration. Since then, we have used the approach in many training and advanced training modules as well as in start-ups. In particular, the combination of intuitive, circular approaches and analytical methods is very instructive. Together with colleagues from industry, we advanced design thinking and other agile methods and offer workshops and courses.

WHAT IS YOUR ADVICE TO DESIGN THINKING BEGINNERS?

Start with yourself! Design thinking is based on a positive attitude. Creativity can only unfold when we as human beings constantly work on our self-efficacy; when we have understood to look at problems from various sides and when we reflect critically on our actions. If you are able to design your own life, you will be able to transfer this mindset to teams, organizations, and companies.

Participate in a number of design thinking workshops with different moderators. Try to learn something from all of them. Do the same as an experienced moderator. Plan your workshops carefully and in great detail. At the same time, stay flexible and have alternatives ready in your mind, for example, an additional warm-up or another tool. Try something new in each workshop.

Larry Leifer

Professor of Mechanical Engineering, Founding Director, HPI & Stanford Center for Design Research

Achim Schmidt

Design thinking coach, graphic recording & visualization expert

RÉSUMÉS

Larry is a Professor of Mechanical Engineering Design and founding director of the Center for Design Research at Stanford (CDR) and of the Hasso Plattner Design Thinking Research Program at Stanford. He is one of the most influential personalities and pioneers of design thinking. He brought design thinking to the world, putting the focus on working in interdisciplinary teams.

Achim has studied industrial design from the bottom up and worked ten years as a car designer. After studying at the HPI (d.school), he worked as a design thinking coach and teaching assistant at the University of St. Gallen. Today, as a design thinking coach, he helps companies develop disruptive innovation. In addition, he is a trainer for elevator pitches for start-ups as well as for sketch notes, visual facilitation, and graphic recording.

WHY ARE YOU A DESIGN THINKING EXPERT?

I have been dealing with design thinking and research in this area for decades. This includes global team dynamics, interaction design, and adaptive mechatronic systems.

In the ME310 program, I was able to observe the cultural differences in a variety of projects and use cases and infer significant conclusions from it for teaching and research at Stanford.

Basically, I've been living the design thinking process and the mindset for over 20 years without knowing at the beginning that it was called that! In industrial design, it is a matter of course to observe the user and find out his needs. My focus is on workshops, both to teach methods and to solve projects and design challenges in industry.

WHAT IS YOUR ADVICE TO DESIGN THINKING BEGINNERS?

Larry Leifer's FOUR simple tips for the design of new market opportunities:
- All innovation is re-innovation.
- All innovation demands from the team radical collaboration and less cooperation.
- All innovation failures are premium learning opportunities.
- Never stop dancing with ambiguity.

Have no fear of making mistakes and just start! It is better to hold a workshop more often with quick readjustments than to hold a major event every few months, to which great expectations are attached. Constantly try new formats and tools. Get active feedback (especially "I wish"), reflect on yourself, thus developing.

Contributors, guest authors and reviewers of *The Design Thinking Toolbox*

Michael Lewrick | Best-selling author, speaker, innovation and digitization expert
Patrick Link | Lucerne University of Applied Sciences and Arts, Trihow AG
Larry Leifer | Stanford University
Achim Schmidt | Business-Playground
Adharsh Dhandapani | IBM
Adrian Sulzer | SATW
Alan Cabello | ETH Zürich
Alice Froissac | Openers
Amanda Mota | Docway
Amber Dubinsky | THES - TauscHaus - EduSpace
Andreas Uthmann | CKW
Andres Bedoya | d.school Paris
Armin Egli | Zühlke AG
Beat Knüsel | Trihow
Bettina Maisch | Siemens AG
Bryan Richards | Aspen Impact + Indiana University's Herron School of Art and Design
Carina Teichmann | Mimacom AG
Christian Hohmann | Lucerne University of Applied Sciences and Arts
Christian Langrock | Hamburger Hochbahn AG
Christine Kohlert | Media Design University for Design and Computer Science
Dahlia Dietrich | Swisscom AG
Daniel Schallmo | Hochschule Ulm
Daniel Steingruber | SIX
Hengartner | Swisscom AG
Denise Pereira | DuPont
Dino Beerli | Young Innovators
Elena Bonanomi | Die Mobiliar
Esther Cahn | Signifikant Solutions AG
Esther Moosauer | EY – Ernst & Young
Florence Mathieu | Aïna
Florian Baumgartner | Innoveto by Crowdinnovation
Gaurav Bhargva | Iress
Gina Heller-Herold | beku-Consult
Hannes Felber | Invacare Europe
Helene Cahen | Strategic insights
Helmut Ness | Fünfwerken Design AG
Ina Goller | Bern University of Applied Sciences

Ingunn Aursnes | Sopra Steria
Isabelle Hauser | Lucerne University of Applied Sciences and Arts
Jean-Michel Chardon | Logitech AG
Jean-Paul Thommen | Professor of Organizational Development and Business Administration
Jennifer Sutherland | Independent Consultant
Jens Springmann | creaffective GmbH
Jeremias Schmidt | 5Wx new ventures GmbH
Jessica Dominguez | Pick-a-Box
Jessika Weber | Breda University of Applied Sciences
Juan Pablo García Cifuentes| Pontificia Universidad Javeriana, Cali
Jui Kulkarni | IBM iX
Julia Gumula | B. Braun
Justus Schrage | Karlsruhe Institute of Technology
Katja Holtta-Otto | Design Factory, Aalto University
Katrin Fischer | Innovation Consultant
Konstantin Gänge | Airbus
Kristine Biegman | launchlabs GmbH
Laurene Racine | Ava
Lena Papasz | Design Thinker | Marketing Consultant
Line Gram Frokjaer | SODAQ
Lucas Bock | Siemens AG
Marc Fetscherin | Rollins College
Madalena Tavares | Porto Design Factory
Malena Donato | ATOS
Maria Tarcsay | KoinaSoft GmbH
Marius Kienzler | Adidas
Markus Blatt | neue Beratung GmbH
Markus Durstewitz | Airbus
Martin Steinert | Norwegian University of Science and Technology
Mathias Strazza | PostFinance PFLab
Maurice Codourey | Unit-X
Mike Pinder | Innovation Consultant
Miriam Hartmann | F. Hoffmann-La Roche
Mladen Djakovic | Q Point

Moritz Avenarius | oose Innovative Informatik eG
Natalie Breitschmid | Sinodus AG
Niels Feldmann | Karlsruhe Institute of Technology
Pansy Lee | MLSE
Pascal Henzmann | Helbling Technik AG
Patrick Bauen | LMtec Swiss GmbH
Patrick Deininger | Karlsruhe Institute of Technology
Patrick Labud | bbv Software Services
Patrick Schüffel | HEG Fribourg in Singapore
Pete Kooijmans | Trihow AG
Philip Hassler | Venturelab
Philipp Bachmann | The University of Applied Sciences of the Grisons
Philipp Guggisberg-Elbel | mm1 Schweiz
Rasmus Thomsen | IS IT A BIRD
Regina Vogel | Innovations and Leadership Coach
Remo Gander | Bosssard Group
Roberto Gago | Generali
Roger Stämpfli | Aroma AG
Roman Schoeneboom | Credit Suisse
Samuel Huber | Goodpatch
Sebastian Fixson | Babson College
Sebastian Garn | B&B Markenagentur GmbH
Sebastian Kernbach | University of St. Gallen
Semir Jahic | Salesforce
Shwet Sharvary | Everything by design
Slavo Tuleja | SKODA AUTO DigiLab
Sophie Bürgin | INNOArchitects
Stefano Vannotti | Zurich University of Arts
Stefanie Gerken | HPI School of Design Thinking
Steffi Kieffer | Revelate GbR
Thomas Duschlbauer | KompeTrend
Thomas Schocher | CSS Versicherung
Tobias Lüpke | EY – Ernst & Young
Ute Bauckhorn | Schindler Aufzüge AG
Vesa Lindroos | Independent Consultant
Waszkiewicz Małgorzata | Warsaw University of Technology
Yves Karcher | InnoExec Sàrl

Actors and contributors to the photo comic strip

Kimberly Wyss (as Lilly)

Alessandro Tarantino
Amela Besic
Beat Knüsel
Benjamin Kindle
Carisa Ruoss
Ceyda Gücer
Cyrril Portmann
Daniele Palermo
Danylo Kharytonskyi
David Würsch
Delia Graf
Fabio Beck
Florian Gerber
Francesco Planta
Gianluca von Ehrenberg
Hannes Gasser
Isabelle Kalt
Janick Blumenstein
Jetmir Arifi
Jonas Bach
Judith Meier
Karen Magdalene Benjamin
Kenny Mezenen
Lars Küng

Lee-Roy Ryhner
Lukas Fischer
Marco Binggeli
Michael Rohner
Milena Nussbaumer
Nicolas Keller
Niklaus Hess
Pascal Schaller
Pascal Scherrer
Patricia Sury
Peter Dober
Philipp Businger
Raffael Frommenwiler
Régis Andreoli
Robin Martin
Roman Bürki
Ronalds Purins
Samuel Graf
Silvan Büchli
Silvan Jason Roth
Sven von Niederhäusern
Thomas Stocker
Ulrich Kössl
Uwe Kortmöller-Scholl

Photography: Nils Riedweg

Many thanks to Patrick Bauen and Nicolasa Caduff for their assistance in creating the templates. Many thanks also go to the Lucerne University of Applied Sciences and Arts, in particular to Michele Kellerhals and Christian Hohmann, Institute for Innovation and Technology Management, for their support.

Making of Design Thinking Toolbook

Sources and index

Sources

- Arnheim, R. (1969, new edition 1997): Visual Thinking. Berkeley, Los Angeles: University of California Press.
- Baars, J. E. (2018): Leading Design. Munich: Franz Vahlen GmbH.
- Berger, W. (2014): Die Kunst des Klugen Fragens. Berlin: Berlin Verlag.
- Beylerian, G. M., Dent, A. & Quinn, B. (2007): Ultra Materials: How Materials Innovation Is Changing the World. Thames & Hudson.
- Blank, S. G., & Dorf, B. (2012): The Start-up Owner's Manual: The Step-by- Step Guide for Building a Great Company. Pescadero: K&S Ranch.
- Blank, S. G. (2013): Why the Lean Start-up Changes Everything. Harvard Business Review. 91 (5): pp. 63–72.
- Brown T. (2016): Change by Design. Vahlen Verlag.
- Brown, T. & Katz, B. (2009): Change by Design: How Design Thinking Transforms Organizations and Inspires Innovation. New York: HarperCollins.
- Buchanan, R. (1992): Wicked Problems in Design Thinking. Design Issues, 8(2), pp. 5–21.
- Carleton, T., & Cockayne, W. (2013): Playbook for Strategic Foresight & Innovation. Download at: http://www.innovation.io
- Christensen, C., et al. (2011): The Innovator's Dilemma. Vahlen Verlag.
- Curedale, R. (2016): Design Thinking – Process & Methods Guide, 3rd edition. Los Angeles: Design Community College Inc.
- Cowan, A. (2015): Making Your Product a Habit: The Hook Framework, website visited on Nov. 2, 2016, http://www.alexandercowan.com/the-hook-framework/
- Cross, N. (2011): Design Thinking. Oxford, Berg Publishers.
- Davenport, T. (2014): Big Data at Work: Dispelling the Myths, Uncovering the Opportunities. Vahlen Verlag.
- Davenport, T. H., & D. J. Patil (2012): Data Scientist: The Sexiest Job of the 21st Century. Harvard Business Review: October 2012 issue, https://hbr.org/2012/10/data-scientist-the-sexiest-job-of-the-21stcentury/
- Doorley, S., Witthoft, S., & Hasso Plattner Institute of Design at Stanford (2012): Make Space: How to Set the Stage for Creative Collaboration. Hoboken: Wiley.
- Dorst, K. (2015): Frame Innovation. Cambridge (MA): MIT Press.
- Duschlbauer, T. (2018): Der Querdenker. Zurich: Midas Management Verlag AG.
- Erbelinger, J., & Ramge, T. (2013): Durch die Decke Denken. Munich: Redline Verlag GmbH.
- Gerstbach, I. (2016): Design Thinking in Unternehmen. Gabal Verlag.
- Gladwell, M. (2005): Blink: The Power of Thinking without Thinking. New York: Back Bay Books.
- Gray, D. , Brown, S., & Macanufo, J. (2010): Gamestorming. Sebastopol (CA): O'Reilly Media Inc.
- Griffith E. (2014): Why Startups Fail, According to Their Founders. In: Fortune Magazine (September 25, 2014). http://fortune.com/2014/09/25/why-startups-fail-according-to-theirfounders/
- Herrmann, N. (1996): The Whole Brain Business Book: Harnessing the Power of the Whole Brain Organization and the Whole Brain Individual, McGraw-Hill Professional.
- Heath, C. & Heath, D. (2007): Made to Stick: Why Some Ideas Survive and Others Die. New York: Random House.
- Hsinchun, C., Chiang, R. H. L. & Storey, V. C. (2012): Business Intelligence and Analytics: From Big Data to Big Impact. MIS Quarterly, 36 (4), pp. 1165–1188.
- Heufler, G. (2009): Design Basics: From Ideas to Products. 3rd exp. edition. Niggli.
- Hohmann, L. (2007): Innovation Games. Boston: Pearson Education Inc.
- Hippel, E. V. (1986): Lead Users. A Source of Novel Product Concepts. In: Management Science, Vol. 32, pp. 791–805.
- IDEO (2009): Human Centered Design: Toolkit & Human Centered Design: Field Guide. 2nd ed. [*Both available on the IDEO home page or at: https://www.designkit.org/resources/*1
- Kelly, T. & Littman, J. (2001): The Art of Innovation: Lessons in Creativity from IDEO, America's Leading Design Firm. London: Profile Books.
- Kim, W., & Mauborgne, R. (2005): Blue Ocean Strategy, Expanded Edition: How to Create Uncontested Market Space and Make the Competition Irrelevant. Hanser Verlag.
- Kumar, V. (2013): 101 Design Methods. Hoboken, New Jersey: John Wiley & Sons.
- Leifer, L. (2012a): Rede nicht, zeig's mir, in: Organisations Entwicklung, 2, pp. 8–13.

- Leifer, L. (2012b): Interview with Larry Leifer (Stanford) at Swisscom, Design Thinking Final Summer Presentation, Zurich.
- Lewrick, M., & Link, P. (2015): Hybride Management Modelle: Konvergenz von Design Thinking und Big Data. IM+io Fachzeitschrift für Innovation, Organisation und Management (4), pp. 68–71.
- Lewrick, M., Skribanowitz, P., & Huber, F. (2012): Nutzen von Design Thinking Programmen, 16. Interdisziplinäre Jahreskonferenz zur Gründungsforschung (G-Forum), University of Potsdam.
- Lewrick, M. (2014): Design Thinking – Ausbildung an Universitäten, pp. 87–101. In: Sauvonnet and Blatt (eds). Wo ist das Problem? Neue Beratung.
- Lewrick, M., Link. P, & Leifer, L. (2018): The Design Thinking Playbook, Wiley, 2nd edition Munich: Franz Vahlen GmbH.
- Lewrick, M. (2018): Design Thinking: Radikale Innovationen in einer Digitalisierten Welt, Beck Verlag; Munich.
- Lewrick, M. (2019): The Design Thinking Life Playbook, Wiley, Versus Verlag Zurich.
- Lietka, J., & Ogilvie, T. (2011): Designing for Growth. New York: Columbia University Press Inc.
- Maeda, J. (2006): The Laws of Simplicity – Simplicity: Design, Technology, Business, Life. Cambridge, London: MIT Press.
- Maurya, A. (2013): Running Lean: Iterate from Plan A to a Plan That Works.
- Moore, G. (2014): Crossing the Chasm, 3rd edition. New York: Harper Collins Inc.
- Norman, D. A. (2004): Emotional Design: Why We Love (or Hate) Everyday Things. New York: Basic Books.
- Norman, D. A. (2011): Living with Complexity. Cambridge, London: MIT Press.
- Osterwalder, A., Pigneur, Y., et al. (2015): Value Proposition Design. Frankfurt: Campus Verlag.
- Patel N. (2015): 90% Of Startups Fail: Here's What You Need to Know about the 10%. In: Forbes (Jan. 16, 2015). https://www.forbes.com/sites/neilpatel/2015/01/16/90-of-startups-willfail- heres-what-you-need-to-know-about-the-10/#5e710a5b6679
- Plattner, H., Meinel, C., & Leifer, L. (2010): Design Thinking. Understand – Improve – Apply (Understanding Innovation). Heidelberg: Springer.
- Puccio, J. C., Mance M., & Murdock, M. C. (2011): Creative Leadership, Skills that Drive Change. Sage: Thousand Oaks, CA.
- Riverdale & IDEO (2011): Design Thinking for Educators. Version One. [available at: http://designthinkingforeducators.com/]
- Roam, D. (2008): The Back of the Napkin: Solving Problems and Selling Ideas with Pictures. London: Portfolio.
- Sauvonnet, E., & Blatt, M. (2017): Wo ist das Problem? Munich: Franz Vahlen GmbH.
- Stickdorn, M., & Schneider, J. (2016): This Is Service Design Thinking, 6th edition. Amsterdam: BIS Publishers.
- Töpfer, A. (2008): Lean Six Sigma. Heidelberg: Springer-Verlag GmbH.
- Uebernickel, F., Brenner, W., et al. (2015): Design Thinking – The Manual. Frankfurt am Main: Frankfurter Allgemeine Buch.
- Ulrich K. (2011): Design Creation of Artifacts in Society, published by the University of Pennsylvania. http://www.ulrichbook.org/
- Ulwick, A. (2016): Jobs to Be Done. Idea Bite Press.
- Van Aerssen, B., & Buchholz, C. (2018): Das grosse Handbuch Innovation. Munich: Franz Vahlen GmbH.
- Vahs, D., & Brem, A. (2013): Innovationsmanagement, 4th edition. Stuttgart: Schäffer-Poeschel Verlag.
- Van der Pijl, P., Lokitz, J., & Solomon, L. K. (2016): Design a Better Business. Munich: Franz Vahlen GmbH.
- Victionary (2007): Simply Materials: Exploring the Potential of Materials and Creative Competency. Ginko Press.
- Weinberg, U. (2015): Network Thinking. Hamburg: Murmann Publishers GmbH.

Goodbye! And have lots of fun solving relevant problems!

"If I had an hour to solve a problem I'd spend 55 minutes thinking about the problem and 5 minutes thinking about the solutions."

Albert Einstein

INDEX

Workshop Planning Canvas:

Planning	Implementation	Follow-up

Design challenge

Agenda

Day 1	Day 2	Day 3	Day 4	Day 5

Result

Participants

Follow-up

Record results (photo), clean up room, minutes, defined next steps

Administrative issues

Room, materials, facilitator, catering, invite users, invite participants, detailed agenda per day

Next steps

Feedback

What needs to be improved?